THE VARIETIES OF SUICIDAL EXPERIENCE

PSYCHOLOGY AND CRIME
General Editors: Brian Bornstein, University of Nebraska, and Monica Miller, University of Nevada, Reno

The Perversion of Youth: Controversies in the Assessment and Treatment of Juvenile Sex Offenders
Frank C. DiCataldo

Jury Decision Making: The State of the Science
Dennis J. Devine

Deviant and Criminal Behavior in the Workplace
Edited by Steven M. Elias

Psychopathy: An Introduction to Biological Findings and Their Implications
Andrea L. Glenn and Adrian Raine

Gender, Psychology, and Justice: The Mental Health of Women and Girls in the Legal System
Edited by Corinne C. Datchi and Julie R. Ancis

Criminal Trials and Mental Disorders
Thomas L. Hafemeister

Criminal Trajectories: A Developmental Perspective
David M. Day and Margit Wiesner

Understanding Police Interrogation: Confessions and Consequences
William Douglas Woody and Krista D. Forrest

Understanding Eyewitness Memory: Theory and Applications
Sean M. Lane and Kate A. Houston

Jailhouse Informants: Psychological and Legal Perspectives
Jeffrey S. Neuschatz and Jonathan M. Golding

Mental Health Evaluations in Immigration Court: A Guide for Mental Health and Legal Professionals
Virginia Barber-Rioja, Adeyinka M. Akinsulure-Smith, and Sarah Vendzules

Violence and Mental Illness: Rethinking Risk Factors and Enhancing Public Safety
Eric B. Elbogen and Nico Verykoukis

The Varieties of Suicidal Experience: A New Theory of Suicidal Violence
Thomas Joiner

The Varieties of Suicidal Experience

A New Theory of Suicidal Violence

Thomas Joiner

NEW YORK UNIVERSITY PRESS
New York

NEW YORK UNIVERSITY PRESS
New York
www.nyupress.org

© 2024 by New York University
All rights reserved

Please contact the Library of Congress for Cataloging-in-Publication data.
ISBN: 9781479823468 (hardback)
ISBN: 9781479823475 (paperback)
ISBN: 9781479823505 (library ebook)
ISBN: 9781479823482 (consumer ebook)

This book is printed on acid-free paper, and its binding materials are chosen for strength and durability. We strive to use environmentally responsible suppliers and materials to the greatest extent possible in publishing our books.

Manufactured in the United States of America

10 9 8 7 6 5 4 3 2 1

Also available as an ebook

CONTENTS

Introduction: Suicidal Violence as a Misunderstood and
Recalcitrant Plague 1

1. Suicide: The Interpersonal Theory of Suicide 49

2. Perverted Virtues Transform Suicide into Murder-Suicide
   and Spree Killing 67

3. Killing Oneself without Killing Oneself: Suicide-by-Cop
   and Related Phenomena 97

4. Suicide Terrorism 116

5. Is Physician-Assisted Suicide Suicide? Is Death
   Row Volunteering? 131

Conclusion: How to Stop a Plague 175

Notes 183

Bibliography 193

Index 203

About the Author 215

Introduction

Suicidal Violence as a Misunderstood and Recalcitrant Plague

An individual intends to kill as many people as he can and knows that in the process he too will die. In advance of the atrocity, the individual explains in writing that his motives are very explicitly nonsuicidal, instead having to do with political, cultural, and religious views that he sees as high-minded, as being worth his own and others' death. Many take him at his word, including reporters and scholars. An animating question for this book is *why*? Why would someone do this? And why on earth would we take a cold-blooded killer of numerous innocent strangers at his word? The question generalizes beyond mass killing scenarios: Shouldn't we have at least a moment's reflection, a moment's doubt, when asked to trust the explanations of someone about to kill anyone for any reason?

Violence takes many forms, a fact that may obscure how many of these forms are of a suicidal variety. Readers may notice that the book's title is an homage to William James's seminal book *The Varieties of Religious Experience* (1902). James believed that there are fundamental commonalities across religious experiences. With regard to suicidal experiences, I make an even stronger claim in this book: that there is a kind of singularity underneath an array of violent behaviors that result in one's own death.

At first take, many violent deaths are such that they may not seem like true suicides. Or, a suicidal element may be apparent, but viewed as somewhat incidental or secondary to other motives and aspects. In all likelihood, however, many of these deaths not only are true suicides but are primarily suicides. The more obvious examples include suicide-by-cop and murder-suicide; less obvious—but, this book argues, no less primarily suicidal—are spree killing, suicide terrorism, physician-assisted suicide, a supposedly dissociative syndrome called amok, and volunteering for execution on death row.

2 | INTRODUCTION

One potentially significant insight of this view is that suicide prevention, perennially urgent and at a potentially exciting crossroads given the ongoing establishment in the United States of a 911-like number and system, 988, specifically for suicidal crises, may prevent suicides as usually understood but, because suicide is at their root, may also prevent atrocities like spree and terroristic killings.

Before situating this perspective within the state of the art and science on suicide prevention, and before elaborating on and defending the view that a number of varieties of violence are at root suicidal, some context is useful. For the most part, there is little or no robust, mature, and definitive *empirical* literature on questions such as whether suicide terrorism is more an expression of suicide than of terrorism; whether murder-suicide is more a variant of suicide than of murder; or whether death row volunteering and physician-assisted suicide are, at base, suicidal. To be sure, there is scholarship on these and related questions, and a small portion of this scholarship is empirical; when it is available, I strive to cover this empirical work, and because it is empirical, I weight it preferentially. What to do, however, when little or no such work is available?

One possibility is to hew only to the empirical, which would result in a very slim book indeed. Another is to mix empirical scholarship, conceptual analysis, and personal insights based on extensive experience studying these dynamics—the approach I take in the pages that follow. Readers are of course invited to disagree with my opinions, analyses, and interpretation of the empirical literature; indeed, dissent is the lifeblood of the academy as it is, or should be, of democracy itself.

In this introduction as well as in chapter 1, I offer a multifaceted, up-to-date, and comprehensive overview of the phenomenon of suicidal behavior per se, by which I mean the kind of suicidal behavior that essentially everyone agrees is clearly suicidal in essence.[1] This introduction takes a deep dive into the subject, covering topics like vicissitudes in the US suicide rate in recent times and various interventions that mitigate suicide risk. A risk of this approach is that it puts the focus on suicide per se—which is, after all, a definite variety of suicidal violence—whereas the overarching aim of the book is to focus on varieties of violent behavior that I argue are fundamentally suicidal. I strive to manage that risk of distraction throughout this introduction and chapter 1. The discussion is important, as a comprehensive summary will better position us to understand various forms of violence, often viewed as essentially nonsuicidal, as in actuality manifestations of suicide.

Why Are Some Suicidal Behaviors Viewed as Nonsuicidal?

As we will see, there are at least a half dozen behaviors that are essentially suicidal in character but that are regularly construed as otherwise; each will be given a separate treatment in the chapters that follow. As to why they are often perceived—*mis*perceived, this book argues—as essentially nonsuicidal in nature, at least two main reasons are operative.

First, as we will see in the chapters that follow, these incidents very regularly injure or kill others. Quite understandably, then, the public's attention and sympathy are drawn to innocent victims. This focus on the injuring and killing of others tends to obscure the fact that the genesis of the entire violent process is often suicide. Second, individuals who have perpetrated such forms of violence and have survived are of course regularly queried by law enforcement, mental health professionals, and others regarding their motives. Such individuals are under great social pressure to dissemble. If their true motive were primarily suicide, and yet they remain alive when others are injured or dead, it is far easier for them to say things like "I didn't intend that," "I lost my mind," or "Something just took me over" than it is to admit the truth.[2]

It is not only suicidal people who misattribute. Other groups do, too, among whom are those bereaved by suicide—easily the most sympathy-inspiring of the groups—who, due to their sense of profound shock and utter disbelief, can gain comfort from the view that their loved one really did not know what they were doing.

A second reason inspires less sympathy: people knowingly alter or omit the true details of a case so that they fit a particular narrative they are advocating.[3] Consider, in this context, the tragic death by suicide of TV news anchor Christine Chubbuck. Ms. Chubbuck died by a self-inflicted gunshot wound as she reported the news live on local TV, an act that she meticulously planned out over the course of several days at an absolute minimum, although it is more likely that her consideration and planning of the event evolved over many weeks or months. Regardless, the evidence is completely clear that Ms. Chubbuck did not die on an impulsive whim. Of the many considerations that make this very

4 | INTRODUCTION

plain, one is that she brought a loaded weapon to the set and placed it in a kind of prop bag that she regularly had with her under the desk as she presented the news—a bag in which she was *not* in the habit of placing a gun, never mind a loaded one. On the day in question, she reached under the desk, extracted the gun, and ended her life, all within the span of a few seconds, and all on live TV.

Moreover, Ms. Chubbuck had told one of her colleagues exactly what she had planned to do. With reference to this last detail, a filmmaker who made a movie about Ms. Chubbuck's life and death purposefully omitted it from the film, explaining that to have included it would not have "worked dramatically."[4] Perhaps, but my retort is that not including it "misled the public."

Returning to the phenomenon of people disavowing their own behavior, a prison psychiatrist who writes under the pseudonym Theodore Dalrymple described such incidents as "and-the-next-thing-I-knew-doctor" events and quotes Tolstoy's novella *The Kreutzer Sonata* thus: "When people say they don't remember what they do in a fit of fury, it is rubbish, falsehood."[5] That there is something to this quote is a cornerstone of my argument in this book.

Dalrymple, who is in reality British psychiatrist Anthony Daniels, has a definite flair for description of such phenomena; he can be read as cynical and misanthropic, but in my opinion that is a superficial misreading. His humor can be cynical, to be sure—not to mention at times very funny—but his animating ethos is an admittedly old-fashioned love and admiration of virtue and truth. In any event, it is certainly the case that a large fraction of Daniels's clinical experience was accrued in prison settings, and it is also the case that this has affected his outlook on topics like human nature and responsibility for one's own behavior.

This book is about suicidal behavior, not criminal behavior, there being a distinct divide between the two, at least nowadays. I therefore rush to emphasize my distaste for implications that suicidal behavior should be in any way criminalized, whether in fact or by insinuation. If I am to be criticized for my views on suicidal behavior, it would not be on grounds that I confuse criminality and suicidality. Rather, it would be on other grounds—for example, that I insist that any and all suicidal behavior is a manifestation of at least one mental disorder of some kind and of some above-zero level of acuity, an important and debatable point to which I will return in more detail later. For now, say what you might about this opinion, but one thing it does not do is attribute suicidality to anything related to criminality. My references to Dalrymple's writings are *not* in any way intended to blur the distinction, nor does Dalrymple blur it.

Dalrymple's clinical experiences have clearly impressed upon him the folly of unadvisedly trusting people's post hoc explanations for their behavior, especially behavior about which they may feel ashamed or regarding which they sense others may disapprove. Referring to criminal, not suicidal, behavior, he writes in his book *If Symptoms Persist* (1994), "In my experience, criminals hardly ever know what came over them. They ascribe their absence of mind variously to drink, drugs, their childhood, stress."[6] He continues in that same essay, again specifically about criminal, not suicidal, behavior, "I have a patient who once stabbed a close friend in the chest. He refers to the occasion as 'the night Bill had his accident.'"[7] A similar distancing of one's responsibility from one's own behavior is on fairly regular display when the context shifts from the criminal to the suicidal, a truth that, although being perhaps uncomfortable, is no less true.

In his book *Man against Himself* (1938), still influential, psychiatrist Karl Menninger reported a case that very likely was an example of outward appearances being deceiving in a scenario involving death by suicide. Menninger quoted a news report from March 1935 that described a man's death by self-inflicted gunshot wound. The man's wife heard the shot and rushed to his side. The man survived for a short while, during which he murmured to his wife that he had been asleep and dreaming, and had removed a pistol from underneath his pillow and shot himself while still asleep and in the grip of the dream. Menninger accepted this account at face value, overlooking that those who have just undergone a massive injury are not necessarily reliable historians about what has just happened to them. Menninger's version is not completely impossible, but it seems far more likely that the man purposefully shot himself while awake and then explained the act post hoc as something he did not mean to do. When one is confronted with the frantic question "What have you done?!," it is a universally human commonplace to exclaim, "I didn't mean to." That reaction depends very little on whether one actually meant to or not and applies equally in defense of behaviors mundane (e.g., a child's hand in the cookie jar) and grave (e.g., self-inflicted gunshot wound).

A December 2017 incident is further consistent with the themes that interior experience and intent can be quite discrepant from exterior appearances, and that this applies both to events that are clear suicides and to events, covered in the chapters to follow, that some view as not suicidal but which I argue herein actually are. A family was in the habit of frequenting a local restaurant together. At one dinner, unremarkably at the time, a young adult family member made an innocuous excuse and left somewhat early. He seemed calm and content, and nothing about his comportment occasioned concern in any of his relatives. Minutes later, he killed his girlfriend and then himself.

To family members in incidents like this, the deaths are not just shocking; they are unimaginable, leaving many grasping for explanations along the lines of "he suddenly lost his mind" or "he suddenly wasn't himself." Complicating matters more, of course people actually *can* become acutely psychotic, and they *can* acutely dissociate. However, as difficult as it can be for family members to come to terms with, a far more plausible account is that the eventual decedent harbored suicidal ideas—and, in the case just described, also homicidal ideas—that were concealed from everyone else. In some instances, such ideas are concealed from *almost* everyone else. A key refrain of this book is that suicidal people know what they are doing even if they do not reveal it to others, and that this applies with equal force to phenomena like murder-suicide, suicide-by-cop, and so on.

It is hardly surprising that people sometimes prevaricate regarding suicidal behavior and related phenomena; what is far more surprising is that professionals have often readily believed these explanations—I do not fully understand why, but I suspect that it has to do with the often admirable but occasionally misleading lack of natural cynicism in many mental health professionals. Such beliefs are easily belied, however, and this book strives to do so. As a further foreshadowing, there are instances of distinct and obvious suicide in which the eventual decedents claimed, sometimes with their dying words and other communications like suicide notes, that their deaths were nonsuicidal. This does not make it so; in the pages that follow I attempt to extend this obvious truth to more nonobvious scenarios.

To do this adequately, it is necessary first to see suicide clearly for what it is—a focused, effortful, determined, intent-driven, and ultimately enacted plan to end one's own life, always or virtually always spurred, at least in part, by some form of mental disorder to include, very importantly, mental disorders' subclinical manifestations. This definition of suicide is regularly obscured by common misunderstandings and myths, and thus a deep understanding of suicide requires an undoing of these entrenched barriers to the truth. In my attempt to convey understanding and to thwart misunderstanding, I stake positions that can be viewed as opinionated; the virtue in doing so is that readers either will be persuaded by my views and take satisfaction in having them articulated and in agreeing with them, or they will disagree, in which case they may derive satisfaction from sharpening their own opinions by dissenting from mine. This particular approach is resonant with a neo-Popperian philosophy of science more generally, which avers that theoretical stances that risk falsification prove informative whether they ultimately are falsified or not.

Suicide Rates

Even as astonishing progress is occurring on fronts as varied as biotechnology, nanotechnology, machine learning, space travel, and the treatment of cancer and various other health problems, and even as more attention and resources are paid to suicide prevention, suicide rates are stubbornly rising in some countries, including until recently the United States. The US rate, reasonably representative of some but not all international figures, rose between the early 2000s and 2018, year after year, for fifteen years in a row.

Importantly, that yearly increase is one way in which US trends are *not* reflective of the international numbers. Indeed, during the same period when unrelenting increases in the US suicide rate occurred, the world rate *decreased*. Much of Europe, for example, has represented a success story regarding lowered suicide rates, a success sustained over decades.

Curiously, this fact, which is in glaring need of exploration and explanation, has garnered relatively little interest from the research community, at least to my awareness. I suspect this disinterest stems from the simple facts that most researchers in the suicide prevention research community live and work in the United States and are interested in trends at home. I share those traits and interests; however, exploring the discrepancy between US and international trends seems to me a chance for deeper understanding of what specifically was driving the American suicide rate upward.

What suicide-related drivers are salient in the American context, but less so around the rest of the globe? I have some specific speculations, which are informed by my views about the virtues and the risks of *rugged individualism*. These speculations have at least some relevance to American violence in general, including self-directed violence. Without a firm understanding of this ethos of rugged individualism, it is challenging to fully understand the history, traditions, and culture of the United States (which is not a claim that rugged individualism is uniquely American). Though I am inclined to produce one and quite capable of it, here I do not intend an American paean, and in no case would I attempt to overlook American evils.

The word "individualism" refers of course to self-reliance, and a "rugged" version thereof, to physicality, among other things. A mindset of physicality-imbued self-reliance served American colonists well, as it did American revolutionaries, other warriors, ranchers, agrarians, explorers, and others. But it has costs.

Consider space exploration. The stunning glory of *Apollo 11* required rugged resolve and came at great expense not only in treasure but also in blood. Just two years before Neil Armstrong and Buzz Aldrin walked on the moon, the three astronauts of *Apollo 1* (Gus Grissom, Roger Chaffee, and Ed White) were killed in a fire that ignited in the main astronaut cabin during a launch rehearsal.

Rugged individualism can foster heroism, but it has inured us. In our history, we have shown a glaring capacity for great cruelty, with ongoing reverberations. In our modern sporting life, the most popular American sport, football, virtually unique to the United States, is among the most violent in human history.[8] Our entertainment, at least since the 1970s, is eminently violent (e.g., in movies), a quality that characterizes twenty-first-century innovations in entertainment as well (e.g., gaming). Our history and culture involving guns, uniquely American, have produced the most heavily and lethally armed population in world history, also applicable to our military. There is evidence to suggest that the coming together of American entertainment and American gun culture—as reflected in the use of firearms in prime-time American television shows—is associated with real-life gun violence.[9] "Rugged" can transform—deteriorate—into descriptors like "violent," "brutal," and "savage."

"Individualism," too, can devolve into alienation, loneliness, and despair, and, when it does, can motivate the void-filling, pain-killing effects of opioids and excessive alcohol intake. The "deaths of despair" phenomenon (e.g., opiate overdose, suicide, and cirrhosis deaths) is at least as much a problem in the United States as elsewhere, probably much more so. Rugged individualism can be admirable, and it has played a significant part in the development of the international and historical marvel that is the United States, but the risk of rugged individualism is that it can blend and has blended into perversions of itself (e.g., savagery, drug-addled despair). Factors such as these—a capacity and the tools for violence, a lethal mindset, alienation—are key drivers of suicidal behavior.

I am making points here that overlap with or are neighboring to those made by Ann Case and Angus Deaton in their book *Deaths of Despair and the Future of Capitalism* (2020) and by Robert Putnam in *Bowling Alone* (2000). Regarding Case and Deaton, as their reference to capitalism suggests, their argument is largely economic, attributing deaths of despair mostly to factors like a decrease in jobs that pay a living wage, particularly for certain segments of the population such as white midlife males, living in relatively urban environments, whose educational attainment was, at most, a high school degree. This is a group, I would contend, in whom the appeal of a rugged individualism ethos would be considerable, but who, in part because of the economic factors and processes identified by Case and Deaton, are struggling to enact it.

Given all this, one can ask how could American suicide rates *not* be increasing, as they did from the early 2000s to 2018? It is typical of some quarters of the suicide prevention community to conclude that we are doing nothing right, but I believe that is the wrong stance. For one thing, US suicide deaths decreased in 2019, and then decreased again to an even larger degree in 2020 (fully reliable 2021 data are not yet available, though it appears there was an increase in 2021), despite the isolation, angst, and grief suffered by many due to the COVID-19 pandemic. My view is that we are certainly not helpless, and that our prevention efforts, though highly imperfect and in need of constant improvement, were likely suppressing increases in the suicide rate between the early 2000s and 2018, taking rates that could have been astronomically accelerating and instead bringing them down to their concerning, but moderate, yearly increases. The years 2019 and 2020 may represent the turning of a corner—time will tell—and if they do, it is a considerable accomplishment in the midst of ongoing drivers like an opioid crisis, a pandemic, and an unchanging or enhanced culture of violence.[10]

Even if 2019 and 2020 represented a genuine turning of the tide— and it is important to acknowledge that they may not have—the US rate needs to be lower still, and that is especially true for specific groups. Indeed, the 2019 and 2020 US suicide decreases were pronounced for individuals who are white, but for people of color, much less so. Our aspiration, in my view, is to drive down rates overall, and to do so across all groups.

A culture of violence was no doubt instantiated early in American history, well before late twentieth-century innovations in media, but the 1970s represented an inflection point, a time when savagery was normalized. When I was a child in the 1960s and the early part of the 1970s, a scary movie did not tend to mean a savagely violent one. Films like *Psycho* (1960) and *The Exorcist* (1973) were most definitely scary but explicitly depicted little savagery. Video games of that early era (e.g., *Pong*, 1972) contained none.[11] Yet within just a few years, brutal person-to-person violence became a commonplace (e.g., *Halloween*, 1978; *Friday the 13th*, 1980), and violence in other media like video games was to soon follow.

I believe that that very inflection point (i.e., approximately 1978) is in part responsible for the rise in midlife American suicide that we witness presently. The cohort born in the mid-1960s went through adolescence, a crucial time of development, at the very time of that violent inflection point. Furthermore, it is that cohort, now in their fifties, that is the first in recorded history to have even higher suicide rates than their older counterparts in their sixties and beyond. There are likely other reasons as well for this unexpected shift in the age structure of suicide, but my sense is that the inflection in our culture of violence was one of them.

We have lessons to learn from success stories like those in much of Europe, but I am wary of a "copy Europe" approach coming across as hopelessly naive. One US-European difference is that within Europe there is more of a culture that values safety in general. Later I expand on the importance of means safety—putting distance and/or obstacles between an at-risk person and the potential means of their suicide—but by a "culture of safety," I am not referring only to means safety. I mean a larger effort that leverages typically American values to encourage safety. Imagine, for instance, an individual or family who fully embraces the American ethos of rugged individualism, to the point of going off the grid and living alone in wilderness (cf. the book *The Stranger in the Woods*, which describes a man in Maine named Christopher Knight who did exactly this for almost thirty years, which of course included almost thirty Maine winters).[12] These individuals and families are obsessed with safety because their survival depends on it. Or consider a pattern in military service members uncovered in the research on gun safety by Mike Anestis. Anestis has found that military service members are not especially interested in home gun safety when it involves their own safety, but when it involves the safety of their families or their fellow service members, they become interested indeed.[13] Protecting one's family or concern for one's comrades is not of course uniquely American, although some lack of enthusiasm for gun safety may be; my point is that such factors might be leveraged to realistically enhance a culture of safety in the unique culture of the United States.

Suicide-Related Interventions

Evidence suggests that our failure to suppress suicide rates, at least in the United States, is not for a lack of trying; rather, it may be for a lack of effectiveness and/or a failure to robustly implement measures that we know do work. As interesting context, Joseph Franklin and colleagues (2017) conducted a meta-analysis of studies of predictors of a suicide-related outcome over the last fifty years. For each decade, they calculated the average ability of the predictors to do their job, that is, to accurately predict the occurrence of a suicide-related outcome such as a suicide attempt.[14]

A cliché that has arisen from this study is along the lines of "prediction is no better than a coin flip," but that is an exaggeration (not to mention an annoyance to those of us with editorial duties at suicide-related journals): prediction was at above-chance levels for all decades, and the number of studies focusing on the issue increased geometrically with time, the only pieces of comforting news that can be taken from the review. The extent to which predictive levels were above chance was not especially impressive; predictive accuracy did not increase from the 1960s to the present time (perhaps reflective of the fact that the field is in a sense very young, with researchers proceeding in a number of directions, some potentially contradictory to one another). This difficulty in predicting suicidality is extreme enough that, as things stand, if one's aim were to maximize predictive accuracy and only that, then one should predict "no suicide" every time (because that is almost always the outcome). This has been known for decades, if not centuries; for example, in 1972, George Murphy wrote, "From the numerical standpoint, the prediction of no suicide in every case would be highly accurate. . . . It would also be entirely unacceptable clinically."[15]

In 1960, psychiatrist Alex Pokorny pointed out a paradox that is regularly overlooked. He wrote, "The psychiatrist is 'predicting' suicide by placing a patient on suicidal precautions, but, at the same time, doing [their] best (and enlisting all other help) to keep the prediction from coming true."[16] This surely erodes predictive accuracy.

The increasing number of studies shows that researchers and others are already bringing a sense of urgency to the goal of suicide prediction and prevention, and this same sense of determination is shared by other quarters of our field (e.g., those with lived experience, the bereaved, public health workers). Yet no matter how admirable such urgency and determination are, the findings of Franklin and colleagues indicate that more is needed.

There are voices in the suicide prevention community who wonder, based on the foregoing, if scientific effort is the way forward. They suggest, rather, that perhaps other approaches are needed—often without clarity about exactly what those would entail, or with some clarity combined with a lack of realism—and that perhaps resources should be diverted from research to other efforts. Notice in this thinking the "instead" logic, as opposed to the "in addition to" logic. If the argument were that we should be open to other approaches *in addition to* prevailing ones, my reaction would be "let all flowers bloom."[17] In other words, novel approaches should be broached and should contend on their merits in the arena of ideas. And these individual approaches and areas may synergize with and leverage one another. A former president of the American Association of Suicidology understood this in naming the 2018 annual meeting "Integrating Science, Experience, and Political Will: Informed Action to Prevent Suicide."

The argument I am contesting is "let this new flower bloom, and only it." In suicide prevention research, there is an understandable yearning for statistical models with perfect or near-perfect predictive accuracy—a yearning, that is, for prospection. In prospection, one "reasons forward" in the prediction of specific events (e.g., an individual suicide, a car crash, a plane disaster), as opposed to "reasoning backward" once something has happened. Each approach has merit, and the one has nothing necessarily to do with the other. In "reasoning backward," we have saved millions of lives by learning from specific events like car and plane crashes, though it remains difficult to prospectively predict individual accidents.

To this, one could counter that suicide rates have gone up, not down, and thus "reasoning backward" has done nothing. But this ignores the fact that rates have gone down worldwide and in the United States in 2019 and 2020, as well as the very real possibility, already noted, that they would have gone up *more* but for our efforts. Clearly, we are swimming against the tide, given factors like the opioid crisis, a clearly more violent culture (not necessarily in crimes but in outlets like media), increased access to ever more lethal guns, and a dissolution of family and community closeness. (How many of your neighbors can you name these days? For readers of a certain age, how many could you name back in the 1960s and 1970s?)[18]

To narrow our ken to only one or a few approaches would lead, over decades, to an atrocity—specifically, to tens or even hundreds of thousands of excess suicides, at a time when we might be approaching or even in the midst of, scientifically and otherwise, a turning point, when we begin to drive rates down. Antiscience views have a truly dismal record of solving problems, and an appalling one of killing people and of

14 | INTRODUCTION

making them sick. Science is far from flawless; it is, after all, a human endeavor, and therefore, like any other human effort, imperfect. Just as democracy is a very imperfect form of government and yet, to paraphrase Churchill, the least imperfect, so science is a flawed way of knowing things and solving problems, but the least flawed. A scientific approach is essential to fostering suicide prevention, as well as prevention of the other suicide-involved forms of violence covered in this book.

Means Safety

Having touched on areas both of slow progress and also of promise in current suicide research and prevention, I turn now to a clear area of considerable progress—means safety, one of the few and perhaps only approach(es) in the suicide prevention community with close to universal consensus behind it.

As alluded to earlier, the term "means safety" refers to a collection of approaches that increase the distance between an at-risk individual and the suicide method—the means—that an individual is considering to bring about death. One of the clearer examples involves barriers at bridges that are high enough that a jump from the bridge results in death. One such bridge is located in the state of Maine, the Memorial Bridge in Augusta, where a barrier was installed in 1983. Before then, at least fourteen suicides had occurred from the bridge, at least six of them by patients from the nearby Augusta Mental Health Institute. The barrier is constructed in such a way that it is virtually impossible to scale, in part because the fence curves inward near the top. My understanding is that there have been no suicides from the bridge since the barrier was erected.[19]

This does not exclude the possibility, of course, that those deterred at the Memorial Bridge found some other site from which to jump, or selected another suicide method. Indeed, exactly this notion was expressed in 2017, again in Maine, this time regarding the possibility of a bridge barrier at a different location, the Penobscot Narrows Bridge. At least two people jumped to their deaths from that location in the first six months of 2017 alone; a barrier would cost approximately $750,000. An official who represents communities on both sides of the bridge proposed a barrier and was told by members of the relevant committee that suicidal people, if prevented from jumping at the bridge, would simply "find another way."[20]

It is not incoherent or implausible that suicidal people may do exactly this. But, in actual fact, do they?

A partial answer and a classic demonstration of the effectiveness of bridge barriers were described by Lanny Berman and colleagues in the 1980s regarding two bridges in the Washington, DC, area. One bridge—the Ellington—was the site from which an average of four people jumped to their deaths each year. At a nearby bridge—the Taft, close enough to the Ellington to be visible from it—an annual average of two deaths by suicide occurred. In early 1986, a barrier to jumping was erected at the Ellington, consisting of an iron-bar fence of a height of about seven feet. Two additional features of the fence are notable. First, its iron bars are arrayed vertically, and thus there are few footholds for climbing. Second, the tops of the bars are curved slightly inward, toward anyone considering jumping, further discouraging the scaling of the structure. Nevertheless, the structure is not all that imposing; in a May 2019 visit to our nation's capital, I happened to drive by it and was struck by the impression that although it is a barrier to be sure, it seems hardly a fail-safe one (but see later discussion). All the while, no barrier was installed at the Taft Bridge; though not purposeful, this allowed for the Taft to serve as a naturally occurring control condition to the now-fenced Ellington.

What happened thereafter? In the ensuing four years after barrier installation in 1986, there were literally no suicides at all from the Ellington. This outcome is worth lingering over; the mere installation of a barrier—to boot one that discourages jumping but does not render it impossible—prevented sixteen suicides in the four years after its installation. Unless, that is, suicidal people who felt thwarted at the Ellington spotted the Taft through the Ellington's iron bar fence—to repeat, the Taft is plainly visible from the Ellington—and decided to simply leave the Ellington, make their way over to the Taft, and there jump to their deaths off the barrier-free bridge. Such a result would be damning to the "nudge" perspective I am articulating here as well as to the larger means safety enterprise.

But that was not the result; suicides at the Taft did not increase. That the rate held steady contradicts the possibility of *means substitution*—a particular suicide method being substituted for another that was restricted. This is a quite remarkable result, because one might expect that as word spread over time of a barrier at the Ellington, suicidal individuals would stop going to the Ellington and instead proceed directly to the Taft or another unrestricted high place. Indeed, there is some evidence for a pattern in this direction from a meta-analytic review conducted by Jane Pirkis and colleagues.[21] Their work revealed a very strong effect supporting the effectiveness of means safety, as well as substantially weaker but nonzero support for means substitution at other local suicide hot spots; the relative strength of the means safety effect and the relative weakness of the means substitution effect are important to emphasize. Overall, then, the Pirkis et al. review indicated a net decrease in suicide deaths due to means safety installations. A likely explanation for this pattern of findings is that means safety deters individuals who choose a specific spot with a barrier—and may deter them from suicide in general—but also that suicidal people who know in advance that a specific spot is restricted may therefore select other, unrestricted spots to begin with, at which suicide rates rise somewhat but not nearly enough to offset the lives saved at the restricted spot.

In this regard, it may be relevant that the research on the Ellington and Taft occurred before the existence of the internet, whereas the review of Pirkis and colleagues included post-internet studies. The internet may be a likely medium through which people, including suicidal people, learn of whether or not a barrier exists at a particular high place; indeed, online searches are now common as a prelude to suicide attempts. For this reason, a pre-internet barrier may not have been as subject to substitution phenomena as would be a post-internet barrier.

The result from the two DC area bridges is consistent with this possibility, as are results from a study on the Golden Gate Bridge published in the 1970s.[22] The study posed a simple but very informative question: Of 515 suicidal people saved by authorities just before a jump from the bridge, where are they now? A perspective emphasizing means substitution would predict that many or even most of these individuals would be dead by suicide, having subsequently chosen a different location or method after having been restrained at the bridge. By contrast, a "nudge" perspective as well as an emphasis on means safety would lead one to expect that most of these people would be alive, years or even decades later. The findings decidedly support the latter view—approximately 95% of the sample had not died by suicide in the years following their suicidal crises at the bridge.

It is important to note that most suicides do not occur at bridges; indeed, approximately 80% occur in people's homes.[23] This underscores how crucial it is that means safety be distributed well beyond bridges.

Means safety is a form of deterrence; another interesting example of deterrence comes from Belgium, where families of suicide decedents who die on railways are by law required to compensate rail companies for the associated expense, such as the cost of repairing damaged trains. It is estimated that the total expense of such deaths between 2013 and 2015 was approximately 2 million euros, which is just over $2.3 million, of which around one-third was recovered by Belgian rail firms from families. The average cost to rail firms per suicide death was approximately 8,500 euros. Belgium's transport minister emphasized that the process of the claims was done "respectfully" toward families, and that ideally claims are handled by third parties like an insurance company so that the family is not directly billed.[24] He added that the law allows the families to be sued for compensation for the emotional stress suffered by train drivers; the latter is, in fact, an issue, as several reports of post-traumatic stress disorder (PTSD) in rail personnel who witnessed suicides have been documented.

Personally, I find this law and approach distasteful. As I will have occasion to point out again, suicide runs in my family, and to imagine a bill arriving in the mail in the midst of the shock and agony of a loved one's suicide is painful. From more of a remove, I acknowledge that the practice may deter one or more suicides; indeed, if, as I contend, a main driver of suicide is the misperception that everyone will be better off, then the realization that one's death will cost one's family thousands of dollars to rail companies, beyond all other costs emotional and financial, may tip the balance toward life. Is the prevention of even one death by suicide worth the additional pain bereaved families may feel by receiving a bill like that? I think it probably is; still, because we were distinctly not at a remove, I would have deeply resented getting a bill like that.

Nudges away from suicide, like those represented by means safety interventions, can be a fraught topic, in part because people have trouble believing that they will work, and even if they will, some may question whether their pragmatic and other challenges are worth the trouble. Indeed, this interplay of concerns was the main reason it has taken decades to proceed with a barrier at the Golden Gate Bridge.

Means safety interventions to prevent deaths by self-inflicted gunshot wounds represent a fraught but essential topic as well. The recent work of psychologist Mike Anestis and others leaves little doubt that gun access is facilitative of suicide (and one need not question the Second Amendment to assert this clear empirical reality). In day-to-day work that goes on at the psychotherapy clinic I direct, this issue arises regularly. For context, it is important to note that the clinic is in Tallahassee, Florida, and that although Tallahassee itself leans politically somewhat to the left, the surrounding region—in which many of our patients currently reside, are originally from, or both—leans to the right, is rural, and has high rates of gun ownership. Initial conversations about gun safety thus tend to be somewhat tense. Soon enough, however, the tension lessens, as the therapist states something like the following: "I'm not really as interested in gun removal or restriction as I am in gun safety, especially during times of suicide risk. What would you say to the idea of putting at least some additional physical distance between you and your gun for now? For example, you mentioned the gun is unlocked, loaded, and within arm's reach in the nightstand next to your bed. What if we altered one or more of those parameters—how about locked instead of unlocked, no ammo instead of loaded, out of arm's reach instead of within it?"

Notice how this phrasing handles two dimensions: the fear messaging and the issue of temporariness. The phrasing is purposefully low in fear messaging and high in emphasis of temporariness. There is reason to believe that this combination is the most likely to lead to the acceptability and effectiveness of gun safety conversations.

The doctoral dissertation of my former student Ian Stanley examined this very issue. Approximately a hundred participants, all with a lifetime history of suicidal ideation and with firearm familiarity (i.e., own a gun, have access to a gun, or desire or intend to obtain a gun in the future), were randomized to one of four groups, all of which were exposed to gun safety messaging. The groups varied across the two dimensions of how *temporary* any needed separation from one's gun would be, and how many *fear appeals* (e.g., "guns are dangerous") participants were exposed to. The four groups were thus (1) temporariness emphasized as was danger, (2) temporariness emphasized but not danger, (3) temporariness de-emphasized but danger emphasized, and (4) temporariness de-emphasized as was danger.

We suspected that either group 2 (with temporariness emphasized and few fear appeals) or both groups 1 and 2 (which both saw temporariness emphasized) would see the greater effectiveness of messaging both right after the messaging and a month later. In fact, both groups exposed to temporariness-heavy messaging stated more intentions to adhere to clinicians' recommendations regarding safety, both immediately after the intervention and one month later. We viewed this as a favorable outcome for a couple of reasons: first, it shows that attitudes toward gun safety are malleable among those relatively pro-gun in their values and attitudes; and, second, a relatively uncontroversial leverage point—namely, temporariness—won out over the more controversial topic of dangerousness. Thus, safety messaging can be enacted in an effective, relatively uncontroversial manner.

Returning to the conversations we routinely have about gun safety in our clinic, roughly half the time these conversations result in at least a little physical distance between the weapon and the patient, at least as reported by the latter, and the goal going forward is to increase this distance in the ensuing weeks, inch by inch if necessary. For the half who refuse to put physical distance between the gun and themselves, it is our impression that the conversations have nonetheless created a form of distance between lethal means and patients—specifically, *psychological* distance. Consistent with a theme of this chapter, suicide is not just physically daunting; it is mentally difficult, requiring focused intent. Thus, just as any physical distance created between an at-risk person and lethal means makes the journey toward death even more arduous, any psychological distance between a vulnerable individual and a suicide method makes the mental journey toward suicide even more effortful.[25]

Intent to die by suicide is a key concept. In fact, though it would be an admittedly hollow thought exercise, if I were limited to one question regarding suicide risk, it would be regarding suicidal intent; the way we often assess it clinically is to simply ask people to rate themselves on a scale from zero (intent is absent) to 10 (extremely high intent). There are other useful ways to assess the construct, as I will discuss shortly. Most people who go on to die by suicide express their intent to do so in the hours and days leading up to their deaths; these communications are often to family, friends, physicians, clergy, co-workers, and the like. In psychiatrist Eli Robins's classic psychological autopsy study of 134 suicide decedents whose relatives, friends, and others were interviewed after the deaths, it was found that approximately 70% of soon-to-be suicide decedents communicated their intent to die. Of course, this means that around 30% gave no indication at all.[26] These kinds of findings were a primary reason that in our own study on physical and psychological closeness we were interested in increases in expressions of suicidal intent.[27] Our study results supported the relevance of both psychological and physical closeness; if anything, effects for psychological distance were more robust than were those for physical distance.

The concept of psychological distance deserves further explication. Just as psychological and physical closeness are nonoverlapping, my group's view of psychological closeness is that it is not isomorphic with suicide intent itself, though it is inescapable that the two concepts are related.[28] Indeed, high intent is rare absent psychological closeness; crucially, however, the obverse is not true. That is, one can feel psychologically close to a method without any suicidal intent whatsoever. For instance, many physicians will endorse a psychological closeness—in the sense of extensive knowledge and thorough familiarity—with methods of death, but have no suicidal intent at all, just as many gun enthusiasts feel psychologically close to weapons, passionately so for some, yet may harbor no suicidal feelings at all. Of course, it is also true that physicians and gun owners prove more lethal than many others, should suicidality develop in them.

Another way to understand psychological closeness regarding suicide method is to consider its opposite, which is a sense that the method in question is unimaginable, alien, or foreign. Regarding such methods, a person asked about them may, with a surprised demeanor, say things like, "I wouldn't even know where to begin." By contrast, methods that seem within the ken, capacity, and comfort zone of a given individual are those with which that individual can be said to feel psychological closeness. This same principle applies to the varieties of suicidal experiences covered throughout the book; if one queries a random person about their potential as a suicide terrorist, for example, one is likely to elicit a reaction including surprise, bewilderment, possibly anger, disgust, and so on. A response completely lacking in all these qualities would be peculiar—except in those pondering just such an act.

Another angle on the concept of means safety is that means safety discussions with clinicians add another voice for life and against death in the ambivalent mental debate characteristic of the suicidal mind. There are usually already voices for life, including those of family members and friends, not to mention the almost if not totally inextinguishable self-preservation motive. The addition of one more voice may constitute a full enough chorus against death to prevent it.

How does means safety work? Some believe the main mechanism involves impulsivity—more specifically, that an impulsive resort to a lethal method may be prevented by distance from that method, allowing the impulse to pass. Perhaps occasionally this is so, but the role of spur-of-the-moment processes in lethal suicidality is dubious.[29] A more likely mechanism involves ambivalence.

Ambivalence is a key concept in a thorough understanding of the suicidal mindset and can help solve mysteries that some suicides appear to present. A deceased man in England represents a potentially illuminating example. His body was discovered in a moor, near Manchester, relatively far from where the man lived, and the circumstances were such that they indicated suicide. He had traveled there by train; very little in the way of identifying information was found on him, with the exception of a train ticket. Police were puzzled by it, because it was a round-trip ticket. Why, police wondered, buy a round-trip ticket if one's intention is to travel just from one place to another to die by suicide? A reasonable answer to this question involves ambivalence; when he bought the ticket, his ambivalence about suicide might have been substantial, and it may have resolved as he traveled, making the return part of the ticket unneeded. One might counter that the case could illustrate the role of impulsivity, in that perhaps the man decided to die in the moment as he traveled on the train. However, the article describing the death noted that it was by strychnine poisoning, which the man had brought with him.[30]

Ambivalence is one reason that means safety works; the latter either keeps the ambivalence going or it resolves it in favor of life. Even among those who are aware that means safety saves lives, however, it is common to imagine that it is applicable only to methods like a self-inflicted gunshot wound. After all, this line of thought goes, things like sharp objects, ligatures, and over-the-counter medications are so ubiquitous that they are impossible to keep safe. However, this perspective overlooks an essential aspect of the suicidal mind, namely, that the intently suicidal focus not on abstract categories like "ligatures," "knives," or "medications" but rather on concrete, specific objects, such as a particular knife, belt, cord, or set of scarves, or a particular container of pills. Although it is true that it is challenging to restrict access to all possible ligatures, medications, and sharp objects, it is also true that it is quite feasible to put distance between an at-risk person and a specific ligature, medication container, or sharp object.

The same logic applies to the method of a jump from a high place. In many areas, such places too are ubiquitous, and yet despite this, a particular high place sees more suicides than do comparable sites nearby. We have already encountered one example of this regarding the DC area bridges. Before a barrier was installed, the annual rate from one bridge was four per year; the rate at a nearby bridge with similar lethality was half that, at two per year. An even more dramatically clear example again involves the Golden Gate Bridge, from which, over the last many years, more than forty lethal suicide jumps per year occurred (and occasional nonlethal ones too, more on which soon, because they are uniquely revealing in their own right regarding the true nature of suicidal behavior). As all these deaths are occurring at the Golden Gate, very few take place at the Bay Bridge, quite close to the Golden Gate, and similarly lethal.

Why do some sites become frequent spots for suicide, whereas other comparable ones do not? There are surely numerous and varied reasons, such as ease of access (relevant in itself to means safety efforts), but a major factor involves the site's demonstrated feasibility as a lethal locale. That is, the implicit message received by at-risk people upon learning of the suicide death of a fellow citizen at a particular place is along the lines of "That person was able to do it there, which means that I could too." Relatedly, people having died at a particular locale may reduce its psychological distance for other at-risk people.

Of course, some deaths from a high place occur from high-rise apartments or offices. Here, too, a usual reaction among even fairly experienced clinicians is that means safety is not possible among people who are contemplating a jump from a high place and who, for example, live in a high-rise apartment. It is an obvious but neglected point that means safety can occur in the form of sealing access to windows and other forms of egress. Might it be impossible to fully restrict access due to things like fire codes? Perhaps, but yet again, any distance between an at-risk person and any form of a suicide method is clinically valuable. At our clinic at Florida State University, for patients pondering a jump from their apartment block, we have counseled at least the consideration of moving to a residence that is not at height, on the logic that a patient here or there might actually move to a lower, safer locale, and for the majority who do not, the suggestion may nonetheless spur psychological distance between patients and the prospect of a jump from a height.

It should be acknowledged that there are some instances of suicide—and also of the varieties of suicidal experience covered in this book—in which it is difficult to detect much if any ambivalence at all. A phenomenon known as "complex suicide" is illustrative.[31] These are suicide deaths in which one method is tried, the person survives, and then another method is tried, and so on, until the person eventually dies. For example, a woman drove her car off the rim of the Grand Canyon, an act that is highly likely to prove fatal. But it did not in the case of the woman because the car's suspension became stuck in an outcropping of rock. The woman next extricated herself from the damaged car and jumped off a ledge, only to find herself alive, conscious, and quite injured, on a lower ledge. Despite her considerable injuries, she forced herself to crawl to yet another ledge and fell off of it to her death.

In cases like these, ambivalence seems to be lacking. Importantly, and consistent with the view that ambivalence almost always characterizes even the most severely suicidal, these kinds of suicides are rare (e.g., approximately three out of one hundred suicides). Some of the varieties of suicidal experience covered later in the book are such that they eliminate or minimize suicide's ambivalent aspect by precipitating others to do the killing (e.g., as in suicide-by-cop or death row volunteering; physician-assisted suicide can be seen as an additional, more controversial example of this phenomenon).

How else, besides assigning killing to another, to eliminate or minimize one's suicide-related ambivalence? In the case, described earlier, of the woman who persisted in her suicide at the Grand Canyon, there is evidence that she had seen the film *Thelma and Louise* approximately fifty times in the time frame before her death; the film's final scene depicts two women driving to their deaths off of a canyon ledge. This amount of desensitization to the prospect of driving off a cliff to one's death—together with other such activities in which the woman might have engaged (e.g., visiting the Grand Canyon previously)—may serve the function of decreasing or possibly even eliminating one's ambivalence about suicide. This possibility, as we will see, would be consistent with the percepts on the interpersonal theory of suicide (as well as other similar models), which will be discussed in chapter 1.

Means safety, or rather its absence, was central to a controversial decision in 2017 by a Massachusetts judge finding a young woman guilty of involuntary manslaughter via her texts and other communications to her suicidal male friend. In the days and weeks before his suicide, like the majority of eventual suicide decedents, the young man expressed ambivalence in numerous ways, including with regard to method choice and the logistics of the specific method of carbon monoxide poisoning in his car. Had the young woman expressed alarm and abhorrence regarding the prospect of his loss, or even dispassionately discouraged consideration of methods, chances are substantial that the suicide would not have occurred. But she repeatedly encouraged method consideration, including suggestions on which device to use and on location of death. Most egregiously, when the young man hesitated during actual exposure to carbon monoxide, even to the degree that he removed himself from it, she urged that he reenter the car and continue with his suicide. Evidence was presented at trial that the two were on the phone as the young man died; the woman did not alert his family or authorities. (The deceased young man's mother filed a civil action against the woman; a judge dismissed the case, but her criminal conviction stands.

The woman's lawyers filed an appeal of her conviction to the US Supreme Court, which the court declined to hear in 2020, leaving in place her conviction.)[32]

The case has spurred controversy, and my own belief is that the controversy arises from two sources, one explicit and the other usually unspoken and perhaps even out of the full awareness of those who dispute the judge's decision. The explicit source has to do with free speech; it is for this reason that the Massachusetts chapter of the American Civil Liberties Union denounced the verdict as a violation of constitutionally guaranteed free speech protections, and also it was on this basis that the woman's lawyers appealed to the Supreme Court. The implicit source of displeasure with this verdict, I suspect, stems from a sense that suicide arises from within the person and that once it does, there is an inevitable quality to its proceeding, one that others cannot affect even if they try.

Were this true, the involuntary manslaughter verdict would be hard to defend, because on this view, the young man along with his illness would be solely responsible for his death. And indeed, the young man and his illness clearly had substantial responsibility in the tragedy, and one could argue that they had full responsibility for his initiating a suicide attempt (though here, too, the young woman encouraged him to attempt). When it comes to his attempt culminating in his death, however, given the marked ambivalence he displayed in word and in deed, I suspect the young man, as anguished as he plainly was, and his illness, as serious as it was, were insufficient to lead him across the threshold of death. The young woman's actions seem partly responsible for leading him across this threshold, according to the judge's decision.

Means safety was also in the news in Colorado in January 2017. The issue was the renovation of nine bathrooms at a state mental hospital, at a total cost of approximately $235,000; the reason for the renovations was to remove the bathrooms' ligature points, an intervention highly likely to prevent multiple suicides by hanging per year in the years after the renovation. By far the main benefit would be the prevention of these deaths, but consider other advantages to the state, such as preventing state mental health workers the stress (often traumatic stress) of discovering a decedent and the frantic travail of calling for help and trying to resuscitate the individual. In legal consulting work, I have seen exactly such scenes recorded by surveillance cameras. Often, both the suicide death itself and the panicked aftermath of the discovery of the body are recorded; both are acutely painful to watch even at a remove, which suggests they are many orders of magnitude more painful to experience directly. Consider further the shielding of the state from increased legal liability, which can be considerable in the wake of suicides in health care facilities. Certain lawmakers, however, questioned the intervention, and its ultimate fate is thus unclear. Their questions were focused on the price tag—indeed, the cost per bathroom was over $25,000—and were the questions limited to that, they might be fair. But they were not; along with budget concerns came doubts of whether such an intervention would be "worth the trouble" and actually prevent any deaths. It would.

Two further anecdotes, one involving a near-death scenario and the other culminating in a very tragic death, are revealing regarding the importance and potential of means safety. The near-death example is representative of the very few people who are fortunate enough to survive the almost-always lethal jump from the Golden Gate Bridge, as did Kevin Hines, author of the book *Cracked, Not Broken* (2013). Mr. Hines writes and speaks convincingly and with passion about his suffering from bipolar disorder; his planful resolve and intent to jump to his death; his feeling of social isolation in the moments before he jumped; his fearlessness as he jumped and in the first second or two as he plummeted toward the waters below; and the gripping, mortal fear and regret that overtook him in the two remaining seconds before impact.[33] The contours of this account square well with those who also happened to survive, and show that fear and self-preservation activate even in the most fearless, and further reveal a deeply tragic truth, namely, that if the few survivors report midair regret and fear, it is likely that those who perished experienced these too.

The other example, this one alas lethal, also involves a mental disorder—in this instance, anorexia nervosa—and also involves the activation of fear and regret even in a resolved and fearless individual. The suicide method was the ingestion of a powerful household cleaning product, one so noxious that for most people ingestion of even a drop would prove so aversive that a teargas-like reaction would ensue and incapacitate them. Incapacitate them, that is, to the point that they would be unable to do much of anything, certainly unable to do something so difficult as ingesting the rest of an entire container of the substance. But that is exactly what the person in question managed to do. What was the very next behavior emitted by this fearless person? It was to call 911 in fear, extreme pain, desperation, and regret. Emergency services got her to the hospital and into the operating room within minutes, but to no avail, as her internal injuries were too extensive.

In both of these cases, means safety measures could have proved pivotal. A bridge barrier at the Golden Gate Bridge might well have halted Mr. Hines's ordeal before suicidal ideation led to suicidal behavior, just as less toxicity in the cleaning solution may have allowed the survival of the woman with anorexia nervosa.

Other Suicide-Related Interventions

The US Department of Defense, if not the world's top funder of scientific research, is among the top few, and it is definitely the world's leading funder of suicide prevention research. Though in need of continued scrutiny and replication, a set of suicide-related intervention techniques stemming from work funded by the Military Suicide Research Consortium holds promise.[34]

One example involves research on improving marital satisfaction, in a somewhat surprising way, by Florida State University social psychologist Jim McNulty.[35] Before describing the surprising approach, it is important to first set the context. Not only has the suicide death rate in the US military worryingly increased in recent times, but evidence suggests that military life can represent a serious stress on relationships with family and with romantic partners, and that one of the most common triggers for death by suicide in the military as elsewhere is strife in romantic relationships.[36] For these reasons, interventions that protect relationships from military-related and other strains are of high interest. However, many current such interventions are time-intensive or otherwise not well suited for the tempo and pragmatics of military service. What is needed is something brief, highly portable, engaging, and in tune (or at least not obviously out of tune) with military life and culture, but that still retains good effectiveness.

McNulty's intervention is to my knowledge one of the leading candidates that meet all these criteria. It involves simple pairings of images of one's romantic partner with positively valenced images like those of ice cream, flowers, babies' faces, and puppies. The surprising thing is that this is all it involves; not only that, but participants who are experiencing the intervention are not necessarily explicitly aware of the pairings. Nevertheless, these pairings have a detectable effect on marital satisfaction, one that lasts for many weeks; that is, as compared to a control condition in which participants saw pairings of images of their partners and neutral things (e.g., a chair), those who experienced the positive pairings rated their relationships as better, across measurement formats and over the course of several weeks. Crucially, in subsequent work, it has been shown that these improvements in relationship satisfaction have "knock-on" effects, leading to lowered suicide risk.

This approach is of interest for many reasons, including that it can be repurposed to target any number of issues. Moreover, given its computerized, easy, and pleasant nature, one could imagine it and other approaches like it being adapted to other delivery platforms. Consider, in this regard, a study led by psychologist Kate Comtois of the University of Washington.[37] The effort can be seen as a twenty-first-century update on and replication of classic twentieth-century work known as the "caring letters" study. In the classic original, psychiatrist Jerome Motto recruited hundreds of participants, all of whom were enrolled in acute care mental health treatment for mental disorders of at least moderate severity.[38] As they were discharged from acute care to treatment as usual in the community, they were randomized to one of two groups: (1) treatment as usual plus a brief, regular mail letter, written by clinical staff to patients every so often, expressing support, caring, and encouragement, and reminding them of access to care; or (2) treatment as usual alone. Patients were tracked for years subsequently, with a particular focus on deaths by suicide.

The bottom line of Motto's study was that there were fewer deaths by suicide in the "caring letters" group than in the comparison group. This would be of interest in any case, but it becomes even more so when it is noted that this difference achieved statistical significance, at least in some analyses, notable when the base rate of an outcome is as relatively low as that for death by suicide.

This remarkable result is among an elite few in demonstrating clinically and statistically significant effects on the downstream target of death by suicide (there have been other trials doing this on the targets of suicidal ideation, and some on nonlethal suicide attempt, but very few on death by suicide).

The Comtois replication project chose as its target nonlethal suicide attempt—though inarguably not as serious as death by suicide, nonetheless a plainly serious clinical issue—and chose as its sample US Marines and soldiers at installations in the Pacific Northwest, a timely choice given the concern about suicidal behavior in those in uniform. The design of the study mimicked the original, except that instead of receiving caring letters through regular mail, participants received caring texts through their mobile devices.

It is interesting to ponder the differences between twentieth-century regular mail and twenty-first-century texting. In a given day in the twentieth century, what proportion of the population wrote more than one letter per day? I have found it challenging to nail down a figure, but, especially given the predominance of the telephone in the second half of the twentieth century and the wave of email that crashed in its last decade, it is hard to imagine the percentage being other than minuscule. In the twenty-first century, by contrast, more than 50% of young people who text send at least fifty texts per day.[39] It follows that texts—in this case caring texts—may be a promising medium for suicide prevention.

In the Comtois study, user parameters (e.g., acceptability, friendliness, ease) were favorable, and reply texts showing high risk were very rare (i.e., only five of more than one thousand). More important, caring texts worked, at least regarding some important targets. As compared with the study's control condition participants (who received treatment as usual via behavioral health care at their installation), those whose usual care was enhanced by caring texts fared better. Over the course of the twelve-month follow-up, the odds of having extreme suicidal ideation were 45% lower, and the odds of a suicide attempt 40% lower, among caring texts than control participants. A relatively small dose of simple caring exerted disproportionately large effects.

As mentioned earlier, participants generally enjoyed the caring texts experience; one could imagine such interventions being developed in an even more engaging way, namely, a gaming environment. Indeed, psychologist Joe Franklin has developed just such an intervention as a way to reduce self-injury and suicide-proneness.[40] Whereas McNulty targeted an issue (i.e., marital satisfaction) by augmenting its association with positive things, Franklin's approach targets an issue (i.e., self-harm) by discouraging it via its pairing with negative things. This approach has promise, in that it has been shown, for example, that media suicide stories based on negative suicide-related images (e.g., images of bodies at Jonestown) were less likely to exert a suicide copycat effect as compared with stories without such images.[41] Regarding Franklin's intervention specifically, it pairs pictures of aversive images (e.g., snakes, spiders) with images related to self-injury (e.g., a blade pressed to the skin, pills for potential overdose). The approach worked so well in reducing self-harm that Franklin and his team had trouble believing their own results, and so conducted two additional studies with similar aims and methodology and with similar findings. One caveat is that effects did not last as assessed at one-month follow-up. Interestingly in the twenty-first-century context of a gaming culture, Franklin and colleagues' intervention resembles a game, and they showed that participants enjoyed the intervention much as they would a game they played purely for entertainment.

Approaches like the marital intervention, caring texts, and the game-like pairing of self-injury and aversive images are simple, and of course that is part of their appeal. The successes of McNulty (marital intervention), Comtois (caring texts), and Franklin (aversive and self-injury images) suggest that minds are malleable across many domains, such as marital satisfaction and reduced suicide risk, and in this, they resemble "nudge"-based approaches to things like automatic opt-ins to retirement savings plans and organ donor programs.[42] That is, small pushes, like simple pairings of things with either positive or negative stimuli, like caring messages, or like "nudging" choice architecture from an active to a passive opt-in, tweak the mind.

These interventions are hopeful. But for any intervention or approach to make a lasting and large-scale difference, it needs to be widely disseminated and implemented. Dissemination and implementation researchers have made a start regarding suicide-related interventions, but these remain very early days. Until this work and research mature—and until we as a society summon the political, emotional, and financial will to conduct a "full-court press" on suicide like we did on cancer in the 1950s and thereafter—US suicide prevention writ large is likely to remain a significant challenge.

The Suicidal Mindset: Misunderstandings and Debates

An intriguing example of misunderstanding relates to the involvement of the misuse of alcohol and other drugs in suicide. Focusing on the exemplar of alcohol misuse, to fully understand its role, the concept of a time frame is essential, because the role varies significantly depending on the particular time frame. If the time frame is the months and years leading up to a death by suicide, then the evidence indicates that alcohol abuse plays a very prominent, probably partly causal role in later death by suicide. One way to understand the mechanism of alcohol abuse's long-term effect on later suicide is in light of the elements of the interpersonal theory of suicide, which will be explored in chapter 1.[43] In a nutshell, the theory predicts that suicide occurs when three factors come together: fearlessness of the prospect of death and (for many methods) fearlessness of the pain involved; the intractable sense that one is a substantial burden on others; and the intractable belief that one is socially alienated. Long-term alcohol abuse and its sequelae like accidents, fights, financial difficulties, legal troubles, and relationship disruption may habituate users to physical hardship, may burden others, and may create alienation from them, all of which, in turn, may spur suicidal behavior.

The story is different, however, when the time frame shifts from the months and years before suicide to the minutes and hours preceding it. Whereas the long-term buildup to suicide frequently involves alcohol misuse, the minutes and hours before suicide tend not to involve alcohol *use*, much less alcohol abuse. My own awareness of this truth stemmed from a postmortem study of suicide decedents who had died by self-inflicted knife wound in the 1980s and 1990s in Stockholm, Sweden. Findings revealed that the vast majority of decedents had very little alcohol in their system at the time of death; in fact, a large number had no alcohol whatsoever in their blood.

It is key to reiterate that I am *not* arguing that substance misuse plays no role in the suicidal process. Rather, I am attempting to be more precise about exactly what this role is and when it is operative (i.e., more in the long-term than in the short-term time frame). Moreover, I am *not* contending that substances are never or rarely involved in the short-term buildup to suicide; rather, I am arguing that, when it comes specifically to *death by suicide* (as opposed to thoughts or nonlethal behaviors), intake of alcohol and other drugs is, more often than not, absent.

I have presented this finding several times in seminars, workshops, and the like and quickly learned that it leaves audiences incredulous.[44] More specifically, beyond simply not believing the result, audience members had reasonable questions as to whether the finding might be specific to Sweden, to deaths involving knife wounds, or to alcohol versus other drugs. In response, my colleagues and I compiled the results of all such studies we could find from around the world across all suicide methods.[45] Our findings confirmed the generalizability of the Swedish study across methods and regarding other drugs; most suicide decedents were not drinking alcohol or ingesting other drugs, much less intoxicated by them, at the time of their deaths. I see our meta-analysis as definitive on this question, as it is to my knowledge the most up-to-date and systematic summary of the entire available literature. It did not of course include studies and reports published subsequently, all of which I have not meticulously tracked. Nevertheless, I have seen a fair number, and it is my impression that they triangulate well on the findings we reported in our meta-analysis.

At first glance, this overall pattern may seem perplexing—how can it be that alcohol is so clearly involved in the long-term lead-up to suicide and yet not as much involved in the short-term time frame before suicide? The answer returns to a key theme of this book: that suicide is hard and that therefore any obstacle on the pathway to suicide looms large. A positive memory of an image of one's romantic partner, a negative one pairing self-harm with aversive stimuli, a caring text, a means safety intervention, a voice advocating for life, or a cognitive load in the form of alcohol intoxication all may represent just such an obstacle. My colleagues and I were not the first to notice this latter reality; a worker in the field in 1928 wrote, "It is altogether possible that the drunken [person] may be less sure of success in [their] attempts at self-destruction than the [person] in complete control of [their] mental faculties."[46]

Another common reaction to the fact that suicide decedents were only rarely drinking heavily in the minutes and hours before death occurs in those familiar with day-to-day work in emergency room settings. Such professionals will often protest the result, saying something like

"But we see so many intoxicated suicide attempters in the emergency room, how can that be right?" My typical reply is along the lines of "You said suicide *attempters*. The finding is not relevant to that group—among whom, by the way, it is true that intoxication rates are sometimes high. Rather, the finding is about suicide *decedents*, who are a distinct group." And, to boot, intoxication levels are not *always* elevated in emergency settings: researchers in Great Britain examined 7,270 consecutive hospital admissions for suicide attempt via intentional self-poisoning. Even though these were all attempters, not decedents, most were negative for alcohol, specifically, 4,636 of 7,270, or 63.8%.[47]

This view of alcohol's role in suicidality will be pondered again later in this book in my discussions of other varieties of suicidal experience. For now, based on the foregoing, a prediction is that behaviors that involve both dying and killing are harder, and therefore alcohol ingestion is unlikely to be involved at the time, whereas behaviors that involve only dying and not actively killing (e.g., suicide-by-cop), though very far from easy, are easier, and thus may be somewhat more likely to be associated with alcohol intake.

There are three other areas of misunderstanding that regularly interfere with a clear-eyed view of the suicidal mind, and that thus deserve attention: impulsivity, selfishness, and the role of mental disorders. Impulsivity—the tendency to act without much or any forethought—strikes many as playing a clear role in suicide, for many reasons. Major thinkers over the centuries have referred to its role. Émile Durkheim, for instance, said of what he called "automatic suicides," "The suicidal tendency appears and is effective in truly automatic fashion, not preceded by an intellectual antecedent. The sight of a knife, a walk by the edge of a precipice, engender the suicidal idea instantaneously and its execution follows so swiftly that patients often have no idea of what has taken place." It should be added that by "its execution," Durkheim was almost certainly referring to a nonlethal suicide attempt, again a different phenomenon than death by suicide. It should be said that some respectable and seasoned clinicians attest to presentations like this, with terms like "extrapyramidal-induced suicidal dysphoria," "nonideation suicidality," "dysexecutive suicidality," and "anaphylactic suicide."[48] Personally, however, I am aware of no documented case of lethal suicide that fits this profile (whereas there are many that do not fit it, and cases in which suicidal ideation was experienced but not expressed). But this idea persists, and one source for its resilience among others is its recurrence in fiction, in characters like Romeo and Juliet and Anna Karenina. Edgar Allan Poe's story "The Imp of the Perverse" states the same view. Poe's narrator says, "We perpetrate [acts like plunging to one's death] because we feel we should not." A principle that pervades this book is that Poe had it precisely backward.

Thus, one source for a prevailing idea that suicide is or can be spur-of-the-moment is fiction and its reverberations into nonfiction. Another is that some people actually do have flash-in-the-pan ideation regarding suicide; this seems to come out of nowhere and thus can be accurately described as impulsive. Indeed, if in referring to phenomena like these Poe had focused on *thought* instead of *action*, he would have been more on target, and the same can be said for some of Durkheim's writings. An essential point is that this effect occurs in suicidal *and* nonsuicidal people alike; in fact, approximately one in four of the latter report that this has happened to them.

The most common setting for spur-of-the-moment ideation is on a high place, and what accounts for it is likely nothing having to do with death or suicide, and everything to do with life. More specifically, it is very probably an automatic reaction of the nervous system signaling danger, which is then misinterpreted in more reflective thought as an impulse to die.[49]

Still another source for the mischaracterization of the role of impulsivity in suicidal behavior is that people who survive suicide attempts, when asked why they attempted, not infrequently reply that they did so impulsively; I noted this kind of reaction earlier and will revisit it in the chapter on suicide-by-cop and amok. And yet another reason for misunderstanding the impulsivity-suicide connection is that about a third of deaths by suicide come with very little warning to others, to whom the deaths seem shockingly sudden and who often describe the deaths' causes using phrases like "from out of the blue." These two true empirical facts—that survivors of suicide attempts sometimes describe the acts as impulsive and that those bereaved by suicide sometimes did not see the deaths coming—accord with a role of impulsivity in suicide but, importantly, also accord with alternative accounts.

Regarding survivors of attempts describing the attempts as impulsive, this may occur for multiple reasons other than the attempts actually being impulsive. For instance, as touched on earlier, if someone who has made a recent attempt is being questioned about it in a judgmental or disapproving manner—as is often the case even in professional settings—one might wish to attribute the attempt's cause to something that seems socially acceptable, such as "I don't know what overtook me, it just happened before I knew it, all of a sudden." Or, because suicidal crises tend to cloud cognition, those in crisis may have trouble accurately remembering or reporting their mental state hours or days after the fact. Or, researchers' assessment methodologies may bias such reporting.

As an example of the latter problem, consider the following response options for an item from a frequently used measure regarding whether or not and to what extent a suicide attempt was impulsive:

1. "impulsive; no premeditation";
2. "considered for < 1 hour";
3. "considered for < 1 day"; and
4. "considered for > 1 day."

This wording tilts answers toward the short term and away from the possibility of extensive planning. Moreover, should an individual plan a suicide attempt in detail during, for example, a past major depressive episode, recover, and then later relapse and attempt suicide without much forethought using the method planned in the earlier episode, which response option to choose? Options 1 through 3 might be applicable in the short term, but the true answer overall is option 4. We will see this same problem involving the retrospective reporting of motives with regard to the phenomenon of *amok*, a state of violent frenzy that I will argue is fundamentally suicidal in motivation (in contrast to its usual explanation as a primarily dissociative phenomenon).

Just as one should be very respectful of and sensitive to those who have attempted suicide and survived, so should one be to those bereaved by people who have attempted suicide and died. In both instances, it is nevertheless possible that retrospective explanations are misleading. Regarding the bereaved, they may be utterly certain that a suicide came

36 | INTRODUCTION

from "out of the blue" and when the decedent was "not himself," "not herself," or "not themselves," and some may be comforted by the idea that the death happened in spur-of-the-moment fashion and thus was not preventable. Still, it is possible for the bereaved to be both comforted and absolved from blame, and at the same time to fully face the facts that suicide stems at least in part from mental disorders (more on which soon); that mental disorders are treatable; that suicide is rarely if ever truly impulsive; and that it is in principle, and regularly though not always in practice, preventable.

The misunderstanding of the role of impulsivity in suicidal behavior may hamper means safety efforts. I have heard credentialed professionals at conferences voice comments such as "Means safety works because it prevents impulsive suicide." I believe this is mistaken. Rather, means safety is effective because it makes a deeply daunting and onerous task even more so, deterring most from enacting their own deaths even when those deaths are very much desired and carefully planned.

To the list of misunderstandings involving impulsivity, means safety, and alcohol should be added the notion that suicide is an inherently selfish act. Here, a key but regularly neglected distinction must be drawn between, on the one hand, the thoughts and feelings of the person who will be dead by suicide in the next seconds or minutes and, on the other hand, the thoughts and feelings of those bereaved by suicide. I speak from direct personal experience that, for the latter, reactions such as "How could he have done this to us?" and "Why didn't she think of us?" are common and very understandable. Suicide *feels* selfish to the bereaved; I could not possibly be more sympathetic.

But, crucially, that is different from suicide actually being selfishly motivated in the mind of the eventual decedent. For the latter, consistent with a tenet of the interpersonal theory of suicide that perceived burdensomeness is an essential causal factor, thoughts like "Everyone will be better off when I'm gone" and "I'm doing everyone a favor" are common. Say what one might about such thoughts—that they are misperceptions, deeply tragic, sad, and so on—one thing that they are not is selfish.

French philosopher Blaise Pascal believed that happiness "is the motivation for all [people's] acts, including [the acts of] those who are about to hang themselves."[50] In my opinion, this statement is mostly wrong, though it does contain one implication that rings true. The true part is that relief or escape from desperation can be a primary motivation for suicide. If by "happiness" Pascal meant this sense of relief or escape, then part of what he said holds some merit. It should be noted that an emphasis on escape from misery does not contradict the concept of perceived burdensomeness, emphasized in the interpersonal theory of suicide. The context for burdensomeness is regularly interpersonal, in that suicidal people believe they are relieving others of an onerous burden, but it can also be about how one's selfhood seems an onerous burden that everyone, including the suicidal person, will benefit from having removed.

Turning to the mostly problematic aspects of Pascal's statement, first, it can be read as prioritizing self-burdensomeness (and relief therefrom) over a sense of burdensomeness on other people. The proper emphasis, however, is vice versa. Second, to suggest that suicide decedents, in the moments and hours before their deaths, are in any way happy is quite misleading. What they really are is anguished, scared of the prospect of death now made real, miserable, and utterly lonely. These emotions predominate even in the relatively few eventual decedents who have derived a sense of calm about the expected relief, and they certainly predominate in all others. In no cases are they happy; in only a few is there visible relief (though in a few more there may be an element of subjective relief; all are in emotional agony and, depending on method choice, many will face physical agony of an extreme intensity).

A successor to Pascal, David Hume expressed the sentiment that no one ever died by suicide while their life retained worth. Even towering intellects can be mistaken, and like Pascal's view, Hume's is wrong. But it is salvageable with a tweak, and that tweak is that people do not die by suicide unless *they think* that their lives possess no value. Some mental disorders can render clearly worthy lives to *seem* unlivable—"seeming," it should be reiterated, can be entirely distinct from "actually being."

To continue the theme of the genuinely suicidal mindset and misunderstandings of it, a final issue involves the role mental disorders play in suicide. Earnest, well-meaning people can and do disagree about such issues; the following represents my own take on it—a perspective shared by one of the greatest minds in the history of mental health, widely underappreciated by modern audiences, especially American ones, namely, the French psychiatrist Jean-Étienne Esquirol (1772–1840).[51] A true fact about which there is clear consensus is that the vast majority of people with mental disorders do *not* attempt suicide, much less die by suicide. It is, however, a mistake in logic to derive from this fact the notion that suicides need not involve mental disorders. Among many other dismal and very fearsome things, suicide requires not just injuring but literally killing an innocent person, as well as stunning dozens of people into a miserable and astonished state of bereavement for months if not years. It also can be viewed as denying the inherent dignity and worth of all people, for if all are inherently dignified and worthy, why would some deserve self-killing?

I would add that if one is a biological parent of a living child, one's suicide kills a child's parent, a parent who committed to that child by the very act of bringing the latter into existence. I know of no truer marker for psychopathology than the unsanctioned killing of a human, even including florid psychosis, extreme mania, and profound catatonia. This is stern language, I acknowledge, proportionate to the act's gravity as well as to my decided opinion on the matter. In no way do I intend this, however, as comfort for the stigmatizers of those who have died by suicide, of those who have attempted suicide, of those confronting mental disorders, or of their loved ones. I understand and acknowledge that such language can be taken as comfort to stigmatizers, but it does not follow that the latter are right or that the language is wrong.

And still, the relationship of mental disorders to suicide is repeatedly debated, sometimes hotly, a debate that tends to revolve around questions of what counts as a mental disorder. To understand just how vast an intellectual spectrum this debate can span, consider the views of a University of Toronto associate professor of adult development and community development. The professor would assert not merely that suicide can occur absent mental disorders, not merely that it often occurs absent mental disorders, but rather that it *always* occurs absent mental disorders. Her perspective flows logically enough from her initial premise, which is that mental disorders do not exist (i.e., suicide, which is plainly real, cannot be about mental disorders because the latter are not real, her argument goes). One might have guessed that such opinions passed away along with prominent proponents like Thomas Szasz (who died in 2012), but no, the professor's views were current as of early 2017; in late 2016, she used her own savings to fund graduate student scholarships to study "anti-psychiatry," and her university's decision to allow for this, on grounds of intellectual and academic freedom, led to a newsworthy outcry.

In a more moderate example, in a book on physician-assisted suicide, Susan Stefan asserts repeatedly that not all suicides involve mental disorders and states, "No one ever really believes that all suicides are the result of mental illness."[52] But at least one credentialed researcher in the field believes exactly that—that researcher is me—and I am certain I am not alone. Again, much rides here on how terms like "mental illness" and "mental disorders" are defined. If they are defined extremely narrowly, as Stefan does, then of course it is true—predetermined actually—that not all eventual suicide decedents will meet the narrow definition, just as it is true that if one narrowly defines the color blue as an extremely specific shade of blue, not all things will be blue, including some things that really are.

With regard to mental disorders, if they are defined as limited to full loss of mental capacity and competence, then what is included are very clear mental disorders such as schizophrenia and bipolar disorder, but only then in relatively severe cases (e.g., people with schizophrenia can retain mental capacity and competence; those with bipolar disorder regularly can too unless they are floridly manic or profoundly depressed). What are excluded under such definitions are some of the clearest and, quite important in this context, most lethal mental disorders, such as major depressive disorder, borderline personality disorder, and anorexia nervosa. The exclusion of such conditions from the category of mental disorder may be useful in some legal scholarship contexts, but the moment one steps through the door of an actual mental health facility, the unworkability of such an approach crystallizes with speed and force.

My colleagues and I examined this issue in a reanalysis of the classic psychological autopsy study originally conducted by the eminent late psychiatrist Eli Robins.[53] If anyone knew a mental disorder when he saw one, it was Robins—he not only was the author of the study in question but also played a large role in the transformation of psychiatric nomenclature into its current, modern state. Robins was conscientious and also fully aware of the inherent limitations of the psychological autopsy approach, specifically, the sometimes substantial gaps in information that can occur when collecting retrospective data on decedents by questioning those who knew them (e.g., family members, friends, clergy, physicians). Accordingly, in Robins's study, if he was unable to obtain abundant information on a particular decedent, he refused to assign a diagnosis and instead assigned the decedent to a "no diagnosis" category. A superficial reading of the study, particularly one biased by opinions that many who die by suicide did not have a mental disorder, will view Robins's "no diagnosis" category as clear evidence of this.

It is nothing of the sort. The "no diagnosis" decedents in Robins's study were, to a person, very unwell. Not only were their suicides demonstrative of this, but in most cases, there is such an extensive amount evidence for mental disorders that it is a credit to Robins's conscientiousness that he refused to diagnose them. For instance, one decedent displayed the following features: morose, tense, irritable, anger outbursts, boredom, restless, talked about suicide for years before death. An even clearer example is a decedent described as follows: nervous, moody, anxious, irritable, severe insomnia, frequently talked about suicide, excessive intake of alcohol on a daily basis, numerous arrests, assaulted his wife and broke her nose, in a separate incident killed his wife in the hours before his suicide. I reiterate: Dr. Robins refused to assign a diagnosis even to this latter person due to insufficient data. Only if mental disorders are defined in ways that exclude these two examples of people who were clearly troubled before their suicides is it defensible to assert that suicides occur regularly in the absence of mental disorders.

In our paper on the Robins decedents, my colleagues and I state, "In discourse on this topic, a common refrain . . . goes along the lines of 'if you had experienced x, y, and z, wouldn't you consider taking your own life, wouldn't that be rational?' X, y, and z can represent many things, but the two most common referents are terminal illness and extremely severe abuse including but not limited to extreme prisoner abuse."[54] An example of this refrain is repeated in the book on physician-assisted suicide mentioned earlier; of an individual she interviewed, Stefan writes, her "thoughts of suicide are not symptoms of her condition manifesting during an episode; they are a thoughtful reaction to the reality and chronicity of her condition."[55] This line of argument neglects the very numerous examples of individuals in highly similar or even worse situations who do *not* have suicidal thoughts. Moreover, as already alluded to, there is an essential difference between having suicidal thoughts and enacting them.

We will have occasion to revisit the mindsets of those who decide to enact suicide terrorism later in this book. For now I note that, at least in one study, more than 70% of those polled endorsed the following terms regarding suicide terrorists: "evil," "irrational," and "psychiatrically disturbed."[56] Of course, the public's opinion on people's mindset can be in error—a refrain of this book; however, as we will see later, here the majority appear to have it right.

Defenders of the view that suicides regularly occur absent mental disorders are misled by another phenomenon, namely, that it is not uncommon for suicide decedents, in the minutes or hours before their deaths, to say or to express, for example in suicide notes, that they do not have a mental disorder. It takes very little clinical experience to understand that such assertions are hardly probative; I have heard such assertions from suicidal people whose mental disorders were very plain to see. Furthermore, I am aware of an example of a person who repeatedly denied having a mental disorder during a span of several weeks that involved a near-death self-injury, a visit to a location with the thought of using the features of the location to enact death, and finally a lethal self-injury. In contrast to the person's self-view, credentialed mental health professionals viewed the individual as having a mental disorder without question, though not to the degree of meeting full clinical criteria for the disorder in question. That the person in this example experienced a subclinical variant of a mental disorder could not have been more clear. This is a sad—and unfortunately not isolated—example of a subclinical variant that, despite being subclinical, proved fatal.

Lest one doubt that this issue recurs and remains problematic, in June 2018, CNN reported on a study by the Centers for Disease Control and Prevention (CDC) on worrying rates of increased suicide over the previous twenty or so years (with, as alluded to earlier, the notable exceptions of 2019 and 2020).[57] CNN noted in passing that the CDC report indicated that less than half of the suicide decedents in the study had a mental disorder. This is vanishingly unlikely. What the CDC intended, and what is more plausible, is that less than half had a *known, formally diagnosed* mental disorder. I contend that if the statistic under discussion is *any existing mental disorder, whether formally diagnosed or not,* the figure is at or near 100%. Within minutes of the CNN article being posted, a prominent listserv was used to voice the notion, utterly unlikely, that less than half of decedents had any sort of mental disorder.

Here I would like to address the roles in suicide of mental disorders, social and economic factors, and two of the concepts of the interpersonal theory of suicide (e.g., burdensomeness and low belonging). The theory emphasizes perceived burdensomeness and low belonging, and it views mental disorders as key distal causal factors that operate on suicidal outcomes via theory variables like burdensomeness and low belonging. It is undisputable that social stressors like unemployment and relationship disruptions regularly play a role in suicides. The theory's logical structure is such that one need not choose between social stressors versus mental disorders versus variables like burdensomeness and low belonging in suicide's sources; rather, each is causally implicated at different temporal locations along the distal-to-proximal continuum.

In the field there tend to be three default positions on this set of issues. One is to attribute causality fully to social stressors and to minimize mental disorders; a second is vice versa, that is, to attribute causality to mental disorders and minimize social stressors. These first two options are unsatisfactory on their face, and they manage to persist mainly because they serve the interests of one guild or faction or another. If I were forced to choose between these clearly suboptimal options, I would choose the account that emphasizes mental disorders, only because I have regularly seen presentations of them that, on their own, without the involvement of social stressors, involve lethally dangerous suicidality, whereas I have never seen social stressors on their own, without the involvement of some aspect of mental disorders, lead to potentially lethal crises (though, yet again, much depends on how one defines mental disorders in this line of reasoning).

The third default option is essentially to throw one's hands up and exclaim, "It's complicated." A more thoughtful variant of this latter option is to appeal to concepts from philosophy, mathematics, complexity theory, and so forth and to mount the case that there is an irreducible complexity to some phenomena in nature, and that suicidality is one such phenomenon.

I roundly reject all of these options. Instead, I prefer to use a mix of basic psychological science, clinical psychology, neurobiology, knowledge of human nature, reflections on the nature of death, and clinical experience to model the processes that lead to suicidality. The modeling that I have done in this way allows room for social factors, mental disorders, and many other key elements. I do not claim that it is fully comprehensive or perfectly accurate; rather, I see it as useful, and I use it as a main conceptual touchstone for this book.

One influence on this ongoing misunderstanding is the eminently understandable desire of those with *lived experience* to be understood, which in the current context refers to those who have been suicidal and may have attempted suicide. It is my impression that this group resents having their complex life experiences chalked up to a mental disorder. Their perspective is, I take it, that their situation is more complicated than that. I believe that they are right, that the larger suicide prevention community can and should do a better job of acknowledging this point, and that others have much to learn from them. However, in addition to emphasizing that they have a point, it is essential to point out that they also make a faulty leap in logic. Their logic is "my suicidality was understandable and therefore not a mental disorder"; mine is that "it is understandable *and* a mental disorder."

There is a relevant literature on the postattempt life trajectories of those who attempt suicide, though there are somewhat contradictory voices within this literature. On the one hand, there are studies that emphasize that, after an attempt, those who attempted suicide generate less income, are less likely to accumulate wealth, and so forth.[58] On the other hand, my colleagues and I reported that future well-being may well be reduced, but is by no means precluded, by past suicide attempts.[59]

Earlier I noted that I see serious suicidal behavior as among the truest markers of psychopathology of all, and that this is due in part to

44 | INTRODUCTION

its involving unsanctioned killing. In a very different context, an anti–death penalty activist profiled in the March 2017 issue of *Harper's* voiced a compatible sentiment: "There is an inherent risk to killing or taking innocent life when you give an error-prone government the power of death. . . . It risks innocent life, and I don't think it's the proper role of government, especially when you have other options." Regarding life without parole, he went on to argue that the risk of wrongful conviction exists there too, but "they have the rest of their lives to prove they're innocent. You execute someone, you can't bring them back from the grave."[60] As we will see, it is not uncommon for people on death row to volunteer for execution.

A coherent though arguable position, one that I happen to endorse, is that a similar logic pertains to suicide; as applied to suicide, the passage might be rendered as follows: mental disorders derange the government of the mind over the person; it is not proper that an error-prone mind be given the power of death, risking an innocent life, especially when there are other options, and especially when suicidal people, on the brink of death, change their minds and are glad for it over the subsequent years and decades. I and others believe mental disorders derange the human mind, sometimes to the point of it inviting death.

I recently saw a screening of a documentary film entitled *The S-Word*, which documents the experience of several people with lived experience regarding suicidality (i.e., each had attempted and survived a suicide attempt). One of the more moving moments in the film is when a man, approximately forty years of age, reflects with anguish on the possibility that his suicide attempt many years before had proved lethal. In particular, the thoughts that his children—all born after his attempt—would not exist and that he would not have the privilege of being father to them filled him with sorrow and also relief that that possibility did not come to pass. I will revisit this same kind of sentiment in the chapter on physician-assisted suicide.

A Note on Language

A word on language and phrasing is in order. Thus far, when describing the act of suicide, my phrasing has used variants of "die by suicide," and this phrasing has become the standard, preferred norm in our field.

There is a sector within the field that is passionate and vocal about this norm, and some people within this sector can be harsh to those who use language and phrasing that do not conform to it. I support, endorse, and use language respecting the norm, but I am not passionate enough about the issue that I harshly call out those who run afoul of it (though I do insist on the norm in my capacity as editor in chief of the journal *Suicide and Life-Threatening Behavior*). The ways in which they do so involve phrases like "commit suicide," "complete suicide," and "achieve suicide completion." An additional adjective or adverb, "successful" or "successfully," can compound the problem, in the sense of a "successful suicide attempt" to describe a lethal attempt, or "successfully complete suicide."

To unpack the reasons this kind of phrasing is outdated and is viewed by many as pejorative or otherwise unfortunate, consider the verb "commit." Its denotation need not suggest anything to do with the commission of a crime, but its connotation certainly does. One modern understanding of suicide is that it is reflective of mental disorder, not of criminality; thus the norm has arisen not to use the phrase "commit suicide." In this book, I do not use it at all when in my own authorial voice; when quoting others, I will use it very rarely if ever.

The verbs "complete" and especially "achieve" are, according to current norms, to be avoided when describing a death by suicide. Interestingly, the reasoning here is, in a sense, from an opposite direction as compared to the reasoning involving the word "commit." Whereas for the latter, the concern was the criminalizing connotation, for the former, the concern is suggesting that there is anything laudable about suicide. In many contexts, completing or achieving something is, in fact, laudable; that is not so in this context.

There are at least two reasons for my position about this phrasing, which is that I adhere to the phrasing but I do not harshly judge or sanction others who do not. First, I am not fully convinced that this issue matters very much in the scheme of things. Those who think it does reason thus: societal understanding about and compassion regarding suicide are badly needed, and relatedly, stigma against suicidal people is a major problem. A change in language and phrasing will help people be more open, understanding, and compassionate. On this view, language is the horse and understanding the cart; that is, language change will pull for increased understanding. My hesitation about this view is that

46 | INTRODUCTION

it may have things backward. It might be that increased understanding is needed first (e.g., from scientific research), and then proper phrasing will arise naturally in its wake. I do not know which of these views is right, and until I do, my own choice is to use the norm's preferred language.

Another variant of this hesitation is that allocating energy and time to language change diverts those resources from other, very urgent efforts, like science on understanding and preventing suicide. I am not sure if this hesitation has merit either, though I am sure that plenty of time and energy are spent on language change issues on various listservs and elsewhere.

My second main reason for the lack of zeal and puritanism I feel regarding language change norms involves my reflections on why the norm violations occur and why they tend to persist in whack-a-mole fashion or, perhaps more apt, like weeds. Regarding the term "commit," suicide was criminalized in many societies for centuries, and remains so in some; something having been written into the law for that long is liable to have lasting impact well after the law has changed.[61] Of course, that does not make the phrasing right, just perhaps a little more understandable.

Furthermore, one animating principle of this book is that death by suicide is extremely hard to enact. When one thinks of the enactment of very difficult things, a phrase like "complete the act" naturally comes to mind as do phrasings involving the words "achieve" and even variants of "success." Many readers of this book will have completed or will be completing an academic degree, such as a bachelor's, master's, or doctoral degree, or perhaps some other challenging life or professional goal. Those degrees and other things are *hard*; once earned, they represent a successful achievement to have completed. Suicide is hard too, and that is the reason such language comes naturally to people regarding it. The key problem, and the reason the language should be avoided, is that the dimension of *laudability* is not factored in; the one thing, degree achievement, is laudable, the other, suicide, is not.

As noted at the outset, this book aims to develop a unified view of diverse forms of suicidal violence, typically viewed as distinct from one another. Suicide, murder-suicide, suicide terrorism, suicide-by-cop, volunteering for execution on death row, rampage killings, amok, and even physician-assisted suicide have been viewed as disparate phenomena, with differing motivations. Although they do have notable differences, this volume argues that they can all be understood as variations— sometimes culturally influenced variations—on one core form of suicidal violence. Conventional and clear-cut suicides and related topics have been the focus of this introduction, setting us up to turn later in the book to less clear-cut phenomena. I am proposing a conceptual shift in the understanding of these latter violent behaviors, asserting that they are driven primarily by an individual's desire to die, rather than primarily by a desire to kill, and that these events are best understood as a type of suicide. In some cases, these incidents develop no further than, and culminate in, death by suicide, but in other cases individuals conclude that their deaths suggest or even necessitate the deaths of others. A goal of this book is to delineate the psychological processes involved in deciding that one's own death has inviting aspects, deciding how and when to die, and in some cases concluding that one's own death necessarily requires others to die too.

A premise of this volume is that a comprehensive theoretical understanding may illuminate numerous aspects of suicidal violence and point the way toward more effective prevention of these calamitous incidents. To be sure, there are many variations in the *expression* of suicidal violence—and these are interesting and important in their own right. Having touched on these, a case will be built that a conceptual unity in *motivation* underlies most if not all of the variations in expression. Just as different sculptors can turn marble into an endless array of forms, so may various factors sculpt the expression of suicidal behavior. At base, however, just as all sculptures from marble are still marble, all deaths by suicide may share the same foundational motivations. A theoretical touchstone for this effort will be the interpersonal theory of suicide, expanded upon in the next chapter, which I and others have articulated and elaborated over the past decade or two.[62]

These phenomena of suicidal violence directly cost the lives of well over eight hundred thousand people each and every year. The mental disorders that spur suicidal violence are common, disproportionately afflict the disadvantaged, are well controlled only by treatments available to the advantaged, and regularly rank among the top worldwide health burdens; they are, however, routinely neglected clinically, by research funding agencies, and societally. Good public health requires advancing mental health, a lesson of which we are brutally and frequently reminded, and yet manage to forget time and again. Suicidal violence needs to be confronted so that it can be combated. The understanding and prevention of these forms of violence may avert the catastrophes that these incidents represent on a very regular basis, which, in turn, would directly contribute to the well-being of humanity generally.

1

Suicide

The Interpersonal Theory of Suicide

A profoundly depressed and desperately suicidal woman bolts from the close monitoring of her family, leaps into her car, and drives at maniacal speed to a lethally high bridge nearby. Meanwhile, the police have been alerted; moments later they locate her car approaching the bridge. At its apex the woman pulls over, exits her car, rather deliberately closes the car door, and walks—not runs—to the railing; at the same time, a law enforcement officer frantically exits his cruiser and sprints toward her. At the bridge's railing, the woman hesitates for just over two seconds, and then she jumps. An instant later, the officer catches her by the arm; she struggles against him to no effect as he lifts her back to safety. Her walking, not running, to the rail, and her hesitation of just over two seconds have allowed the officer barely enough time to get to her and to grasp her in midair. His courage and skill averted her death; absent his physical strength, they both well may have perished as her falling weight pulled them together to their deaths below.

At roughly the same time on the other side of the planet, a woman paces outdoors, aimlessly and in an agitated fashion. She monitors the railroad tracks nearby, looking every now and then into the distance for any fast-approaching trains. Eight days earlier she had been admitted to inpatient psychiatry, an admission occasioned by her intent to place herself in front of an oncoming train and thereby cause her death. Upon discharge, her suicidal intent and planning had abated noticeably, but within hours they roared back. She spots in the distance a train hurtling toward her; she approaches the tracks and kneels between them, facing the train. As she kneels, her gaze is momentarily pulled downward; when she looks back up and sees what is coming, she throws herself flat with less than a second to spare, still between the tracks. Cruel in its length, the train takes many seconds to pass over her despite its considerable speed. At last it does, and the woman stands, psychologically stunned but physically unscathed, not even a scratch on her.

Both of these individuals had fully resolved in their minds to enact their deaths, and both performed actions involving substantial physicality to do so. In the crucial moment, however, both their bodies departed from the mind's script, both lost their staring match with death, both blinked, both flinched, and it saved them. Those we lose to suicide, by contrast, manage to overcome this ancient, instinctual, and powerful will to live; the same applies to varieties of suicidal experience emphasized throughout this book. This insight is one basis on which I constructed a prominent model of suicidal behavior called the interpersonal theory of suicide, which this chapter describes in detail.[1] My reasoning is that a viable and useful model of suicidal behavior will be a helpful starting point from which to discuss several varieties of self-directed violence. The unity in these varieties can be understood in part with reference to the concepts of the interpersonal theory (and the similar models it has spurred, such as David Klonsky's three-step theory and Rory O'Connor's integrated volitional-motivational model).[2]

An underappreciated truth of human nature is that, as much as we fear death, we may fear killing even more.[3] Suicidal violence is unique in that it combines two of our deepest fears, dying and killing, felt in our cells and in our souls. As alluded to earlier, not all forms of suicidal violence do this to the same degree; murder-suicide, for example, does for sure, whereas suicide-by-cop, for example, less so because the killing element is elicited from a law enforcement officer by a suicidal individual.

That something as deadly as high suicide risk is at all amenable to the kinds of tweaks I mentioned in the introduction to this book opens a window on suicidality itself. "You may toss out nature with a pitchfork, she will still come back upon you." Originally from the *Epistles of Horace*, but repeated regularly since (e.g., in John Adams's *Memoirs* [1794]), this line expresses the sentiment that come what may, instinct will emerge and have its say. Notwithstanding the notions of Dr. Freud et al., we have no death instinct, but we have an irrepressible draw toward life; many suicidal people have tried to tame this force with their proverbial pitchforks, and while some tragically do so, many are gainsaid by this force that can "come back upon" them. It is true that some may incline toward the Freudian view, and decidedly true that I am not one of them. In the battle of ideas that inheres in the work of Darwin and that of Freud, the victor could not be clearer, and one reflection of that is the explanatory depth and reach of a concept such as survival of the fittest (which presumes a self-preservation instinct in all or almost all circumstances), as compared to that of a death instinct, which strikes many as puzzling and morbid.[4]

I confess that I am uncertain of the original provenance of the Freudian concept of the death instinct, but I suspect at least two sources. First, conversations with suicidal patients do at times suggest an instinctual aspect to suicide; for example, such patients will at times remark that the idea for suicide "just comes to them." That an idea arises suddenly does not necessarily make it instinctual, however. More, an idea that occurs to one quickly and seems to be instinctual in the present may have an origin in ideation months or years before that was deliberative. Second, "flash in the pan" suicidal ideas, even among the nonsuicidal, are not rare. As was discussed in the introduction, however, there is evidence that, far from reflecting a process related to death, the phenomenon is likely related to the self-preservation instinct.

Further to this point, both of the real-life examples that opened this chapter were characterized by both reflective thought and instinctual action. In both cases, one involving a jump from a bridge, the other involving an oncoming train, the individuals had deliberately thought through the suicide plan for weeks at least, probably longer. Nothing involving their planned deaths had an instinctual character. There was, however, an instinctual element to their actions, and it was their last-instant, unreflecting, automatic behavior—hesitation in the bridge incident, throwing oneself flat in the train example—that was lifesaving. Nothing about the death elements was instinctual; everything about the lifesaving reactions was—plainly contradictory to Freud's death instinct ruminations, and fully in accord with Darwin's achievement.

To actually die by suicide—as opposed to thinking about it or talking about it or planning it out, or even attempting it in nonlethal fashion—requires an orientation toward death that is unnatural and exhausting, much as is holding a very heavy barbell over one's head, to take a relatively trivial example. The latter is not hard to discuss, contemplate, or plan, nor is it especially difficult to initiate. But the full and sustained doing of it is; most of even the very intent are stopped before they even begin, and the remaining minority are thwarted seconds into the act. For these latter individuals, their determination may rapidly deteriorate under physical load, and for the very few for whom it does not, they are physically constrained within seconds via sheer muscular exhaustion. In those few seconds, an otherwise minor irritation or distraction may loom large and may become a substantial obstacle to persistence—put differently, a nudge away from persistence.

Suicide is much harder still because, unlike lifting a heavy weight, it flies in the face of evolved, finely tuned self-preservation instincts, sculpted by natural selection over eons. From this perspective, it is incredible that anyone enacts it, which, in turn, argues for the force of the underlying psychopathology.

Our heritage wards us off not just of death and dying, but of killing as well. It is hard to kill, certainly psychologically but also logistically, a fortunate truth that saves lives every day. In an example from late 2017, a New York City man cut a gas line in the basement of his home, hoping to trigger an explosion that would take his life. In fact, there was a small explosion, but it was not of sufficient intensity to kill anyone, including the man in question. The latter was hurt, sustaining a minor injury to his leg. No one else was harmed, though this is far from assured when a gas explosion occurs in the middle of a very crowded city.

This same principle was at play in a far more harrowing incident, namely, the Columbine school shooting. To be sure, many were killed: to be exact, fifteen died, including the two adolescent perpetrators, who killed themselves after murdering the others. As ghastly as it was, it was less so than what the perpetrators had planned. Prior to the shootings, they had rigged the school buildings with bombs, hoping to fulfill their perverted dreams of outkilling Timothy McVeigh. The latter took the lives of 168 people in the Oklahoma City bombing, and the Columbine toll may well have exceeded even this number had the bombs not all malfunctioned. For each of the hundreds of students and school personnel who might have perished on that day, the fact that bombs are logistically difficult to deploy saved years and in many cases decades of life.

That bombs are very difficult to work with is a fact that will recur when we turn to what I consider as the plainly suicidal element of suicide terrorism. Some of the most revealing studies of this phenomenon involve would-be perpetrators whose bombs malfunction at the crucial moment, sparing their lives and those of many others, with the additional benefit that the failed perpetrators are alive and can be interviewed about their motives, mindsets, and histories.

In a related example, also from late 2017, a man rammed his car into the headquarters of Germany's Social Democratic Party. At first blush, the incident seemed like a politically motivated terror attack, but subsequent investigation convinced authorities that it was a suicide attempt only. The man was only slightly hurt; no one else was. As we will see in the chapter on suicide terrorism, there are documented incidents of planned suicide terrorism with these same contours; that is, the perpetrator survives, no one else is hurt, and it turns out that a main motive of the perpetrator was likely suicide, with hurting and killing others as secondary.

These kinds of events, incidentally, do get mistaken for pure and primary attempts at violence on others. I was involved as an outside witness in an attempted murder trial that was of just this kind.[5] A young man was in a conflictual romantic relationship; the problems escalated, to the degree that, in a fit of despair and rage, the man decided to take his own life. To do so, he drove his vehicle at maximum acceleration across several lanes of busy traffic, expecting to be hit and killed in the ensuing accident. His vehicle threaded the eye of a needle and was untouched by other cars, but at the far side of the lanes of traffic was a row of buildings, into which the man's vehicle crashed head-on. The specific building impacted was a business in which there were several people at the time of the incident. No one in the building was injured; the man himself was, but his injuries, though substantial, proved non-life-threatening. Prosecutors charged the man with attempted murder, with a possible prison sentence of more than twenty years.

His lawyer's defense was simply that it was a suicide attempt and nothing more, and my role was to affirm that the young man's history and behavior and the incident itself indeed bore many signatures of a suicide attempt scenario (e.g., the man's psychiatric status at the time resembled that of the prototypical person who attempts suicide much more so than the prototypical profile of the attempted homicide perpetrator).

Returning to the principle that suicide is difficult because our nature warns us away from killing and dying, it should be the case that homicide (which of course involves "only" killing) should, in a sense, be easier than suicide (which, with few exceptions like suicide-by-cop and death row volunteering, involves both killing and dying). I am aware of an incident of murder-suicide in which the perpetrator showed full resolve and no emotion about the murder element along with considerable ambivalence about the suicide element; I will have occasion to mention this case in a different context in the chapter on murder-suicide. It may then follow that there are more nonfatal suicide attempts than nonfatal homicide attempts; my reasoning is that more suicide attempts are nonlethal because the fear of dying interferes more with suicide than with homicide.

In his book *The Murderer Next Door*, psychologist David Buss wrote, "For every 'successful' murder, there are more than three attempted murders that fail because of successful medical intervention."[6] This three-to-one ratio of homicide to attempted homicide may represent a considerable underestimate, as it does not account for unreported and/or untreated nonlethal assaults intended as homicides. Even so, there is reason to think that the same ratio involving suicide is even more skewed; nonlethal suicide attempt rates are notoriously difficult to establish definitively—in large part because numerous attempts are known only to the individuals who have attempted—but a reasonable if somewhat conservative estimate is twenty-five nonlethal suicide attempts for every one suicide death.[7] Again, it is important to note that many homicide attempts go undetected too, but overall there is reason to believe that more nonlethal suicide attempts occur than do nonlethal homicide attempts—a pattern that would be consistent with the principle that suicide is, in a sense, harder even than homicide.[8]

On the logic that suicide is harder than homicide, there should be documented instances of murder–attempted suicide in which the one who is killed is lost but the one who plans to die by suicide does not do so. A similar logic should apply to some suicide pacts. In a 2016 suicide pact in Pennsylvania, a husband and wife had mutually agreed on suicide, but the wife found that she could not carry through and asked her husband to kill her. He did, and then cut his own wrists and ingested numerous painkillers, but in neither case to a fatal degree.

This is a ghastly but not uncommon outcome of suicide pacts: one person dies, but the other survives and is left to deal with the physical and emotional aftermath. In this light—and in light of one of the world's highest suicide rates—it is not hard to see why South Korea has moved to outlaw suicide pacts, specifically making the organizing of them a criminal offense. This move is one part of a larger set of measures approved by the South Korean president's cabinet in January 2018; another of the measures is to make annual health checkups mandatory for all people in their forties, fifties, sixties, and seventies—the age groups responsible for the vast majority of South Korean suicides—and to mandate that depression examinations be part of the health checkups.[9]

The capacity to stare down death or, more generally, to unflinchingly do hard things might be usefully dismantled into the literal ability to do so, as opposed to one's subjective belief that one can do so. Once one develops the literal ability to do something hard, the belief that one can do so may harden and may remain fixed even as the literal ability fades with time. As one personally resonant example, I played football for most of my first two decades of life (and still would if I could), and it contributed to a knowledge that I can do hard things to this day. However, reflecting now on the shocking collisions I both inflicted and absorbed, I wonder if I could perform or endure them now without flinching. My mind believes so, but does my body still? This same kind of process may explain flinch-like, lifesaving reactions during suicide attempts even in people who are convinced of their ability to enact death.

The main point of this chapter is to summarize and update the theory of suicide I originally developed in the book *Why People Die by Suicide*.[10] This line of work was originally intended to at least partly explain suicide in its conventional, uncontroversial denotation. Yet as I will attempt to show throughout this book, and as is often true of useful scientific theories, the interpersonal theory has explanatory reach, in that it sheds light on other suicide-related phenomena too.

An important point at this juncture is that even within the category of conventionally defined suicidal violence, others beyond the suicidal individual are sometimes killed, as they can be in the varieties of suicidal experience covered later in the book. There are documented cases, for example, in which someone who intends suicide by jumping from a high place lands on a pedestrian and causes the latter's death as well; in which someone who intends suicide via chemical exposure accidentally exposes and kill others as well; and in which an individual who intends suicide by self-inflicted gunshot wound uses a powerful enough weapon

56 | SUICIDE

that the shot eventuates not only in the individual's death but also in the death of someone nearby (e.g., someone sleeping in the bed on which the suicidal individual sits when firing the weapon).

Still on this same subtopic of accidents within suicides, in Florida in July 2016 a suicidal woman intended to kill only herself, in the garage of her family home. To do so, she started the engines of two cars inside the garage; she was later found there, dead by carbon monoxide poisoning. The carbon monoxide exposure generated by the incident was extreme enough that everyone else in the home was killed as well; the evidence is clear that the woman's lethal intentions were specific to herself.

These tragic examples are painful to ponder. Doing so, however, paints a vivid picture that is one animating theme of this book: that suicidal violence is a bane when one considers just the loss of the suicidal individuals themselves; it is even more so when one considers not just the searing pain of the bereaved but also that suicidal violence may kill others, sometimes unintentionally—as in the woman's suicide in her garage—other times intentionally, as depicted in chapters that follow.

* * *

Suicide combines killing with dying, amplifying the taboo quality of each, which may account for suicide's entrenched stigmatization. As unnatural and difficult as unsanctioned killing of another is, suicide may be even more so, in that it involves all of the following aspects: the frequently brutal killing of an innocent; the state of mind that death has inviting properties; others' potential deaths via suicide contagion, not to mention the occasional actual deaths of bystanders; the deprivation of choice and life to one's future self; the deprivation of choice and future care and comfort to loved ones; and the decision to devastate dozens of people into a shocked state of often lasting bereavement.[11] Any one of these is suggestive of psychopathology; their conjunction is a clear exemplar of psychopathological functioning. Some may view this depiction of suicide as unsympathetic, but I respectfully disagree, and I remind readers that death by suicide runs in my own family. My perspective is at a minimum plausible and, if correct, positions us to be clear-eyed in a fight against suffering and death.

Killing (including killing oneself) is a daunting task that requires high states of energy and arousal; it simply will not happen otherwise.[12] But suicide involves dying too, and the prospect of death is fearsome and alarming and therefore is also arousing.[13] Those who are about to die by suicide may act and feel as if someone is about to kill them simply because someone *is* about to kill them. It may not matter, in terms of triggering a mindset of alarm, that they are their own killer. This chapter will explore the highly unusual states of mind produced in those who are simultaneously killers and victims.

The principle that killing a human is against our natures, including if that human is oneself, is helpful in understanding the lives and deaths of individuals who show preoccupation with a specific form of death over the course of years, and then die by suicide in exactly that fashion. For instance, a man found in a shower stall dead due to self-asphyxiation by ligature stated eight years before his death that if he were forced to go through a particular experience, he would "hang himself in a shower stall." Three years before his death, he said of a similar kind of experience, "I'd rather hang myself in a shower stall." A year later: "I am so depressed right now I just want to hang myself in the shower." And a year after that, approximately one year before his death, he was quoted as saying something virtually identical.[14] Many of these remarks were said in an offhand manner, in a way that others likely took as jests, and perhaps in part they were. But, in addition, they showed preoccupation over time with a very specific form and location of death, and this kind of preoccupation may be necessary for or at least facilitative of the capacity to do something as difficult as self-inflicted death.

The theory I developed in the book *Why People Die by Suicide*, mentioned earlier, was formalized in 2010.[15] It was then combined with an evolutionary perspective in 2016, and then integrated with models of automatic cognition in 2022.[16] As an overview, the initial statement of the interpersonal theory of suicide boils down to a fairly simple postulate: that an individual is most at risk to die by suicide when they want to and can.[17]

Of course, this statement requires unpacking regarding what constitutes wanting suicide and being able to enact it. With regard to suicidal desire, the model's conjecture is that it is made up of seemingly intractable social disconnection (thwarted belongingness) and the perception of being a burden on others (perceived burdensomeness). An emphasis of the theory is that even those who are overwhelmed by such states and who thus desperately desire death are simply unable to enact it, because doing so is so difficult, daunting, and fearsome. This emphasis squares well with anecdotes like those that opened this chapter, in which highly suicidal people hesitate, flinch, or desperately make last-instant grasps for survival in a crucial moment during their suicide attempt, and thus survive despite their original suicidal desire.

According to this conceptualization, the capability for suicide includes fearlessness of death, tolerance of physical pain, and familiarity and comfort with specific means of suicide (this latter facet is frequently referred to as "practical capability"). Though to my knowledge this has not been empirically arbitrated, my expectation would be that those who die by suicide always have elevated fearlessness of death as well as above-average practical capability regarding their means of suicide; I expect that they frequently have high physical pain tolerance as well, but am less certain about this aspect for the simple reason that not all means of suicide can be characterized as physically painful.

Van Orden and colleagues furthered these ideas by rigorously formalizing them, leading to several specific, empirically testable predictions. These predictions involve a causal explanation for stages of severity of suicidality (e.g., passive suicidal ideation, active suicidal ideation, suicide intent, near-lethal or lethal suicide attempt). One prediction involves thwarted belongingness and perceived burdensomeness as "proximal and sufficient causes of passive suicidal ideation."[18] That is, the existence of passive suicidal ideation requires either considerable perceived burdensomeness or substantial thwarted belongingness, but not both.

What accounts for the progression from passive to active suicidal ideation? According to the theory, the answer is the simultaneous occurrence of thwarted belongingness and perceived burdensomeness, both deemed to be permanent and intractable. The role of hopelessness (i.e., permanent intractability) deserves highlighting, as, according to the theory, the most dangerous forms of suicidal ideation occur when thwarted belongingness and perceived burdensomeness are deemed to be lasting and unchangeable.

According to the interpersonal theory, suicidal desire, although in itself distressing and a barrier to optimal functioning, is not lethal without the capability for suicide. This concept has been touched on already, but its specific role in the interpersonal theory's prediction requires elaboration. The model conjectures that active suicidal desire enters the realm of imminent risk as it progresses to suicidal intent, manifested by the additional presence of fearlessness about death, a key component of suicidal capability.

Finally, the most dangerous, severe level of suicidality is lethal (or near-lethal) suicide attempt. This represents a rare outcome, as it involves the simultaneous presence of suicidal intent (composed of hopeless interpersonal views and lowered fear of death) and elevated physical pain tolerance. Most important, for this final hypothesis—the theory's overarching one—the presence of high pain tolerance is necessary for suicidal intent to develop into suicidal behavior, as the pain involved in most suicide attempts must be endured. One potential limitation of the theory is its silence regarding the role of physical pain tolerance in suicides that do not involve extreme pain.

To summarize, the primary hypothesis of the interpersonal theory of suicide pulls together the multiple constructs (hopeless thwarted belongingness and perceived burdensomeness, and the facets of capability) and describes the interplay of each as necessary for attempts to die by suicide. These four hypotheses described within the framework of the interpersonal theory provide a testable and falsifiable explanation for the development of suicidality, spurring well over one hundred distinct empirical investigations (more on which soon).

The interpersonal theory of suicide focuses on near-term causal factors for suicidality within the individual; however, given that it is a theory of one form of human death—a form that appears to fly in the face of evolutionary principles—it would be intellectually satisfying if it could be plausibly integrated with evolutionary thought. In reaction, my colleagues and I developed the argument that suicide derives from a derangement of a self-sacrificial behavioral module that was adaptive in the ancestral environs.[19]

This framework hinges on the idea that humans are one of several species that have evolved adaptive, self-sacrificial behavioral modules— adaptive in that they increase the fitness of the self-sacrificing individual's *genes* even as the individual itself is sacrificed. As applied to suicidal behavior in humans, the derangement of the tendency toward self-sacrifice revolves around the concept of perceived burdensomeness. That is, the individual miscalculates that death is more beneficial to their community (family, friends, large society, etc.), and therefore self-sacrifices. The essence of this perspective is that human suicide is a misfiring of an evolutionarily adaptive behavioral suite; the suite is adaptive when self-sacrifice really does maximize fitness—a rarity in the modern but not in ancestral environs and not in several nonhuman species to this day—and is not just maladaptive but disastrously so when self-sacrifice occurs based on a misperception of actual benefit.

Earlier I mentioned the more than one hundred empirical examinations of the interpersonal theory of suicide. In a meta-analysis conducted by Carol Chu, myself, and other colleagues, we found general but moderate support for the interpersonal theory's hypotheses as formalized by Van Orden and colleagues.[20] More specifically, as the theory would expect, suicide ideation severity was significantly correlated with higher levels of perceived burdensomeness and thwarted belongingness. Further, also as the theory would predict, suicide attempt history was significantly associated with higher degrees of the theory variables (i.e., perceived burdensomeness, thwarted belongingness, and the capability for suicide).

In addition to the general assertions of the theory, the meta-analytic results provided support for some of the theory's "out on a limb" hypotheses. For instance, the crucial interaction between thwarted belongingness and perceived burdensomeness in predicting suicidal ideation received support, as did the even more essential three-way interaction between thwarted belongingness, perceived burdensomeness, and capability for suicide in prediction of suicide attempts.

Despite these findings demonstrating general support for the hypotheses of the theory, some key limitations were identified. A major one involves measurement imprecision, a problem in the suicide literature as a whole. With regard to the interpersonal theory, its main purpose is to describe the development of lethal or near-lethal suicidal behavior, a relatively low base-rate occurrence. Vanishingly few studies have assessed suicide mortality as an outcome within the framework of the theory. Furthermore, the theory distinguishes between passive and active suicidal ideation, and suicide intent and attempt. Due to very real logistical challenges in obtaining robust data on such outcomes, these distinctions are usually neglected in the literature—including, I acknowledge, in my own research program—limiting the direct assessment of theory hypotheses. We researchers neglect these not out of ignorance but due to the pragmatics and ethics of studying a rare and lethal behavior. Further still, and as alluded to earlier, the importance of the sense of intractability for perceived burdensomeness and thwarted belongingness is highlighted within the theory but is often overlooked in empirical research, as the standard measure (namely, the Interpersonal Needs Questionnaire, developed—again admittedly—by my group) assessing these variables does not include perceived intractability (though a newer one developed by my former PhD student Chris Hagan does).

Another issue that may account for supportive albeit moderate effect sizes in the literature on the interpersonal theory involves potential suicide subtypes. The theory stipulates that subtypes of suicides do not exist and, rather, addresses suicide as one unitary phenomenon (albeit one with gradations of severity). Some support for this stipulation comes from a study that attempted subtyping of a series of forty-four deaths by suicide based on Durkheim's subtypes (i.e., anomic vs. altruistic vs. egoistic).[21] This attempt failed, simply because the differentiations were not clear. Subtypes may exist, however (again, as famously asserted by Durkheim), and if so, it is possible that the interpersonal theory is relevant to only one or some type(s) of suicide.[22]

Perhaps because of issues like these, the synthesized results indicated generally modest effect sizes. The meta-analytic findings of Chu and colleagues shed light on the falsification, or lack thereof, of the interpersonal theory of suicide.[23] The theory is generally supported, albeit with modest effect sizes. Despite their modesty, I view these effect sizes as approaching the ceiling of what is possible in the context of very imperfect tests of statistically intricate postulates. Through this lens, Chu and colleagues' results provide clear support for the theory; through another lens, modest support.

Beyond measurement imprecision as already noted, additional explanations for these modest effect sizes may include that the theory is inaccurate. While this may be so, results to date, including the meta-analytic findings of Chu et al., tend not to support this conclusion, as research seems to generally support the theory, despite the limitations mentioned earlier (and more extensively by Chu et al.). It is also possible that the theory may be incomplete, and I turn now to one potentially promising way to redress that.

It involves implicit, automatic psychological processes (those operating out of an individual's conscious awareness but nevertheless influencing, or potentially influencing, behavior). The current version of the interpersonal theory is silent on that topic—its emphasis is almost entirely on explicit processes—but there is reason to suspect that implicit processes are involved.[24] For example, psychologist Matt Nock and colleagues used a test of implicit psychological processes to show that automatic associations between oneself and death predicted later suicide attempts.[25] More recently, it has been demonstrated that automatic affective responses (as opposed to one's thoughtful, deliberative responses) to the perception of one's spouse better predict long-term marriage outcomes than do explicit attitudes toward one's spouse. As touched on earlier, McNulty and colleagues conducted three longitudinal studies showing that these same automatic affective associations involving one's spouse (partner-good) protected participants from subsequent suicidal ideation.[26] An implication of such work is that past research on the interpersonal theory of suicide has returned supportive but moderate effects in part because it has neglected implicit processes, and focused on explicit ones alone.

The interpersonal theory constitutes one lens through which to see suicide, which the rest of this book contends is the fundamental basis for a variety of forms of violence. To summarize, overall the interpersonal theory, which emphasizes concepts like capacity, intractable loneliness, and hopeless perceptions of burdensomeness, has been reasonably well supported by a corpus of well over one hundred empirical tests. Nevertheless, for the reasons summarized earlier, it should be viewed in the context of limitations, many of which are being addressed currently in ongoing theoretical and empirical work.

* * *

On the point of profound and intractable states of loneliness—an emphasis of the interpersonal theory—it is worth reflecting on our social natures, and the corresponding power of even very small doses of interpersonal rejection, and of its flip side, feeling cared for, as already noted. In addition to things like caring letters and texts, memories of caring and being cared for can be powerful antidotes to suicide. Years before her tragic accidental death, Princess Diana considered suicide in the wake of unflattering coverage by the media. She drove to England's suicide hot spot, cliffs called Beachy Head off which a jump is fatal; the princess intended to jump "only to be drawn back by thoughts of her two sons."[27]

Just as caring memories and the like can be powerful even in tiny doses, so can small doses of social ostracism prove painful, in seeming disproportion to their true, rationally considered consequences. This truth is vividly illustrated by an experimental paradigm from social psychology called Cyberball. Cyberball is a video game, somewhat similar to the classic game *Pong*, which was a simple, two-player ball-batting game. Cyberball is a ball-tossing game, but with three players essentially playing virtual catch. The person in the social psychology experiment believes they are playing the game along with two other players more or less like them (e.g., fellow undergraduates), for that is what participants are told. But it is a deception; the other two players are actually under the control of the investigator. A typical game involves forty throws of the ball, of which the first two include the participant. Afterward, however, the participant is excluded from the game; that is, the other two "players" throw the ball back and forth between themselves, leaving the participant out.

Note the scale and true social consequences of this dose of ostracism. The participant is not face-to-face with anyone, including the experimenter, who really is in another room, and the other players, whom the participants believe are also in another room. The participant loses nothing really, certainly nothing material. The slight logically cannot be personal, because the supposed other players know nothing about the participant.

But it certainly *feels* painful, and compelling evidence exists suggesting it is painful, perhaps even literally physically so. It is possible to construct a Cyberball apparatus such that participants play the game while undergoing magnetic resonance imaging of their brains. Research has shown that, in response to social exclusion in Cyberball, one of the most clearly affected brain regions is the anterior cingulate cortex. This is truly intriguing, because this very same brain area is a main seat of the processing of physical pain. As humans evolved, it is possible that social ostracism represented a mortal threat, and thus the physical pain centers were recruited in the course of natural selection to make social ostracism physically painful and thus to be avoided and, when experienced, repaired.

People definitely are motivated and work to restore social connection after experiencing ostracism in Cyberball, an effect underlain by another brain system. This latter system is more neuroanatomically diffuse than the somewhat more localized pain-focused anterior cingulate cortex (though, as with most things brain, pain too is a more complicated story than just that one area in the cingulate). The system involved in restoration of social ties relies largely on socially relevant neuropeptides like oxytocin, which is implicated in many key social behaviors (e.g., mother-infant bonding and breastfeeding, romantic love).

In collaboration with neuroscientist Liz Hammock, my former PhD student Carol Chu and I have found that the system appears to markedly malfunction in people with past suicide attempts, certainly as compared with healthy control participants, and even as compared with nonsuicidal but depressed individuals. We administered a set of questionnaires to all participants and took a blood sample from everyone. All participants then underwent the Cyberball procedure, after which we took more blood and questioned them. Needless to say, we also rigorously took care of everyone afterward, acutely aware that even a small dose of social exclusion can be viewed as perilous for vulnerable individuals.[28]

Based on our post-Cyberball questionnaires, everyone clearly felt the pain of it; that is, it operated in its intended fashion. But their blood levels revealed another story.

In healthy controls, blood oxytocin levels robustly increased post-Cyberball, presumably to fuel the ensuing social reparation response. We observed a similar response in nonsuicidal depressed participants; though it was somewhat blunted, these participants too experienced a post-Cyberball oxytocin surge. In stark contrast, people with past suicide attempts not only did not show an increase in blood oxytocin levels but showed a noticeable decrease.

One may wonder whether this effect might be related to accurate perceptions of the slight. Perhaps, that is, some participants were not attending to the game well and/or were engaging in psychological denial about the experienced ostracism. We assessed accuracy by asking the participants to estimate the percentage of throws on which they were included. There is a correct, reality-based answer to this question of course, and it is 5%, because the participants were included on only two of the forty throws in the game. Interestingly, it was normative in the overall sample to overestimate inclusion—the overall sample average estimate of inclusion was 9%, almost twice the actual rate. This is consistent with some inattention but could also relate to any number of things, like denial or, my favored candidate, participants' disbelief that exclusion could be as profound as 95% of the throws. In any event, participants understood that they were excluded but underestimated how much.

This was particularly true for the healthy controls, who thought they were included about 13% of the time. It was true of the nonsuicidal depressed controls, but less so, in that they believed they had participated around 9% of the time, approximately the overall sample mean. It was true as well of the participants with past suicide attempts, but even less so; their estimate was just under 7%, not far off from the actual reality of 5%.

What I take all this to mean is that these latter participants most accurately understand what has happened and thus should if anything have the most robust oxytocin increase. That they have the least, and an actual decrease to boot, may reflect just how dysregulated that social brain system has become in them.

If a rejection as minimal as that in Cyberball can be noticeably painful, what of interpersonal rifts that are far more impactful? Consider divorce in this regard. It is worth stating the obvious that there is a wide array of outcomes following a divorce. Nevertheless, status as divorced versus married is a quite robust risk factor for suicidal outcomes, consistent with the importance of social connectedness and the pain inherent in losing it.[29]

* * *

This chapter has touched on several concepts, methodological issues, and associated research directions relevant to the interpersonal theory of suicide. A measured and dispassionate view on this strand of work is that it is useful (clinically and otherwise), reasonably empirically supported, and generative; it is also clearly imperfect, in need of more scientific and conceptual development, and vanishingly unlikely to be the theoretical pinnacle in work on suicidal behavior. On this latter point, my own view of progress in science is that it accrues in stepwise fashion, with some steps being bigger than others. The interpersonal theory was a step; I will leave it to others to decide how big a step or, better yet, to build more steps in the progression toward a full understanding of—and thus a significant reduction in—suicidal behavior.

2

Perverted Virtues Transform Suicide into Murder-Suicide and Spree Killing

There is little ambiguity as to whether murder-suicide is in part suicidal; plainly it is, by definition. Confusion exists, however, on what is primary, murder or suicide. Incidents such as two mass shootings occurring in 2017 in Las Vegas and at a church in Sutherland Springs, Texas, draw one's attention to those who are killed by the perpetrator. One's sympathies lie with the victims; beyond feelings of contempt, one's emotions do not linger much over the perpetrator. Nor should they, in one sense, that sense being that he committed an utter atrocity. In another sense, however, understanding of the perpetrator's motives, which requires interest in if not sympathy for the killer's mindset, may produce insights to head off such incidents in the future.

I would be very surprised if the Las Vegas and Texas killers did not harbor long-standing suicidal thoughts—ones that temporally preceded plans for murder. My reasoning here has to do with my efforts, while writing a book on murder-suicide (*The Perversion of Virtue*), to identify cases in which perpetrators of murder-suicide evinced no suicidal thinking, at least not initially, and instead were preoccupied with murder all along.[1] I delved into this work with the expectation that there would be many such instances, an expectation that was disproved. What I encountered instead were incidents that on first blush appeared from media reporting to be entirely about murder, which, upon deeper reading, proved to have originated in suicidality.[2] I would rush to reiterate that such reporting is of course understandable when many innocent people have been brutally murdered.

I referred in the previous chapter to the violence that occurred at a high school in Colorado. Dave Cullen's book *Columbine* is an exemplar of how deep investigative reporting can gainsay initial media reports (and of how hard-won, rare, and valuable such reporting is; the project took many years for Cullen to complete). Many of the latter painted a picture of the two adolescent perpetrators' psyches as flooded with resentment over being bullied by other students; on the night of a school shooting in February 2018, this one in South Florida, I heard precisely this misunderstanding repeated about the Columbine event on a national news network. Stipulating that it was true that the incident was motivated by being bullied—as we will see, it was not—then it follows that the shootings could have been revenge-fueled. As Cullen convincingly showed, this is a profound misreading of the Columbine tragedy.

First, an emphasis on revenge and murder neglects an inescapable fact: in addition to the incident being a violent atrocity, it involved two suicides. Revenge in general is a fairly rare spur for suicide at any age, but when it does occur, it is almost always in the context of a highly conflictual marital-romantic context. Revenge toward peers is not an especially common motive for adolescent suicide (though it is somewhat more common in workplace murder-suicides in adults).

Which leads me to a second point that questions an emphasis on vengeful murder: the boys involved in the Columbine violence *began* as depressed and suicidal, and then over time their suicidal depressions grew in scope to involve the deaths of others. The violence perpetrated upon others captured public attention, and as noted, that is only as it should be. But it does not change the fact that had these boys not been suicidally depressed in the first place, the violence would not have occurred. As to how suicidal depression grew in scope to become the Columbine killings, I believe a psychological process I termed the "perversion of virtue" was at play.

Which brings me to a final point as to why it is misguided to view the Columbine perpetrators as revenge-seeking: The virtue that these boys had in mind as they planned and carried out the incident was *not* justice—had it been, revenge as motive would have been more plausible—instead, as jarring as it may be to read, it was glory. In the months' worth compendium of journals, audiotapes, and videotapes which the boys left behind and over which Cullen combed meticulously, the perpetrators-to-be expressed at length their opinions that they would be remembered heroically, gloriously. If more were needed, a clue as to their deranged mindsets comes from the fact that they believed Oklahoma City bomber Timothy McVeigh was remembered in this way, and that therefore the boys' goal was to kill more people than the 168 innocent souls for whose deaths McVeigh was later executed. As noted earlier, the Columbine perpetrators may well have done so had the bombs they prerigged throughout the school not all malfunctioned. This latter detail is essential to understanding the tragedy and its basis in a perverted view of glory and heroism, but it too tends to be overlooked or forgotten—I had forgotten it myself until I read Cullen's book, and I am under the impression that large percentages of audiences to whom I sometimes speak on the incident have forgotten it as well. Here again, this seems only natural, in that front and center in one's mind are the thirteen *actual* gun-enacted murders (and two suicides), much more so than any *potential* bomb-related killings. The latter, however, could have numbered in the hundreds, and represented the Columbine perpetrators' main motives, goals, and plans, carefully developed over many months.

Yet another facet of the tragedy that tends to be overlooked or minimized is the particular misery of the two perpetrators' families. There is a sense, here yet again, that this is only as it should be, given the plight of the thirteen other bereaved families, and this is not even to mention the physical and psychological damage that was inflicted on those at the school that day who survived. Having emphasized this, the agony of the families of the two perpetrators warrants a moment's reflection. They, too, are bereaved by the deaths of their children, but also endured years of severe anger, contempt, and disgust directed toward them, mixed with a set of emotions that I believe may be literally indescribable, but involves a deep blend of sorrow and guilt.

As it happened, I had the opportunity to affirm this view in a phone conversation with Sue Klebold, the mother of one of the perpetrators. At the time, Ms. Klebold was writing a book on the tragedy, her son's role in it, and the acutely painful aftermath.[3] She had seen my book on murder-suicide, in which I discuss numerous such incidents, including a dispassionate description of her son's role in the atrocity, and she wanted to discuss it with me. I thus approached the call prepared to be upbraided, steeled by the belief that I had had a privileged opportunity to say my piece (in print and in enduring form), and now it was only proper that I listen to Ms. Klebold's.

I need not have worried. Not only did she convey her agreement with my description of the boys' glory-based motives, but she did so in a kind and gentle way, still clearly tinged almost twenty years on with palpable sorrow for her son's actions. She has said thereof, "I'm not trying to downplay the viciousness he showed at the end of his life. I'm trying to understand how his suicidal thinking led to murder. . . . I have come to believe that his involvement in the shootings was rooted not in his desire to kill but in his desire to die."[4]

Two adolescents, initially depressed and suicidal, became more than that, via the perversion of a virtue, in their case heroic glory. I claim that all or virtually all genuine murder-suicide events conform to this same pattern, although the specific perverted virtue in question may vary. That is, a careful tracing of the trajectories over the months and years preceding authentic murder-suicide incidents, I predict, will reveal an initial origin in a depressive episode tinged if not saturated with suicidality; from there, the progression will involve mentation along the lines of "Wait a minute, as long as I am going to be dead, isn't it the reasonable thing, the right thing, the *virtuous* thing, for so-and-so to be dead as well?" Over time the perpetrator-to-be decides this question in the affirmative and is deluded to believe that murder will serve one or more of four virtues: justice, mercy, duty, and/or glory. Who "so-and-so" is is often meaningfully associated with which virtue is perverted; in justice-motivated incidents, the victims are mostly former romantic partners or employers and employees at a workplace from which the perpetrator was fired, and in mercy-motivated events, the perpetrators are often desperately depressed parents who believe that their suicides absent their child's death would be unmerciful.

Why focus specifically on only the four virtues of justice, mercy, duty, and glory? Are there not others (e.g., honesty, service, loyalty)? I have two main answers to these questions.

First, justice, mercy, duty, and glory cover the territory of human virtue well. Most if not all other virtues can be subsumed under or at least related to these four; for instance, service to duty, and honor to glory. Second, these four virtues are essential not only to the modern human mind but also the primate and indeed the mammalian mind in general, and likely to the ancestral human mind as well. Regarding nonhuman primates and other mammals, virtues like justice and mercy are plainly key to their natures; a monkey will react angrily if it is unjustly deprived of a grape when its cagemate receives one, as will a rat react mercifully by working diligently to free a trapped cagemate (this behavior has notes of duty too).

Regarding the ancestral human mind, we lived in small groups and in a constant and often desperate struggle for survival. It is admittedly speculative, but nonetheless it seems reasonable to imagine that everyone was essential, thus the importance of duty; freeloaders were potentially deadly, thus the importance of justice; the truly vulnerable deserved mercy; and glory was accorded to extraordinary acts of accomplishment, sacrifice, and valor.[5]

* * *

It is interesting to ponder the progression from suicide to murder-suicide further, in particular with regard to the course of depressive symptoms within it. As already stated, notable depression is the common origin point, but what of the course of symptoms thereafter? I am aware of no systematic, definitive study on the topic, but from reading numerous anecdotal accounts of this phenomenon, I have developed a clear intuition, and it is at least as unsettling as the view that murder-suicide represents a perversion of virtue—namely, that preoccupation with and the planning of a murder-suicide can serve as an antidepressant.

Allow me to unpack that perhaps startling assertion. The planning of a momentous event of any kind (even including a murder-suicide, disturbingly) gives one a sense of purpose, meaning, and mission; these, in turn, ward off symptoms like apathy, anhedonia, concentration difficulties, and worthlessness. It may be more accurate to say that this represents a partially effective antidepressant, in that the symptoms mentioned are reduced, but the process nonetheless culminates in death by suicide.

There is some evidence, though here too it is not fully definitive, that a process like this was operative in the Aurora, Colorado, movie theater shootings perpetrated by James Holmes. This atrocity was not a murder-suicide, it should be noted, though Holmes was aware of and uncaring about the likelihood of his death in the course of the shootings. As thoroughly documented in psychiatrist William Reid's book *A Dark Night in Aurora*, Holmes murdered twelve theatergoers and injured numerous others, many very severely. In the time frame leading up to the shootings, Holmes had experienced the dissolution of what appears to be his life's only romantic relationship, and Reid writes of Holmes, "He had been depressed for a time, and the loss of his hope for a relationship made it worse. I asked him if anything brought him hope. He replied, '. . . just the mission . . .' 'The mission' was Holmes's budding plan to kill as many people as he could. He believed strongly, but somewhat vaguely, that committing homicide would somehow stop what he had called 'depression.'"[6]

This raises the possibility that there are instances in which the planning of a murder-suicide serves as a fully effective antidepressant, in that not only are symptoms reduced but the plan for murder and for suicide is dropped. Pondered but not enacted murder-suicides are an even more underresearched topic than enacted murder-suicides, analogous to the situation with interrupted and aborted suicide attempts as compared with deaths by suicide.

Lest this seem far-fetched, I have high confidence that a companion process occurs with regard to suicide (though I acknowledge that this confidence is partial).[7] On the podcast *WTF* in May 2018, comedian Marc Maron observed that earlier in life he found a kind of solace in knowing that suicide was an option. More than a few suicidal patients report that they find the existence of a suicidal option not just calming but buoying. I have come to regard the key word in these kinds of expressions as "option"; that is, there are no options for the lethally suicidal mindset other than death itself. To imply more than one option, as some suicidal patients do when they refer to suicide as *one* option, suggests a mindset that has not progressed to full lethality (though such patients are clearly at nonzero risk).

If a murder-suicide is considered, which in turn and paradoxically serves as a kind of antidepressant, leading to the abandonment of the murder-suicide plan, there is likely no evidence of it left other than in the memory of the person who considered it. We thus may know exceedingly little about a phenomenon that, while probably fairly rare, is still far more common than usually understood. In such scenarios, the abandonment of the plan is complete, in that no element of it is enacted.

Partial abandonments are possible too, either of the suicide element of a murder-suicide plan or the murder element. Regarding the latter— murder-suicide plans that end as suicides only—in the documentary film *Kingdom of Us*, the reactions of the members of a large family to the suicide of the family's father were recounted. There is evidence that the man had pondered his suicide for many months or even years. Moreover, there were indications that he may have pondered the murder of his entire family as a part of the process of his own suicide. For example, he installed mechanisms on the doors of each of the family home's bedrooms that would lock the rooms from the outside, locking anyone in the bedrooms inside. This occurred more than a year before the man's eventual suicide and had confounded the family members as to why he had done so. The answer arrived only after the man's suicide: the locks were part of a plan for the murders of the entire family (e.g., by fire or natural gas), to be followed by the man's suicide.

What altered the plan, such that it culminated in only one death (i.e., the man's suicide)? I have a speculation: as I suggest happens with the perpetrators or potential perpetrators of all murder-suicides, the man first decided on his own death and subsequent to that, reasoned that under a scenario in which he would be dead by suicide, his family members would be better off if they were dead too—thus the plan for the family's murder as a prelude to the man's suicide. In the man's mind, this "family better off" notion likely involved an appeal to virtue, such as duty or mercy, but needless to reiterate, this perceived virtue is in reality a perverted distortion of a virtue.

Thus far, the account tracks that of the usual murder-suicide perpetrator. However, I think the case in question involves a third mental step beyond the decision, first, to kill one's self, necessitating (in the individual's mind), second, the need to kill others. The man had decided to be victim (via suicide), then decided to be killer (via murder), and then third, decided to become rescuer, not of himself but of his family. This same phenomenon occurs in suicide, when people decide to be victim and killer, and then at the last minute instinctually save themselves. As we have seen, the concept of ambivalence is essential in understanding such scenarios.

There are yet other possible reasons why the murder element of a murder-suicide plan might be abandoned. One is simply that the perversion of virtue aspect is reconsidered, and the individual changes their mind about whether it really would be the (seemingly) virtuous thing to first kill others. Another possible reason is that the person persists in believing that murder would be virtuous but decides including it would just be too difficult. Such a decision would be compatible with a thesis underlying this book that killing of any sort is extremely difficult. It also would be consistent with the logic of means safety (i.e., killing is hard, placing obstacles and/or distance between a potential killer and victim[s], harder still).

As already noted, the latter emphasizes placing distance and/or obstacles, whether actual or psychological, between an at-risk person and the means of risk. In murder-suicide plans that become suicide only, perhaps the individual comes to view actually killing others as too far a reach, too difficult. If that is right, one wonders how many gun-involved murder-suicides would have been suicides only were it not for the relative ease of killing others with a gun versus with other means (e.g., knife, ligature).

Murder-suicide plans absent the enactment of the murders exist more than we realize; similarly, murder-suicide plans absent the suicides may too. Earlier I mentioned the school shooting that occurred in February 2018; it was in Parkland, Florida. In this incident, seventeen people were killed, all murdered. There was no suicide, leading media commentators to speculate, therefore, that this may be some kind of distinct violence, unlike earlier events in which the perpetrator clearly planned and enacted his own death. Perhaps, but I am not fully convinced.

First, we know that the perpetrator did not kill himself, but we do not know that he did not plan and intend to kill himself. As we have seen, it is a fairly regular occurrence for even very seriously determined suicide intentions not to be fully carried through, with the individual stopping just short of enacting suicide in the crucial instant or seconds before a lethal attempt. I do not know this to be the case in the south Florida tragedy, but it is a possibility. Second, the perpetrator was put on suicide watch immediately after his capture. Third, perhaps more convincing and relevant, the perpetrator has a long personal history of serious mental health problems, including but not limited to depression. It is the relatively rare depression that does not involve at least some suicidal thinking, and indeed, news reports indicate that, in numerous visits to the shooter's home in the years before the shooting, law enforcement documented incidents of self-cutting. The family with which he was living at the time of the shooting (his parents were deceased) described him as "depressed" and "lonely." The facts are not definitive, but it is possible that this perpetrator too matched the profile of an originally suicidally depressed person adding a murderous element to suicidal thinking.

The February 2018 incident in Florida differed from previous, similar crimes in at least two ways, and I suspect that these differences may be closely linked to one another. One of the differences, as alluded to earlier, is that the perpetrator did not kill himself (though he might still have been suicidal). A second difference occurred in the days and weeks following the Parkland shooting; I am referring to the quality of the resulting discourse over guns in America. On the one hand, it is usual for there to be outrage and calls for change, followed by very little change indeed, and it is unsurprising that that was pretty much the outcome yet again; on the other hand, the pulling away of numerous prominent sponsors from the National Rifle Association seemed a qualitatively new development. This, too, essentially amounted to much ado about nothing, but stipulating for the moment that the discourse was, at least for a time, of a qualitatively different nature, it is interesting to ponder the reasons why.

Is it the number of people who were killed? Clearly not, as the incidents in Las Vegas and in Newtown, Connecticut—to take but two possible examples—caused more deaths. Is it that youths were killed? Probably not, in that the atrocity at Newtown not only took more lives but also took the lives of twenty young children (and six administrators and teachers, and the perpetrator's mother, and the perpetrator).

Another possible difference, however, relates to the fact that the shooter is still alive. Could it be that, when the perpetrator kills himself, it facilitates quick dismissal of the incident as "merely" mental illness? And when the perpetrator survives, it interrupts the reflexive and dismissive attribution of the incident to mental illness, allowing reflection on other issues, such as the role of American gun policy and our violent culture in general?

If so, it would suggest that stigma toward the suicidal has laid the groundwork for grotesque killings of innocent people, including children. That is, as a society we do not reflect on these incidents much if they can be quickly attributed to mental illness. Furthermore, if my speculation has merit, it would point to an irony: discourse may have moved beyond a reflexive "that guy was just crazy" line of thought in the

Parkland shooting, even though the individual in question is unmistakably mentally ill.

The February 2018 Florida school shooting occurred in the midst of data collection for the dissertation project of my former PhD student Ian Stanley. The project was focused on gun safety, and though its methodology was highly quantitative and involved a full experimental design, qualitative data were also collected in the form of free-form written statements from the project's participants, many of whom—being young college students at Florida State University—were recently Florida high school students, similar to the shooting's victims.[8] The tragedy plainly affected the project's participants in that before the shooting, it was rare for them to write much if anything in response to the free-form prompt, whereas afterward, it was noticeably more common, and many of the participants referred specifically to the incident in their writing. Some of the writing expressed more openness to gun safety initiatives, even among some participants who had previously not been especially open to it.

Yet another school shooting (this one again in Texas, in May 2018) involved an explicitly suicidal person who planned to perpetrate a murder-suicide, motivated, it appears, by a sense of perverted justice. For months he had pursued a female classmate, was rebuffed, but did not relent. A week or so before the shooting, she publicly declared to the class that she was not interested in him. This likely plunged him into despair, triggered his plan to kill himself, and then, on further thought, led him to think that justice required that she die first.

He certainly did perpetrate murder—he killed ten of his fellow students, including the girl in question. In the words of the Texas governor, speaking on television, "He gave himself up [to authorities] and admitted at the time" that his plan was to die by suicide, "that he wanted to take his own life earlier." The governor added that the perpetrator wrote about his plans for suicide "in journals on his computer and his cellphone." As in the Columbine incident, mentioned earlier, this individual had seeded the school in advance with explosives that ultimately failed to detonate, showing, among other things, how extensively this perpetrator had planned and premeditated the incident.

My suggestion overall with regard to this shooting as well as the earlier Florida shooting is that they were planned as murder-suicide and enacted as murder only; this is very clear in the Texas example, and I assert likely in the Florida one as well. There are occasional incidents that operate in the opposite way—that is, a planned murder-suicide that culminates in suicide but not murder. One such event occurred in Ohio in February 2018. A seventh-grade boy formed an eight-step plan for a school shooting; the plan, developed over several weeks at least, was later discovered by law enforcement officers on the boy's phone. The boy expressed admiration for the Columbine perpetrators and wrote, "I'm going to die doing it . . . when they interview my parents and ask how they didn't see the signs they should know it's not them it's me and it's because of how I see the world. . . . I'd hurt and destroy something bigger but my school's an easy target." The boy did indeed bring a loaded weapon to school, where he (and he alone) died, by a self-inflicted gunshot wound.

The note further stated that the school shooting would be "bigger than anything this country has ever seen" and that "I will never be forgotten, I'll be a stain in American history."

This latter detail may be revealing, in that it shows a slightly different mindset than that at play in the Columbine perpetrators, for example. The latter did not view themselves primarily as "a stain" but rather thought what they were planning was heroic (i.e., they perverted the virtue of heroic glory). That the young Ohio adolescent viewed himself in negative terms perhaps played a role in his decision not to kill others, only himself.[9]

* * *

As noted earlier, approximately 2% of suicide decedents perpetrated a murder in the time frame before their own deaths. That is a seemingly small number, but here, as elsewhere, looks can be deceiving. In 2017, over 47,000 Americans killed themselves; the 2% rate for murder-suicide indicates, then, that well over 900 innocent American souls were murdered as a prelude to these suicides. This would be the case even if in each of these incidents a single individual were the victim, but in a sizable fraction, more than one person was murdered before the perpetrator died by suicide.

This 2% statistic is fairly robust in general (e.g., in FBI reporting) but also across different subgroups of suicide decedents. For instance, Pamela Wible, writing in the *Washington Post*, described her compilation of suicide deaths among physicians. A physician herself and an advocate for suicide prevention and mental health for physicians, Wible noted that of the 757 cases in her files, 15 also involved homicide, a rate of 1.98% and quite consistent with the 2% statistic cited here.[10]

Wible's case series follows other regularities of murder-suicide as well. Given that a murder-suicide has occurred, chances are very high that the perpetrator was a man, true in people in general as in Wible's series of physicians in particular. Given that a man has perpetrated a murder-suicide, it is likely that the victim was his female romantic interest, true generally as in Wible's physicians; this was the case in seven of the fifteen murder-suicides in this series.

In a somewhat parallel fashion, should an individual decide on their suicide and then reason that that fact necessitates the death of the family, the modal set of decedents includes the spouse and all of the children. There are, however, occasional incidents in which a particular child or a subset of the children is spared. It is my anecdotal impression about these incidents that, should a parent plan and enact a murder-suicide of the family but spare one or more of the children, the age range of those spared is regularly between sixteen and twenty. One way to understand this pattern is that the older the child, the more likely they are to escape or self-defend in a lifesaving manner. This is certainly plausible, and it has happened, but I believe it is not the prevailing reason for this pattern.

My understanding of the primary reason is informed by my view of murder-suicide as a perversion of such virtues as duty and mercy. In the perpetrator's mind, it is either the dutiful or the merciful thing, or both, to kill younger children because the perpetrator is under the impression that the children will suffer too much without them. If the child is sixteen or older, on the other hand, the perpetrator may conclude that the child is old enough to be all right on their own—that duty has been discharged, that mercy is not apt (the spouse, usually the wife, is killed out of a similar perversion of mercy and/or duty, or a perversion of justice—a "she caused all this, so why should just I and the children die?" type of thinking, if it can be called thinking). I emphasize that this is merely my anecdotal impression (but based on many incidents), and empirical scrutiny of this idea is needed.

* * *

In an incident in Brazil, a bride-to-be betrayed her fiancé with the latter's best man.[11] Unbeknownst to the tryst participants, the groom-to-be discovered the affair and decided in despair to take his own life. But then he had a subsequent thought, along the lines of "If I just kill myself, they will live on, unpunished, perhaps together; that would be unjust; I have to kill them first." He proceeded to do so at the wedding reception, and then died there by self-inflicted gunshot wound.

In an incident in the rural United States, a socially isolated dairy farmer developed a plan to end his life but then had a further thought, along the lines "If I just kill myself, no one will know for days or possibly even weeks, and the milk cows, unmilked that long, will suffer intensely; that would be unmerciful; I have to kill them first." He proceeded to do so, sparing all non-milk cattle, and then died by his own hand (this is, of course, not a murder-suicide given that no other people were killed, but the relevant psychological processes can involve the killing of pets or farm animals).

My book *The Perversion of Virtue: Understanding Murder-Suicide*—in which these specific examples are mentioned—documents case after case of this type and builds the argument that all genuine murder-suicides have this character: they begin as suicides but then morph into something more through a psychological process termed the "perversion of virtue."[12] This mental process makes it seem obvious and compelling to the eventual murder-suicide perpetrator that to only die by suicide would be unvirtuous, and that the virtuous thing to do is to kill others too. That to do so is far from virtuous underscores the distorted mentation involved. Consistent with the theme of the current project, my work on murder-suicide sees suicide as foundational in the phenomenon, with all else developing from it.

It can be remarkable how different instances of depravity and tragedy share underlying commonalities, given a clear conceptual grasp of them. Consider three: the Germanwings disaster, Jonestown, and Heaven's Gate. To varying degrees, each can be viewed as a murder-suicide, in which a suicidal individual justified murder via an appeal to a perverted virtue.

In the Germanwings air incident, a depressed and suicidal pilot flew his passenger jet into the side of a mountain, causing his death and the murders of everyone else on board (the total death toll in the incident was 156). Though his motives are somewhat obscure, my speculation is that the pilot, previously angered by his employer and/or aviation authorities, decided on his suicide and then reasoned that should he crash one of the industry's planes it would accomplish both his death and the enactment of justice. He may also have been aggrieved by past treatment by passengers and thus believed that they deserved justice too (at least his version of it). Though it is not readily apparent at first blush, the Germanwings disaster is a workplace murder-suicide, much as are incidents in which a disgruntled former employee returns to a workplace and kills people there before killing himself; despite media coverage, workplace settings, not schools, are the modal place for these kinds of events to occur.

The Jonestown and Heaven's Gate tragedies, both mass suicides enacted under the influence of a persuasive but deeply troubled leader, can be viewed as having happened at workplaces too. In both cases, the people's deaths occurred at the place that they saw as their life's work. In Jonestown, people literally worked at the site; in Heaven's Gate, members mostly left the house the group rented (and where the suicides took place) to do various jobs to fund the group, but they also worked in the home on such tasks as the house's upkeep and food preparation.

In the case of Jim Jones, especially as the catastrophic day approached, his mental state was disturbed enough that it is somewhat perilous to speculate about it; he may, however, have really believed that his own death was inevitable and furthermore that, given his death, it would be the wrong thing to do to leave his followers behind to suffer. Here, unlike in the Germanwings incident, the motive was not disgruntlement but something akin to mercy or duty. Suicidal parents who kill their children before taking their own lives regularly engage in just this line of thought, thinking that they are being merciful to the children by not leaving them behind.

Another element appears to have been involved in Jones's mindset as well. In a last speech to the group on the day of the tragedy, Jones claimed that "revolutionary suicide" was the only option left for the group, and that they should embrace it as way of "protesting the conditions of an inhumane world." I have recently heard almost these exact same words from those emotionally asserting that suicide need not involve mental disorders because it can be a last resort of protest against injustice. Though this idea is thought-provoking, I beg to differ, as my earlier remarks on the role of mental disorders in suicide would suggest. I would add that it would give me pause if I, like those who have recently argued for a "revolutionary suicide" notion, were on virtually the same wavelength as someone as clearly unwell—and as clearly responsible for the awful deaths of hundreds of innocents—as was Jim Jones.

In Heaven's Gate—an incident in which thirty-nine people killed themselves (and two others of the group later died too) in the belief that they would depart their bodies for a higher plane of existence on a spaceship trailing the Hale-Bopp comet—the leader, Marshall Applewhite, seemed genuine in his fervent belief about the spaceship and may have felt that it was his duty or the merciful thing to "spare" as many people as he could. The "exit videos" taped by the group members in the buildup to their suicides plainly show that many of them fully endorsed Applewhite's beliefs and were convinced they would live on once aboard the spacecraft; very tragically, some of the members seemed less certain of this belief, and in a few cases frankly terrified, but they died too.

Here, the phenomenon of decreased blink rate in the moments preceding suicide deserves mention. There is some reason to suspect that this sign is a regular marker of imminent suicide, a visible manifestation of the inner focus, concentration, and resolve suicide requires.[13] Insofar as I am arguing that murder-suicide is a subspecies of suicide, the same sign should appear in the buildup to murder-suicide incidents. One of the incidents that first alerted me to this effect occurred as a man was videotaping himself in the woods as he planned the murder of his family and his subsequent suicide. In unemotional tones and with little facial expression, he described his ideas for this crime. As unsettling as this is to watch, it becomes even more so when one notices that the man's blink rate is very abnormal; he barely blinks at all in the course of nearly a minute (when, based on population averages, he should have blinked approximately twenty times in a minute).

I view lowered blink rate as a nonspecific warning sign for suicide in general, not just the subcategory of murder-suicide; I refer to it as nonspecific because there are other factors that can lower blink rates (e.g., opiates, some neurological conditions) and also because, taken in isolation, lowered blink rate alone may not be especially clinically informative. However, when paired with other ominous warning signs (e.g., suicidal intent, agitation), lowered blink rate is potentially worrisome.

The Heaven's Gate goodbye videos afforded another opportunity to further explore this phenomenon. My team and I, led by my former PhD student Mary Duffy, carefully counted the blinks per minute in the videos and compared them to the blink rates observed in comparison groups. We chose four comparison groups: one group included individuals who, like the Heaven's Gate members, were talking into a video camera but, unlike the cult members, were talking about relatively mundane things (i.e., product reviews); a second group included individuals who, like the Heaven's Gate members, were talking into a video camera and also were talking about a provocative topic (going through the Ice Bucket Challenge, which involved pouring ice water over one's head in a promotional campaign to fight amyotrophic lateral sclerosis [ALS]) but, unlike the Heaven's Gate members, were not talking about their own deaths. Two other comparison groups included depressed individuals, one group with no or very little suicidality, the other with some suicidal ideation but no or very little suicidal intent. The comparison groups allowed us to rule out that an altered blink rate is merely due to talking into a video camera, even about something involving a physically provocative experience, or merely due to depressive phenomena in general.

A benchmark number to keep in mind is the resting, unobtrusively observed blink rate in the general population, which is approximately twenty per minute. When a person is speaking into a video camera, that rate is slightly higher, up to around twenty-six per minute. In our comparison groups, participants' blink rates were around or well above thirty per minute. By contrast, the blink rate average for the Heaven's Gate members was approximately twenty per minute, despite their being videotaped, and despite the fact that they were talking about something quite provocative. In fact, the provocative thing about which they were talking—their own deaths—is specifically the reason we think they showed a relatively lowered blink rate, in that they were in a sense staring down death.

The average figure of twenty blinks per minute in the Heaven's Gate group is a little deceptive, in that a few of these individuals had a very fast blink rate, and thus elevated the overall group mean. These individuals tended to be the ones, referred to earlier, who, unlike the rest of the group, were deeply afraid of what was coming.

One may counter that the Heaven's Gate members were not genuinely suicidal, in that they expected to live on in a higher plane of existence. This is debatable, and in fact, the members were devoted to their ideals in very much the same way that people can be extremely dedicated to more orthodox religious ideals.[14] It is also the case that the group's members had much in common with (other) suicide decedents: like many suicide decedents, Heaven's Gate members believed they would be better off after death and were alienated from and to a degree disgusted with their bodily, worldly existence.[15] They gave away possessions, thought about and planned their deaths for months, and communicated their intent to die to others.

Furthermore, I would suggest that the facing of death registers upon ancient, visceral, and instinctual lower-brain circuitry, and that this is the case regardless of any religious, philosophical, or other rationale. Staring down death engages lower-brain circuitry and can suppress blink rate, and this appears to have been the case in the Heaven's Gate group.

* * *

Elsewhere in this book, I have emphasized that taking post hoc rationalizations for suicidal behavior at face value is regularly a mistake; for a host of reasons, people can be motivated to obscure their motives after a suicide attempt. A candidate for an ironclad, formulaic law of human behavior is that there are no such laws; even very useful rules of thumb—like that when someone nearly takes their life, there is above-zero conscious intent to do so—are not always entirely applicable. This complicates matters, but it should be no surprise that human behavior and affairs more generally are complicated.

An unfortunate incident that occurred in November 2017 in Pennsylvania is illustrative. It involved an attempt at murder-suicide in which, mercifully, no one was hurt, much less killed. The attempted perpetrator was a mother, and the intended victims were her two young children. By all accounts, the mother was in an extremely desperate state and needed help. Her way of arranging for it, evidence later suggested, was to insert a garden hose into the tailpipe of her car and run the hose into her car,

84 | PERVERTED VIRTUES TRANSFORM SUICIDE

with her children and her inside. She had texted her mother on the same day to indicate that she desired suicide.

She later claimed that this was not a genuine murder-suicide attempt but merely a "cry for help," one that was "harmless." She later stated, "I truly thought I would gain a sympathetic ear. I thought my act was harmless. I truly did."

Throughout this book I caution that one's default stance in the face of such claims should be extreme skepticism, and that would be my counsel here, though key aspects of the fact pattern give at least some pause. First, a bus driver happened on the scene, and later reported that the car was not running, which of course is necessary for it to be deadly via carbon monoxide poisoning.[16] Second, there was indeed a garden hose in the tailpipe, and there was in fact a garden hose leading into the car, but crucially, two garden hoses were involved—one in the tailpipe and one in the car—and the two were not connected. One might ask, why were there hoses anywhere in the car to begin with? The woman's work was such that it involved garden hoses.

Far less persuasively, her lawyer argued regarding her having paid that month's rent that day, asking, "Why would you pay rent if you're killing yourself?" But things of this very nature often occur in the lead-up to actual and very clear deaths by suicide, very likely attributable to the profound ambivalence that is inherent in even the most severely suicidal mindset. That is, when one momentarily wavers toward life and away from death, one decides to pay rent, make dinner plans with a friend for the next day, and so forth, only to die hours later if things waver finally toward death.

The overall fact pattern fits the defense's theory that the woman truly did not intend to kill anyone and really was just attempting to elicit help. But it fits another theory too, and this one is very consistent with a recurring theme of this book: suicide is a daunting and fearsome enough prospect that some suicidal individuals, convinced in their minds not only that death is the right thing for them but also that they will be able to enact it, cannot enact it, even though they are in the process of attempting. Their fear of death and pain disarms them.

Two other mental factors are also at play. First, death is so momentous that it can fully preoccupy the mind, leaving little mental power left to do other things, sometimes including carefully planning and enacting the steps of a lethal suicide plan. Second, though many different mental disorders are contributors to suicide, most decedents are experiencing some form of depression at the time of their deaths. A cardinal symptom of depression is impaired concentration; concentration is one of the very things required if one is to conceive and enact a complicated or difficult plan. The combined effects of the incapacitating fear of death, death's fully preoccupying nature, and depression's impaired concentration make it somewhat surprising that anyone is able to die by suicide.

This phenomenon thus leads to *aborted* suicide attempts, referred to earlier, which are in-process suicide attempts that the individual ceases before the full plan is enacted. It is of interest to consider a distinction within the domain of aborted suicide attempts, namely, those that are intentionally aborted versus those that are stopped unintentionally due to error or other such factors.

In the case of the mother and her two young children, it is quite possible that she fully intended that she and her children die, and was attempting to enact their deaths, but did not, due to mental errors like forgetting to start the car or to attach the two hoses. If so, the incident would represent an unintentionally aborted murder-suicide attempt.

The case does have some signatures of a genuine attempt at a murder-suicide involving the perverted virtue of mercy. The two children in question were the biological children of the woman and a man with whom she was in an on-again, off-again relationship. She later gave birth to twin boys fathered by another individual; she put them up for adoption because they were allegedly "targets of abuse of" and "hated" the first man. She had other children besides the twins, and continued to fear for the safety of these children from this man's violent behavior; she thus took out a restraining order against him.

At the time of the incident in the car, this man was in jail. The woman therefore had troubled romantic relationships, had two children adopted away, had a romantic partner who she feared might harm her remaining children, and was often parenting alone. Though it is speculative, this list of stressors may have combined with preexisting risk to overwhelm her to the point of deciding on suicide, at which point she then may have reasoned that should she die, her children must also, else they would be subjected to ongoing danger without her, on top of mourning her loss.

In other words, her perversion of the virtue of mercy may have led to her decision to include her children in her plan.

Under either theory of the case—an unintentionally aborted genuine attempt or an effort that was not really an attempt but a cry for help—it could be argued that the woman's culpability was above zero, in the sense that at a minimum she put her children, the bus driver who chanced upon the scene, and emergency responders through an ordeal. State prosecutors indeed argued thus, and a jury returned a unanimous verdict of ten to thirty years in prison, to be followed by ten years' probation. Notably, a previous jury had deadlocked, perhaps reflecting that though some culpability is hard to dispute, this is a case with ambiguous features.

That the plan was genuine and the rationale of a cry for help a post hoc dissimulation—as can be true in such situations—represented the prosecuting attorney's opinion. He stated of the woman's after-the-fact explanation, "I think it's garbage. I think it's an excuse she came up with only after she realized that prison life is miserable."[17]

The Germanwings disaster mentioned earlier is but one example of suicidal people killing others as part of enacting their suicide. A July 2016 bus crash in Taiwan took the lives of twenty-six people, mostly tourists from mainland China.[18] Investigators rapidly determined that the incident was more than just a tragic, accidental bus crash; the investigation revealed that the driver had doused his seat in fuel and deliberately set himself on fire. He intended to kill himself, and then events that occurred as a consequence of his actions killed many others. His motives were not clear, but psychological processes involving the perversion of virtue strike me as likely, as they do in the Germanwings incident.

Of course, these kinds of events are rare, but they occur more frequently than is often realized. Since the 1970s, at least ten such incidents have occurred involving airplanes, with fatalities ranging from a single death to 217. In a series of nine such incidents the average number of people killed was close to fifty, highlighting that although rare, these events are catastrophic, with an average death toll higher than that of almost all rampage shootings.[19] In at least two of this series of airplane incidents, the pilots had taken out substantial life insurance policies on themselves, reflecting the planned nature of the events and also a "death-worth-more-than-life" mindset (the typical life insurance policy will indeed pay following a death by suicide provided that the death occurs two years or more after the policy is bought). There is convincing evidence that the disappearance of Malaysian Airlines Flight 370 in March 2014 was a murder-suicide incident with many similarities to the Germanwings tragedy.

Spree Killing

On July 22, 2011, Anders Behring Breivik detonated an explosive device that killed eight of his fellow Norwegians; later that same day, he killed sixty-nine more, shooting the majority of the mostly teenage victims multiple times, often at close range, often in the back of the head as they fled. One of the last victims Breivik killed was a fourteen-year-old girl; he later stated he had no difficulty at all in executing her. Another of his teenage female victims was found in such a condition as to indicate that Breivik had shot her at very close range in the back of the throat through her open mouth as she screamed either in terror or for mercy, the height of evil perpetrated by an unfeeling and savage monstrosity.[20]

Given this level of savagery, it is notable that about an hour earlier, Breivik had had to overcome considerable reluctance to murder the first of his shooting victims. Of Breivik's rampage, a biographer wrote, "His body was fighting against it, his muscles were twitching. He felt he would never be able to go through with it. A hundred voices in his head were screaming: Don't do it, don't do it, don't do it! I must either let myself be caught now or carry through with what I have planned, he thought. . . . He forced his right hand down to his thigh, unfastened the holster, took hold of the pistol."[21] Moments later, his first shooting victim was dead. Interrogated later, Breivik said of his experience murdering the first victim, "It felt absolutely awful. The first shot was the worst. . . . It's a nightmare that I don't think you can understand until you've carried out . . . it was sheer hell. Taking another person's life."[22]

Throughout this book I have cautioned against putting too much faith in after-the-fact explanations, and if anyone deserves skepticism, it is a deplorable individual like Breivik. And yet, in these statements and in numerous others of his regarding what he did, Breivik is not rationalizing or prevaricating. All of the considerable evidence accords with his unapologetic statements, and his description of killing his first victim squares well with similar accounts from other spree killers.

This fact of Breivik's first reaction to killing should be lingered over: an individual who had already killed eight people in a bombing incident, who had prepared very carefully to kill dozens more, who would subsequently do exactly that, who shot a screaming teenage girl in the mouth from a range of about two feet, and who concluded his atrocity, with some relish, with the brutal execution of a female child—*even he* initially blanched at the prospect of shooting a fellow human. That is because, in addition to being detestable, deranged, and depraved, he is human, and as we have seen, humans—all humans—have an inherent reluctance to kill.

Interestingly in light of research by Skeem and colleagues showing a lack of a strong tie between psychosis and violence, a pair of forensic psychiatrists concluded that Breivik was psychotic, a conclusion that may have led to a verdict of not guilty by reason of insanity.[23] However, a second pair of psychiatrists independently evaluated Breivik and found, almost certainly correctly, that he was not psychotic but rather had a marked and very severe personality disorder with prominent narcissistic and antisocial characteristics. Accordingly, Breivik was found guilty and assigned the maximum sentence (extremely likely to equate to the rest of his life in prison, though Norwegian law does allow for an evaluation after twenty-one years in prison of whether the individual represents an ongoing danger to society).

Having murdered dozens of people, and understanding that the authorities were at last in pursuit, Breivik seriously considered suicide. He ultimately decided against it, believing that he could do more for his political agenda by living on (that agenda being an incoherent and puerile mishmash of the "de-Marxification" and "de-Islamization" of Europe; he targeted the camp not because of its ties to Islam but because of its ties to liberal politics). Still, his remarks immediately after his capture suggest a quasi-suicidal mindset: "I have sacrificed myself. I have no life after this."[24]

Like Breivik, many spree and mass killers either consider suicide or fully expect to die as part of their heinous plans. Timothy McVeigh was very clearly prepared to die in the Oklahoma City bombing (which, as a disturbing reminder, killed 168 people, including 19 children in the site's day care center).[25] Had he been twenty to thirty seconds further behind his schedule, he almost surely would have (in the event he was blown off his feet by the blast as he walked away, but was unhurt; of course his actions eventually did culminate in his death via execution). Some would doubt that McVeigh's actions had a suicidal motive. It is arguable, but one underappreciated fact is that months before the atrocity, McVeigh was in a deep suicidal depression over his failed aspirations in the military and his struggles to find work and relationships in civilian life. He called a suicide hotline for veterans in the midst of this depressive episode.[26]

Spree killing can be viewed as a generalized case of murder-suicide; the differences between them are relatively few. One candidate for a difference is that spree killers are not always suicidal, whereas murder-suicide perpetrators are. Even here, however, there are issues: for example, spree killers are not always as *obviously* suicidal as murder-suicide perpetrators, but some of them who seem nonsuicidal may well harbor suicidality that they have revealed to no one. It is also true that not all spree killers kill themselves, but the same is true in attempted murder-suicide scenarios in which a perpetrator plans murder-suicide, enacts the murder element of the plan, but then balks when it comes to the suicide aspect of the plan. Another potential difference is that in spree events, personal knowledge or connection between perpetrator and victims is rare, whereas in murder-suicide events it is the norm. In incidents that seem intermediate between spree and murder-suicide—the Columbine tragedy is one possible example—on the one hand, there was indeed a spree element in that the two teenage perpetrators shot people at their school with indiscriminate abandon, but on the other hand, the boys knew many of the people at the school.

Regarding the potentially suicidal aspect of murders, a study of 104 cases of murder or attempted murder in the United States is informative. One geographic area was studied, and the work focused on non-gang-related incidents in the years from 2000 to 2012. The 104 cases were selected for there being multiple victims within each incident. The victims in each murder were unrelated to one another, and for each incident, at least one of the victims was not related to the perpetrator. Almost 90% of the cases ended either with the perpetrator's suicide (42.3%) or with the perpetrator being subdued violently (47.1%), in some cases lethally, by authorities at the scene. Only 10.6% of these attacks ended with the surrender or fleeing of the assailant.[27]

The selection criteria for the study excluded murder-suicides occurring within families, it should be noted. Had those been included, the suicide rate following murder by definition would have been even higher within the overall series of incidents. In fact, in a study of thirty-three murders occurring mostly within families in Switzerland, sixteen ended in the perpetrators' suicide (48.5%).[28] Interestingly, these tended not to be motivated by revenge (cf. justice) but what the authors termed "perversions of loyalty," motives that I might recast as perversions of virtue such as duty and mercy.

In a separate study of thirty mass murders committed from 1949 to 1998, 56% of the assailants died by suicide or attempted suicide before capture, 10% were killed, and 33% were captured alive.[29] Murder does not necessarily involve suicide, but how commonly it does is not well appreciated.

* * *

Some of the examples discussed in the book thus far show the dynamic, fluid trajectory of desires to die and kill in suicidal people. It is very common, and on reflection not at all surprising, that the will to live and the revulsion to kill reemerge and squelch any thought or plan to die and/or kill. Even in suicidal people and in those harboring murder-suicide plans, defined by their will to die and in a subset by their murderousness, it is the norm that the will to live and the imperative to not kill prevail. What is vexing, disturbing, and tragic is that they do not always.

These same processes and vicissitudes play out in spree killers, and I will have a little more to say about them, their suicidality, and their violence toward others at the end of this chapter. Before ending this chapter, however, it is valuable to explore the emergence, fading, and reemergence of desires to kill and die, not just in spree killers but in suicidal people generally, and the potential long-term consequences for people going through these phases and surviving them. Vicissitudes in desires to die and to kill certainly occur in those who are the focus of this chapter, namely, those who perpetrate murder-suicides and spree killings followed by suicide, but there are relatively few data on them—even anecdotal data—and so the following examples open the lens to suicidal people in general before returning again to spree killers in particular.

Vicissitudes in Desires to Die and to Kill in Suicidal People

Of those who have jumped from the Golden Gate Bridge, 1% or so survive. To review, interviews with these fortunate few reveal that a typical scenario contains the following features: complete and unwavering intent to die; lack of hesitation in jumping; lack of fear for the first second or two in the air; and a gripping fear of death and deep regret at having jumped in the remaining two seconds before impact.[30] As has been noted, this suggests, tragically, that a large proportion of those who perish at the bridge go through this same sequence of mental events but do not live to tell of it.

Those who survive of course suffer months or years of physical consequences, but the mental consequences bear reflecting on too. Some are positive, such as the relief not to have died and gratitude for having more time to live. Some are negative, including the development of PTSD regarding the terror with which they were directly faced for a full two seconds in midair, as well as that which occurred in the waters below (e.g., the fear of drowning, a real and regular outcome). Given the terror, one might expect that a robust and extensive literature on PTSD following a suicide attempt exists; after all, this is certainly the case regarding forms of terror like natural disaster, assault, and combat. Together with my former PhD student Ian Stanley, I learned that this is just not the case regarding suicide attempt. For one thing, neither the fifth edition of the *Diagnostic and Statistical Manual of Mental Disorders* (*DSM-5*) nor standard clinical interview instruments on PTSD specifically mention suicide attempt as an index trauma; the same holds for self-report assessments of PTSD. For another, we searched the literature, and though it is possible that we missed something here or there, the first mention we could find of the phenomenon occurred at the relatively late date of 1993. This contribution was a conceptual consideration of the possibility that a suicide attempt could serve as an index trauma for PTSD; the authors opined that it could, but that in their clinical experience, only rarely so. They asked, "Is PTSD following a suicide attempt actually rare, or just rarely noticed?"[31]

My guess is that it is both to some degree. It is definitely rarely noticed, as the paucity of literature on it shows. But it is also probably somewhat rare because, with some important exceptions to be considered shortly, people have direct control over what happens in their suicide attempt. They plan it, they initiate it, they enact it, and should they choose, they can abort it (a not uncommon phenomenon, as we have seen). None of these parameters apply, or apply as much, to index events such as natural disasters and assaults. In these latter situations, people can feel both surprised and powerless to handle whatever they are surprised by; the elements of surprise and powerlessness make the development of PTSD far more likely. Many suicide attempts contain neither element, making PTSD after a suicide attempt somewhat rare.

I believe, however, that the field may have overgeneralized this sensible principle, leading people to the view that postattempt PTSD almost never happens, accounting, in turn, for the lack of a literature on the topic. It is a mistake to view all suicide attempts as lacking the qualities of surprise and powerlessness. It is certainly the case that the vast majority of those about to attempt suicide *think* they know what will happen. But, to reiterate, thinking does not make it so.

This is very easy to see in jumps from a height. In midair, surprise—terror would be more accurate—spikes, and the powerlessness is total. In the water some degree of power may return for some individuals, but for most their injuries have rendered them powerless and hypothermia will do so as well; the terror of drowning is stark. In ligature scenarios, few are fully prepared for the terror of a restricted airway; we have ancient "alarm"-type systems that activate in reaction to asphyxiation, and the subjective experience of such an activation is mortal terror. Even in overdose examples, a method that some see as relatively nonviolent and thus less likely to involve terror or helplessness, such states nevertheless emerge due to unexpected, and indeed inherently unpredictable, physical reactions to the overdose agent in question.

Can there be any doubt that such scenarios characterized by grave terror and intense powerlessness result in PTSD, in at least some instances? Incidentally, resources like the *DSM-5* do mention one suicide-related phenomenon as a potential index trauma, namely, the suicide attempt of another person. Presumably this is included, although one's own suicide attempt is not, based on differences in powerlessness (the former involves powerlessness, whereas one's own attempt supposedly does not). As we have seen, however, at least in some cases, this is folly. The one empirical study we found that directly and specifically addressed the topic is consistent with this being folly and would suggest that scenarios in which PTSD develops about a suicide attempt actually are not all that rare.

Bill and colleagues studied thirty individuals (66.7% female); all had major depressive disorder, all had a history of suicide attempts, and all had been recently discharged from inpatient psychiatry.[32] As assessed by clinician-administered semistructured interviews and patient self-report questionnaires, participants were assessed for PTSD involving nonsuicidal index traumas as well as PTSD related to a suicide attempt. Nearly half of the thirty participants (46.7%) developed suicide attempt–related PTSD, and an additional 10% reported a subclinical variant of suicide attempt–related PTSD.

We have already encountered Kevin Hines, author of the book *Cracked, Not Broken*, who recounted his near-death suicide attempt from the Golden Gate Bridge. To my knowledge, he was not formally assessed for PTSD in the weeks and months thereafter, but from hearing him describe his experiences on multiple occasions, I believe he may well have qualified for at least a subclinical variant of PTSD (subclinical meaning a partial, not a full, manifestation of the condition in question). For months after the incident, Hines reports having frequent nightmares of falling to his death, a clear example of the PTSD symptom cluster known as "reexperiencing."

A potentially lethal suicide attempt can be punishing to live through even without subsequent PTSD, and certainly with it. However, should PTSD develop regarding a particular suicide method, going forward into the future the individual will fear that method and thus be unlikely to repeat it. This may lead people to other suicide methods; on the other hand, fear can generalize and may do so to suicide in general. The suffering inherent in PTSD should not be minimized, but one element of that suffering may include some protection from future suicidal behavior.

In the context of nightmares about one's suicide attempt, I would add that clinically I have been struck by the relative rarity of dreaming about one's suicide *before* an actual suicide attempt occurs. I do not mean to suggest that this never occurs, but in abundant clinical experience, I cannot recall having encountered it, and a search for the literature on the point comes up mostly empty. I find this somewhat surprising because that which preoccupies us during waking hours tends to appear in our dreams as well; as I have contended throughout, imminently suicidal people are certainly preoccupied by their pending suicide attempt.

Why might it be that pre-attempt dreams about an eventual suicide attempt may be rare? A speculation involves the function of nightmares in general. Cross-culturally, most nightmares are about being chased or attacked. Nightmares may have evolved in the ancient, ancestral past as a way for the mind to solve the problem of predator threats. This would be consistent with why they are pervasive in humans, and why they have clear commonalities (being pursued or attacked) cross-culturally despite other, very clear cultural differences. Further, providing the mind with a solution to the problem posed by the nightmare tends to eliminate the nightmare. This is the operative principle behind the leading treatment for nightmares, called imagery rehearsal therapy.

As the name implies, the essence of the treatment involves rehearsal, several times per day, of a particular image; the image in question is a revision of the nightmare's crescendo moment such that, in the new image, one has control or mastery over the situation in the nightmare, as opposed to the original crescendo moment in which one was victimized or chased. This revision and rehearsal process is essentially the entirety of the therapy, and it is a prime example of the truth that simple behavioral-cognitive interventions can be extremely effective, in seeming disproportion to their lack of complexity. Image rehearsal therapy is the most effective known treatment for nightmares.[33] This is the case whether the nightmares occur within the context of PTSD or in the freestanding condition known as nightmare disorder (as the name implies, this condition is characterized solely by frequent nightmares, which is not to say it cannot be highly distressing and impairing). No other treatment rivals it, including the best-characterized medication for nightmares, the blood pressure drug prazosin. There is some evidence for this drug's effectiveness, although in a recent, very impressive and large clinical trial evaluating it for PTSD-related nightmares, it did not outperform a comparison condition.[34]

If it is the case that nightmares evolved as a means to problem-solve predator threats, and if suicide-related nightmares and dreams are indeed rare preceding a suicide attempt, it may be that suicide death was not a threat in the ancestral environment. Suicide is clearly an ancient problem, in that we know of examples dating back to early civilizations. But that is not the same as saying it was an ancestral problem; the time since the existence of those civilizations (approximately five thousand years) is but a mere blink of an eye in the ancestral, evolutionary context.

If suicide was not an ancestral problem, incidentally, that does not necessarily mean that some aspects of current suicidality have no evolutionary basis. As noted earlier, my research group has suggested that what may be implicated evolutionarily is a usually adaptive tendency involving protection of others even at the cost of danger to oneself. This is and/or could have been adaptive, in that such behavior can save copies of one's genes that reside in others, enough or more copies to compensate for those lost in one's own death. Modern suicide may be a derangement or misfiring of this behavioral module.[35]

* * *

The reemergence of the reluctance to kill is not limited to self-directed violence; it occurs with regard to other-directed violence too, such as spree killing and other forms of homicide. For example, drifter Joseph Duncan attacked a family of five, brutally murdering the mother, her partner, and one of three children.[36] He kidnapped the other two children, engaging in depravities I do not care to describe; he later killed one of the children, and as he was in the act of killing the third child, he had what he described as "an epiphany" that killing is wrong. He then took the child to a restaurant, where they were recognized and the police summoned.

People like Duncan, with a grotesque combination of antisociality and narcissism, tend to attribute insights like "killing is wrong" to some supernatural force like God, overlooking how improbable it is that God would single out someone like him with whom to communicate, and insinuating that God, having made this first mistake of choosing Duncan, compounded the error by getting the message to Duncan late, after four people had died in extremely cruel fashion. "Killing is wrong" was not placed in Duncan's mind by God or any supernatural process; it was there already in Duncan's deranged but still human mind. A number of things muted the message, among them Duncan's savagery and towering narcissism as well as his experiences with past violence, the extent of which is unknowable, probably even to Duncan, but unquestionably considerable. That the message arrived at all in a mind like Duncan's verges on the miraculous (not in the religious but rather in the probabilistic sense) and is reflective of the ingrained and powerful character of the reluctance to kill.

* * *

It can seem peculiar, even off-putting or callous, to emphasize that murder-suicides and even most spree killings are either fundamentally suicides or at least contain a very substantial suicidal element. This strikes many as discordant because of the injustice perpetrated against innocent victims by someone who seems either completely inscrutable or selfish to such a degree as to be a monstrosity (such as is Breivik, for example). The victims and their families do deserve our sympathies, of course. Future victims would as well, but I think they deserve something more, something that past victims deserved too: an effort to understand these tragedies in advance so that we are positioned to thwart them. To do so requires a dispassionate, intellectual understanding of what may produce such events, and a dispassionate process is virtually by definition discordant with the natural emotional reactions involved. These incidents thus demand that we hold two things in mind at the same time: a dispassionate determination to understand so as to prevent, and a deep sympathy for the victims of atrocity.

3

Killing Oneself without Killing Oneself

Suicide-by-Cop and Related Phenomena

Ordinarily, I possess a somewhat allergic attitude toward weaving fictional material into nonfiction. However, a medium like film can represent a reflection of public opinion, and how different it is or can be from the actual reality. That difference is very relevant to this book's thesis; in fact, in a way it *is* the thesis.

In most cinematic references to suicide-by-cop, for example, people who later die by suicide-by-cop are portrayed as especially dangerous; specifically, in a study of such films, researchers reported that 77% of eventual suicide-by-cop decedents had killed someone before their deaths, whereas the actual percentage is approximately a tenth of that.[1] This same study reported that in film, there was no instance of someone who died by suicide-by-cop having previously attempted suicide, whereas in reality this is common. The same pattern applied to history of chronic depression: only 6% in the movies, but many times that in the real world.

We observed a similar phenomenon in a previous chapter describing the on-air suicide of a news reporter. The reality was that the reporter meticulously planned her death; in the movie version, that did not "work dramatically" for the filmmakers so the facts were changed to fit a made-up impulsive suicide scenario. I am not qualified to determine what does or does not work dramatically, but distortions like this—legion in film, literature, and so on—warp public opinion. This is no small matter, as public opinion is one of the key arenas for success concerning matters of public health (cf. smoking and tobacco, the key drivers of change regarding which were grassroots activism, science, funding, and legal battles, a many-decades-long campaign that profoundly changed public opinion). We will encounter such distortions again, for example, regarding suicide terrorists, romanticized by those who recruit them as well-functioning,

98 | KILLING ONESELF WITHOUT KILLING ONESELF

heroic martyrs when in fact many of them are marginalized, depressed, and otherwise vulnerable.

* * *

Much as it was informative to consider some demographic aspects of murder-suicide, so may it be to briefly consider some similar facts regarding suicide-by-cop. For example, studies show that at least 10% of officer-involved shootings are suicide-by-cop incidents, and some studies have returned rates of approximately 25%.[2] As another example, those who die in this manner are overwhelmingly male, around 95% male to be specific (e.g., in one study, 96%; in another series of fifteen, only one was female).[3]

This is no surprise, for a few reasons. First, *any* form of death by suicide tends to be male-linked; in the United States, the ratio of male-to-female suicide decedents is roughly just under 4 to 1. That is, approximately 75% to 80% of American suicide decedents are male.[4] Second, the figure of 95% substantially exceeds even the high rate of 75% to 80% male decedents, very likely having to do with the violence involved in suicide-by-cop incidents. Involvement in any form of violent event is a very strongly male-linked phenomenon. If this line of reasoning is valid, one would expect that other suicidal scenarios involving direct violence would have similar male involvement as does suicide-by-cop, and consistent with this, suicidal violence like murder-suicide, suicide terrorism, and amok are also male-linked, with 90% or more of perpetrators being male. Similar logic would apply to most forms of suicide covered in these pages, with the possible exception of physician-assisted suicide, which does not have the pronounced gender discrepancies that other forms of suicidal death display. Proponents of access to physician-assisted suicide may see this as evidence that it is really not suicide, and that is one viable interpretation. I incline toward another, namely, that physician-assisted suicide procedures are carefully designed to minimize or eliminate the potentially violent aspects of suicide and death, and thus one would not expect gender disparities. On this latter interpretation, the lack of gender disparities in physician-assisted suicide does not bear on whether or not it constitutes suicide.

Related to the potential for other-directed as well as self-directed violence in suicide-by-cop incidents, the roles of firearm ownership, past involvement with law enforcement, and past violent behavior all deserve emphasis. Each of these is more common in men than in women, and each of these is frequent in those who instigate suicide-by-cop incidents.

To say a little more about the role of firearms in suicide-by-cop, of men who die by suicide-by-cop, approximately half (specifically 48%) brandished a firearm. This detail lends itself to more than one interpretation; one is that suicide-by-cop is fully about suicide and is not often intended to harm the officer in question (if it were, it might more frequently involve lethal weapons like various firearms). Moreover, and also consistent with this interpretation, of the 48% who possessed a weapon, 14% confronted an officer with an unloaded weapon. Let me rush to reiterate the danger and difficulty that these scenarios present to law enforcement officers; they of course do not know in advance exactly who possesses what and, if it is a gun, whether it is loaded. Officers need to make very rapid life-or-death decisions that are extremely momentous at the time but also for years and decades afterward for everyone involved, including the officers. The fact remains, however, that in suicide-by-cop scenarios, odds are fairly high that the individual does not possess a loaded weapon.

Almost all of those who confront officers without a gun do so either with no weapon at all or with a knife. It could be argued that the latter choice (a knife) is patently suicidal; the chances of harming an officer with a knife are relatively low, and yet being threatened with a knife will elicit lethal force reactions from officers fairly reliably.

As alluded to previously, suicide-by-cop in women is rare, but when it does occur, the woman is almost never without a weapon of some kind. Fully half of these weapons are firearms—slightly *more* than the corresponding rate in men—but only a third of those guns are loaded (whereas those of men are more frequently loaded). I interpret this fact pattern to mean two things: first, women generally have fewer guns than men, and thus their having them at least as frequently as men in suicide-by-cop provocations suggests at least as high intent to die as in men; second, the relatively lower rate of females' guns being actually dangerous to others (i.e., loaded) is consistent with female distaste for violence (for the most part, a very enviable quality). Further to these same points and interpretations, almost one in five females in suicide-by-cop incidents had no weapon at all but simulated or feigned a brandished weapon in a threatening way to an officer.

Two other descriptive details regarding suicide-by-cop scenarios deserve discussion. First, 87% of those in these scenarios declare their suicidal intent clearly, either prior to the incident or during it, and sometimes both. The corresponding rate in suicide is approximately 70%. The very high rate of suicide intent communications in suicide-by-cop provocations is on the one hand unsurprising. For one thing, communication of intent to die by attacking an officer can be a part of the provocation of the officer; for another, the incident is by definition occurring in the presence of another person, where any intent communications are more likely to be heard if voiced. The very high rate of suicidal intent communications is suggestive of the patently suicidal aspect of suicide-by-cop phenomena.

Approximately 35% of those in suicide-by-cop incidents are under the influence of at least some alcohol at the time. Long experience has taught me to go to some lengths to remind readers of a distinction that, once considered, is very obvious, but that nonetheless is easy to lose sight of. It is the difference between having ingested some alcohol (e.g., one glass of wine) versus being intoxicated by alcohol (defined in the United States as having a blood alcohol content of 0.08% or more; for some non-American readers, 0.08% is equivalent to 80 mg/dL). The figure of 35% of those who engage officers in suicide-by-cop scenarios is *not* with regard to intoxication but rather with regard to having ingested any alcohol whatsoever.

Those who imagine that alcohol ingestion is a primary driver, in the moment, of suicidal phenomena, may consider a statistic like 35% to be supportive of their perspective. It is nothing of the kind. This figure means that more than six in ten of those in suicide-by-cop incidents have no alcohol in their systems whatsoever at the time; another two or three of those ten have a little; and only a few are intoxicated—intoxicated, in the sense of exceeding a threshold like 0.08%, not necessarily in the sense of approaching incapacity. This latter state is virtually never seen in such incidents.

As noted elsewhere in this book, there has been an informative meta-analysis of much of the literature on usual blood alcohol content at the time of suicide death in general (not suicide-by-cop specifically). The general rate found by psychologist Mike Anestis and colleagues in that 2014 analysis is 26.86%. For comparison, the same report indicated that in accident victims, the corresponding rate was 31.7%, and in homicide victims, 37.7%. Of those dying from these three sudden causes, suicide decedents had the *lowest* blood alcohol content, and this was true to a statistically significant degree.[5]

This strikes many as surprising and unexpected, but from another standpoint, it stands to reason. That is, if purposeful, self-inflicted death is as difficult and effortful as I have claimed it to be, it makes sense that only a minority of suicide decedents ingested alcohol in the time frame before their deaths, alcohol being an agent that actively interferes with difficult, purposeful efforts. This perspective may explain the difference in blood alcohol levels between suicide decedents in general (26.86%), suicide-by-cop decedents (36%), and homicide victims (37.7%): the two groups who are not faced with the prospect of killing (only of being killed) have ingested more alcohol than the group that has to confront both killing and being killed.

* * *

In Israel, there has been a recent spate of knife attacks, the perpetrators of which are often Palestinian youths, and the targets of which are often law enforcement or members of the Israeli Defense Forces. These incidents are frequently lumped together with suicide terrorism. On the one hand, that makes a certain amount of sense, in that I am contending that at root, they are similar because both are fundamentally suicidal. On the other hand, the distinction between suicide terrorism and suicide-by-cop is a useful one, and there is reason to view these knifing attempts as suicide-by-cop more so than as suicide terrorism.

Interviewed by the *Times of Israel* on January 31, 2016, regarding such incidents, Israeli professor Ariel Merari—whom we will encounter later in connection with his eye-opening work in this area—stated that Islam's forbidding attitude toward suicide is key in understanding them. Merari argued that if an Islamic person in Israel died by suicide, "[their] family become outcasts." If one really wants to die, he contended, the current political climate encourages suicide-by-cop as a solution, because "the entire society will say, 'how wonderful, he is a shahid, he is a hero.' They will not say he committed a religiously forbidden act."[6]

A stipulation of the model of suicide I described in earlier chapters is that death by suicide is fearsome and daunting, so much so that many of those who genuinely desire death cannot enact it. Those involved in killing are often reluctant and are significantly affected by it; this certainly includes officers involved in suicide-by-cop incidents. The reluctance to kill can be seen in numerous phenomena. For instance, killing another is an egregious enough violation of our nature that many perpetrators, even those who later go on to relish depraved killing (e.g., Jeffrey Dahmer), are literally nauseated by their first killing.[7] Sanctioned killers often refuse to kill or are later very disturbed that they did not refuse; examples include the many combat soldiers who have been trained and intend to kill but who cannot do so, combat soldiers who killed and are marred by the experience for years or sometimes decades, and physicians haunted regarding their participation in physician-assisted deaths.[8]

Specific to suicide-by-cop, law enforcement officers who kill in these incidents often develop PTSD as a consequence.[9] Regarding those who induce officers to shoot them, numerous accounts of suicide-by-cop incidents demonstrate that those who instigate these events want to die but are unable to kill themselves.[10] For example, in a recent suicide-by-cop incident, an individual left multiple suicide notes, including one for the police stating they "ended the life of a man who was too much of a coward to do it himself." There is a sense in which this anecdote is unfortunate, in that it affirms an entrenched notion that suicide is inherently cowardly—I have argued strenuously here and elsewhere that that is a profound misunderstanding of the phenomenon—but the anecdote vividly shows that at least some of those who die in suicide-by-cop scenarios do so because they cannot overcome the reluctance to kill. And, it should be added, the individual who left the note about being unable to directly kill himself did nevertheless arrange for his killing. Many descriptors leap to mind for someone who has arranged their own violent demise, "coward" not being one of them.

Another incident illustrates both truths that the officers involved are frequently deeply affected by the incidents, and that the incidents regularly stem from suicidal people being determined to die but simultaneously being unable to enact death. In this event, a woman approached a Los Angeles County sheriff's deputy in a polite manner. The officer sensed that something was amiss and asked the woman how he could help her; they were standing just a few feet apart. The woman extracted a weapon from her purse and aimed it at the officer's chest, giving the latter no choice but to draw and fire his weapon at her. She died at a nearby hospital soon thereafter.

A note was found in the woman's car, and it read as follows: "Please forgive me. My intention was never to hurt anyone. This was just a sad and sick ruse to get someone to shoot me. I'm so very sorry for pulling innocent people into this. I just didn't have the nerve to pull the trigger myself." The note included the names and address of her parents and concluded, "I am very sorry for this."[11]

Like suicide, this suicide-by-cop event involved planning and intent, awareness and regret that the event will negatively affect others, and a grappling with the self-preservation instinct. Like suicide notes in suicide, the note in this suicide-by-cop incident featured pragmatic detail (here, the names and address of the woman's parents). Such features illustrate the usual qualities of the suicidal mindset, and in this particular instance, show that such regularities frequently apply to suicide-by-cop events, consistent with the perspective that, at bottom, they are suicides. Further consistent with this view, the woman who was killed shared commonalities with all those who die in suicides; for example, she struggled with a combination of depression and chronic, severe physical impairments, and had attempted suicide multiple times before the day in question.

This example also is revealing about the effect on the officers involved. The sheriff's deputy who shot the woman stated that he was regularly reminded of the shooting, and that it was and remains intensely painful for him.

* * *

Unsurprisingly, most officer-involved shootings do not involve suicide-by-cop features, but neither is it a vanishingly rare phenomenon. As alluded to earlier, approximately 10% of police-involved shootings are suicide-by-cop incidents, and on occasion rates of approximately 25% are found. As also noted earlier, in many of these incidents, it is later documented that the weapon brandished at the officer was either unloaded or not an actual gun (e.g., a toy gun purposely embellished to look realistic).[12] This detail understandably complicates the officers' later emotional processing of such incidents, in that they have to come to terms with the fact that they shot an unarmed individual. The fact that they could not have known that is of course relevant but does not necessarily resolve the complex emotions involved for the officers. Second-guessing is common among such officers, especially when they learn that decedents were intently suicidal and also unarmed.[13]

Another factor relevant to officers' later emotional processing has to do with how regularly these incidents rapidly escalate. It is not uncommon for an officer in one moment not to be tracking a particular individual and, within seconds, for that same individual to confront the officer with a weapon. When this happens, the potential for a phenomenon called "sensitization" is significantly increased, which involves lasting fear being instilled regarding a provocative thing introduced into awareness not gradually but all of a sudden. Regardless of the provocation, when sensitization occurs, the prospect for the development of PTSD is substantial; indeed, as noted, many officers do suffer from PTSD related to suicide-by-cop incidents.

To get a vivid sense of why, consider the following true example. Officers are called to a residence regarding a man threatening to kill everyone in the residence, including himself, with a rifle. They find the man in a back room; the man sees the officers, hesitates for a second or two, lunges for the rifle on the bed beside him, and almost instantly levels it at one of the officers. The officers fire of course.

It initially appeared that the man was uninjured, though he did release the gun. Having secured the weapon, the officers cuffed the man, asked if he was hurt, and got no reply. On further examination, the officers found a small entry wound in the man's chest, one that would prove fatal within minutes. The man then looked at one of the officers and asked, "Why did you shoot me?" The officer replied, "I told you to drop the gun." The man answered, "I wouldn't have shot you!"

Of course, none of this matters procedurally; there was simply nothing else for the officers to do given the circumstances. But years later, the man's words haunt the officer interviewed about the incident, as does the fact that the rifle in question was unloaded, adding validity to the man's words.

*　*　*

Many of those who initiate suicide-by-cop incidents have previously attempted suicide, as was the case in the example of the woman mentioned earlier, and some have even attempted suicide-by-cop in the past. A man's suicide-by-cop in Arizona received publicity because a video of the man, who reportedly had Asperger's syndrome, went viral. The video had nothing to do with the man's death; it was from some time earlier, and depicted him being comforted by a service dog. In a YouTube video posted a while before the incident, the man stated that he had tried suicide multiple times, including once by cop, with a gun.

Little else is known about this previous attempt, and I suspect that that is more or less the norm regarding such incidents that police successfully defuse, in that, in contrast to lethal suicide-by-cop events, they are rarely reported on by the media. This creates an unfortunate situation for law enforcement officers because the considerable successes of de-escalating potentially lethal situations go unreported, whereas incidents in which officers' hands are forced (and which they would very much prefer go otherwise) are regularly more publicized.

The risk officers face in situations like these is obvious, in that the events are initiated by the brandishing of weapons toward them. There are more risks still, as shown by a tragedy that occurred in Maryland, in which an officer was killed and the instigator was not. A trio of brothers had decided to "go out in a blaze of glory" by opening fire on a police precinct, an act they video-recorded on their phones. A four-year veteran of the force, a narcotics detective, rushed to the scene to return fire; he was in plain clothes. Other officers responded as well, and one shot the plain clothes officer, likely mistaking him for one of the brothers.[14] A second officer was shot in the incident as well. All three instigators survived.

* * *

Suicide-by-cop is suicide, but unlike most suicides, it evades direct killing, passing that onerous task on to others. As we have seen, these others are usually law enforcement officers, but they need not be. When a suicidal individual confronts someone known to be armed, and furthermore known to be quite willing to use the weapon, and when the reason for the confrontation is a hoped-for culmination in one's own death and one is in fact killed, suicide is clearly the apt term for the death. All parameters save one are identical to suicide-by-cop scenarios, the one difference being that a police officer was not involved. The main consequence of this difference is merely that the specific term "suicide-by-cop" is not applicable, leaving options like "suicide-by-other" or "dyadic death" that are more inclusive but are not as clear or descriptive.[15] Another term is "victim-precipitated homicide," covered in a later section; we will see there that this may not be the best choice of term, in that this form of death appears to have several distinct features from the varieties of suicide covered throughout the book.

A colleague recently described a case to me that she believed qualifies as "suicide-by-other," but that I believe actually illustrates a boundary between genuine "suicide-by-other" and a very tragic homicide. The example was of a mother whose adult son had a particularly severe and chronic presentation of schizophrenia. Doctors struggled and mostly failed to control the illness with varying combinations of medications at various doses. It is *not* the case that most or even many people with schizophrenia are violent, but there is no doubting that this young man was. His mother was acutely aware of the fact as well and had mentioned on multiple occasions to friends and others that she feared her son might kill her. Reasonably enough, many reacted to this with the urgent counsel that she should distance herself from her son, but her response was a placid appeal to her love of and duty to her son. Very sadly, her loyalty did indeed cost her her life.

My colleague's read on this awful tale was that the mother was inherently suicidal; why else, reasoned my colleague, would she repeatedly subject herself to what she plainly knew could be lethal violence? But there is a clear answer to this question having nothing to do with self-destruction, quite the contrary actually: in a phrase, motherly love. The woman's *intention* was not to die but rather to care for her struggling adult child, and the latter instinct was strong enough that she was willing to face potentially deadly violence to enact it. This hearkens back to a previous chapter's discussion of the roles of death instincts versus life instincts. There I questioned the very existence of a death instinct and gave examples in which everything regarding death was highly planful and far from instinctual or impulsive, and in which an instantaneous, instinctual, last-instant reaction was lifesaving. In the example of the mother and her son with schizophrenia, her instincts had nothing to do with death and everything to do with life (i.e., nurturing life, as parents do).

One can imagine relationship violence scenarios ending in death that *do* have a suicidal aspect. For example, consider an escalating domestic violence scenario involving a man and a woman; the man has a history of extreme violence, the woman, a history of suicidal depression. Having decided to end her life, the woman provokes the man when he is in a state very likely to culminate in extreme violence, with her death as a result. In this example, the signature of suicide qua suicide—*all* suicides—is operative, that signature being resolved intent to die. This leads us to the phenomenon of *victim-precipitated homicides*.[16]

Victim-Precipitated Homicides and Other Boundary Phenomena

In the imagined anecdote in the previous paragraph, the motive is clearly suicidal. Although this appears to occur from time to time, the majority of such deaths seem not to have a genuinely suicidal element. Consider, for example, this series of actual incidents described by Marvin Wolfgang, an early leader in this area of research:

— A husband accused his wife of giving money to another man, and while making breakfast, he attacked her with a milk bottle, then a brick, and finally a piece of concrete block. Having had a butcher knife in hand, she stabbed him during the fight.
— A husband threatened to kill his wife on several occasions. In this instance, he attacked her with a pair of scissors, dropped them, and grabbed a butcher knife from the kitchen. In the ensuing struggle that ended on their bed, he fell on the knife.
— In an argument over a business transaction, the victim first fired several shots at his adversary, who in turn fatally returned the fire.
— The victim was the aggressor in a fight, having struck his enemy several times. Friends tried to interfere, but the victim persisted. Finally, the offender retaliated with blows, causing the victim to fall and hit his head on the sidewalk, as a result of which he died.
— A husband had beaten his wife on several previous occasions. In the present instance, she insisted that he take her to the hospital. He refused, and a violent quarrel followed, during which he slapped her several times, and she concluded by stabbing him.

108 | KILLING ONESELF WITHOUT KILLING ONESELF

— During a lover's quarrel, the male (victim) hit his mistress and threw a can of kerosene at her. She retaliated by throwing the liquid on him, and then tossed a lighted match in his direction. He died from the burns.
— A drunken husband, beating his wife in their kitchen, gave her a butcher knife and dared her to use it on him. She claimed that if he should strike her once more, she would use the knife, whereupon he slapped her in the face and she fatally stabbed him.
— A victim became incensed when his eventual slayer asked for money which the victim owed him. The victim grabbed a hatchet and started in the direction of his creditor, who pulled out a knife and stabbed him.
— A drunken victim with knife in hand approached his slayer during a quarrel. The slayer showed a gun, and the victim dared him to shoot. He did.
— During an argument in which a male called a female many vile names, she tried to telephone the police. But he grabbed the phone from her hands, knocked her down, kicked her, and hit her with a tire gauge. She ran to the kitchen, grabbed a butcher knife, and stabbed him in the stomach.[17]

I would argue that in none of these examples is the motive plainly suicidal, but let us consider the two that are at least debatable. The first involves an intoxicated man beating his wife, giving her a knife, and daring her to use it on him; the wife indicated that she would do so if he struck her again. After her husband did so, she responded by stabbing him. In the second example, a drunken man threatened someone with a knife; the person displayed his gun, and the man responded by daring him to use it on him, whereupon he was shot to death.

I see neither of these two incidents as suicidal because I do not believe that the intent is to die. Rather, I believe it is to dominate by forcing someone to back down from a dare. The intent is thus to assert social rank and is in this sense reputational—and it backfires completely. We will see reputational motives at play again later.

Before turning to other violent scenarios that also involve reputational miscalculations, I have two additional comments about the Wolfgang work from the 1950s. First, these deaths very regularly involve alcohol, ingested both by the killer and by the victim. In fact, the figure provided by Wolfgang is 74%, approximately three times the rate observed in suicides.[18] This represents another reason to view these deaths as nonsuicidal in character, in that they do not conform to the parameters of genuine suicides.

Nevertheless, two years later, Wolfgang published "Suicide by Means of Victim-Precipitated Homicide," which used the same series of violent incidents as in his previous paper.[19] Perhaps the author had changed his mind on reflection, or perhaps he is construing any death in which the victim precipitates the cause as at bottom a suicide. The latter line of thought shares similarities with this book's thesis, with the key caveat that I do not view most victim-precipitated killings as suicide.

Research on victim-precipitated violence continues.[20] I am aware, however, of few convincing data that indicate it is predominantly suicidal in nature. Moreover, there are a number of conceptual, definitional, and other problems (e.g., can be seen as victim blaming) with the concept.[21]

Turning to another boundary phenomenon, in Russian roulette, a bullet is loaded in one of the six chambers of a pistol, the chamber is spun, and then one aims the gun at one's head and pulls the trigger. People do indeed die in this fashion; researchers uncovered seventy-one such deaths in CDC data from 2003 to 2006 in several US states.[22]

As with victim-precipitated homicide, I hesitate to include Russian roulette within the category of genuine suicide of any variety. My hesitation involves two issues. First, in genuine suicide, as I have noted frequently, intent-to-die ratings equate to or verge on 100%, whereas they are at most one-sixth that in Russian roulette. Second, unlike, for example, in suicide-by-cop and death row volunteering, I am not sure Russian roulette at bottom really is about suicide. It may be primarily about reputation and the lengths to which one will go to earn and display it. That reason, if correct, sets Russian roulette apart from the other forms of self-directed violence.

A timely form of self-precipitated death involves overdose of substances like opiates and fentanyl. There are such deaths that clearly are intentional suicides (e.g., with a note or video to that effect, a massive overdose, etc.). Many are clearly accidental (e.g., when one believes one is ingesting heroin but is instead ingesting something more powerful, such as fentanyl).[23] Some of these deaths may have that same reputational element as Russian roulette, but I suspect that is relatively rare, and regardless, as noted earlier, reputational and suicidal motives seem to me distinct.

* * *

This chapter has described suicide-by-cop as best understood as a variant of suicide. Fundamentally, the features and principles that attach to suicide thus attach to these incidents too, though the "by-cop" element can distract from that truth. To be sure, the "by-cop" element deserves attention and understanding, as the law enforcement officers caught up in these deaths are often deeply affected, as documented earlier. As important as this is, it does not change these incidents' essential nature as suicides; in these incidents, as unnerving as it is to state, the decedents' suicide method is "the cop," whereas in suicides in general it is ligature, gunshot, and so on. There are no fundamental differences between suicide and suicide-by-cop other than this method difference, just as there are no differences between suicide by ligature and by self-inflicted gunshot wound other than the method difference. As in suicides more generally, those who die in suicide-by-cop incidents are deliberate and knowing in their actions. In those instances in which an individual attempts suicide-by-cop, is wounded, but survives, the individual's postincident explanations tend not to involve assertions of an "and-the-next-thing-I-knew-doctor" quality. This stands in marked contrast to a phenomenon I turn to in the next section—amok, an allegedly dissociative state in which one violently runs wild—in which such post hoc claims are common.

Why this difference between suicide-by-cop and amok? In a phrase, the presence of a law enforcement officer. That is, in suicide-by-cop, those involved know that their behavior, verbalizations, inferred motives, and so forth are being observed by a trained authority; not so (often) in amok.

In both phenomena I assert that people know what they are doing, and in both cases, should they survive, they are tempted to say something along the lines of "I don't know what came over me" or "I lost it for a while." This temptation is referred to in psychological research as "demand characteristics," in that if a particular experimental setup demands a specific response, it is hardly illuminating that that response occurs. The demand characteristics for disavowal post-amok are intense indeed, and thus it is not informative when disavowal occurs.

Consider, however, the effects on disavowal-related demand characteristics of a law enforcement officer's presence. A trained authority's presence is likely to mitigate disavowal, though hardly to zero, as officers themselves would readily attest.

This line of thought produces predictions that are empirically testable, at least in principle. One simple prediction is that disavowal and, relatedly, claims of dissociative states are likely to be noticeably more frequent in amok than in suicide-by-cop incidents. Another is that in suicides in which one person induces another to kill them, and the person induced to kill is *not* a law enforcement officer, disavowal, dissociation claims, and the like should be at similar levels as those found in amok. An exception to this rule may involve cases, such as that referred to earlier instigated by three brothers in Maryland, in which an officer is killed and an instigator survived. In this scenario, demand characteristics for "I-don't-know-what-came-over-me" kinds of explanations are considerable, and thus appeals to dissociative states—either by the instigator or by his counsel—may be more likely.

Amok

A psychological scientist was recently quoted as follows: "High-profile mass shootings capture public attention and increase vigilance of people with mental illness. But our findings clearly show that psychosis rarely leads directly to violence."[24] The researcher and her colleagues studied more than eleven hundred violent offenders who had been discharged from psychiatric facilities. From this group, they focused on the highest-risk subgroup consisting of offenders who had been involved in at least two violent incidents in the year following discharge from a psychiatric facility. The goal of the work was to characterize the offenders' mental state during the incidents of violence. The researchers found that a very clear majority of incidents had nothing to do with psychosis-related states like dissociation.[25]

Violence is sufficiently against our nature that, when it occurs, one of the first rationales that crystallizes in people's minds is along the lines of "he must have lost his mind." For example, the mother of Anders Behring Breivik (who murdered seventy-seven of his fellow Norwegians), after learning of the atrocity, stated, "If it does turn out to be Anders, he must have been unconscious when he did it."[26] Later interrogation and evaluation of Breivik revealed that he was in no way unconscious, nor was he psychotic, at the time of the murders.

Similarly, the phenomenon of amok is often attributed to dissociation, but there is substantial reason, in addition to findings like those on the violent offenders and examples like Breivik, to doubt the connection. Like suicide, amok is perpetrated, often by a man, after a period of social withdrawal, brooding, and agitation. Like murder-suicide and sometimes suicide-by-cop, amok frequently results in the murder or attempted murder of at least one other person. A sizable proportion of amok perpetrators (sometimes called "amok runners" in the literature) are killed during the episode, either by their own hand or by others. One of the first descriptions of amok in the West came from Captain Cook in 1770, and the phenomenon was first described in the academic literature at the turn of the twentieth century.[27] The behavior of "running amok," though, had been well known in Malaysia for several centuries.[28]

In recent decades, amok was largely viewed as a culturally unique dissociative disorder, and indeed it was described largely in that way in the fourth edition of the *Diagnostic and Statistical Manual of Mental Disorders* (*DSM-IV*; the edition previous to the current one, *DSM-5*).[29] However, some of the earliest recorded observers of amok described it, I think quite rightly, as a form of suicide.

I have already alluded multiple times to the "and-the-next-thing-I-knew-doctor" phenomenon, in which people distance themselves from responsibility for their own behavior, and I have pointed out that in suicide-by-cop, this line of defense is complicated by the fact that a trained law enforcement observer was present for the incident. That is often not the case in amok scenarios, leading, as touched on earlier, to three potentially testable predictions: (1) there will be more claims of "I didn't know what I was doing" in amok scenarios than in suicide-by-cop incidents; (2) within amok events, the extent of officer presence will correlate with the (lowered) likelihood of "and-the-next-thing-I-knew" explanations by amok runners; and (3) within amok incidents, the timing of officer presence will correlate with the likelihood of post hoc excuse making, such that claims of "I lost my head" will be less likely the earlier in the amok run the officer is present. The logic regarding this latter prediction is that once an amok run is well underway, and, as is often the case, multiple people are already killed or injured, the "lost my mind" defense seems more plausible than if the process has just started or not progressed much.

The *DSM-IV* described amok and similar other behaviors found in Laos, the Philippines, Polynesia, Puerto Rico, and Papua New Guinea and among the Native American Navajo as "a dissociative episode characterized by a period of brooding followed by an outburst of violent, aggressive, or homicidal behavior directed at people and objects."[30] It also noted that episodes tended to be preceded by a perceived insult and were prevalent only among males. However, while multiple reports of amok contain dissociative features such as perceived loss of agency and localized amnesia, it is probably inaccurate to categorize it primarily as a dissociative disorder because it necessarily involves premorbid brooding (a brooding that is likely knowingly focused on what the perpetrator-to-be is about to do) and indiscriminate homicidal violence. As other authors have remarked, the only evidence of dissociation that has been reported in amok is from perpetrators who have survived their attacks, and who may have considerable reason to feign symptoms of dissociation and amnesia as rationale for their behavior.

Additionally, historical patterns in amok, chiefly the drastic reduction in cases of amok following Britain's shift to rapidly punish amok by execution, indicates that people are able to control their urge to run amok in many cases, and that it is not an uncontrollable dissociative phenomenon.[31] I argue that, based on reviews of case studies of amok and recent research conducted on individuals who commit mass murder, it is not a culture-bound disorder but rather a universal behavioral syndrome that manifests with some differences across the globe. I propose that amok is better described as a phenomenon related to murder-suicide or suicidal spree killing than as a culture-bound or dissociative disorder as it has been in the past, most notably by the American Psychiatric Association in the *DSM-IV* (interestingly, *DSM-5* omitted the condition altogether).

Attacks occurred in the spring of 2018 in Toronto that had features highly reminiscent of an amok episode. Specifically, a man killed ten people and injured fourteen others in a rampage in which he drove his car through a crowded area. There is every indication that he understood exactly what he was doing and that he was not in any sort of dissociative state at the time of the assault. For example, just before he perpetrated the attack, the man posted to social media the line "All hail the Supreme Gentleman Elliot Rodger!" The reference is to an individual who carried out a very similar attack in California in 2014, the motive for which was a hatred of women; women specifically were targeted by Rodger and were likely targeted in the Toronto incident as well. The same social media post stated "the incel rebellion has already begun." "Incel" is an abbreviation for "involuntary celibacy," which the California killer Rodger believed was unjustly forced on him by women. In fact, in the Toronto incident 80% of the decedents were female, consistent with similar beliefs. The perpetrator in California killed himself just after the attacks; in the Toronto case, it is possible that the offender expected to be killed, though it is unclear. He survived and is now incarcerated.

The psychological processes operating in these two cases display, among other things, *blame externalization,* a very true marker of forms of externalizing psychopathology like antisocial personality disorder. In each case, a self-centered individual feels deserving of—one might say entitled to—female attention and, not receiving it, makes the classic mental move of the externalizer: "The problem is with them, not with me." Instead of considering the extremely likely possibility that they themselves are behaving in off-putting, uninteresting ways, the men blame women's supposed conspiracy of "incel." One glaring problem with their viewpoint—that obviously some men do receive female attention—does not escape them, but neither does it alter their beliefs. They simply attribute the fact to some men's inclusion in women's conspiracy against them.

When these kinds of psychological processes are at work in suicidal individuals—in these two cases, one man was plainly suicidal, the other may have been as well—murder-suicides can result. Assuming for the moment that both of these examples contained suicidal elements, I would speculate that each incident represents a "perversion of the virtue of justice" murder-suicide. That is, the mental processes proceeded as follows: "This is all hopeless in the face of this relentless female conspiracy against me; I am going to kill myself. But I am not to blame; women are. Therefore, it would be the just thing, the virtuous thing, for some of them to die if I am to die too."

Related states that do *not* contain a suicidal element may serve as interesting and useful boundary markers for what is and what is not, at bottom, primarily suicidal. I have already examined phenomena like victim-perpetrated homicide and Russian roulette in this context. As another example, Norse literature describes a war-related phenomenon of "berserk." Warriors who experienced berserk (known as "berserkers") fought in a trancelike fury with both great abandon and considerable effect. In contrast to amok runners, berserkers were not particularly likely to die, and descriptions of their suicides are vanishingly rare; rather, they are described as invulnerable and superhuman. An interesting side note is that some have attributed berserk to the ingestion of large amounts of alcohol and/or psychedelic drugs; similar claims (at least regarding alcohol) are frequently asserted regarding suicide. With regard to suicide, such claims are not empirically supportable, as the majority of suicide decedents have blood alcohol levels at or near zero, as noted earlier.[32] It would surprise me if the same pattern did not apply to berserkers, the logic being that both death by suicide and highly effective mortal combat are daunting and difficult, and that alcohol intoxication, far from being facilitating, actively interferes with the performance of daunting and difficult behaviors.

In his book *Achilles in Vietnam*, Jonathan Shays described phenomena similar to berserk in both Homer's epic poems and the Vietnam War.[33] However, Shays's depiction can be viewed as intermediate between the suicidal amok runners and the nonsuicidal berserkers, in that Shays views these states as highly conducive to later PTSD, which in turn elevates suicide risk.[34] Shays's points on the toll killing can take on killers of any sort (including those who kill in combat) bear similarities to points I have made in this chapter regarding suicide-by-cop incident and to points I will make in a later chapter about the effects of killing on physicians who directly assist in suicides.

4

Suicide Terrorism

A well-educated, slight, middle-aged man, described as stern, easily offended, and threatened by sexual intimacy, brooded over his future on a cruise ship from Egypt to New York. He was preoccupied not just with his own future but with that of what he saw as his civilization, which he worried Western civilization would subsume and destroy. Once in New York, he wrote to a friend back in Egypt of his desperate loneliness. He later wrote in letters home of his feelings of "estrangement" in the midst of having withdrawn from all the classes he was taking.

His disposition seemed at least in part genetic, in that all his brothers and sisters shared these same traits of touchiness, intimacy fears, humorlessness, and tendencies toward withdrawal, aloneness, and rumination. They also shared his very strong feelings about religion.

His name was Sayyid Qutb, and he was a founder—if not the founder—of the kind of thinking that eventually, decades later, produced the atrocity of September 11, 2001. Qutb was put on trial for plotting to overthrow the Egyptian government; he was found guilty and was executed in August 1966. He received his death sentence gratefully. "Thank God," he declared.[1] Like the prisoners on death row whom we will encounter later who very willingly volunteer for execution, there is reason to consider Qutb's death a suicide. It is not just that he was very willing to die, and not just that he had been preoccupied by death for years; additionally, he had a clear opportunity to escape death, and declined it. Specifically, an offer was made to him by Egypt's leader Gamal Abdel Nasser of a commuted sentence; Nasser was even willing to offer him a post in his government of minister of education (Qutb was an accomplished intellectual). All that was required was that he appeal his sentence. Qutb's sister Hamida, who was also in prison, was brought to him. "Write the words," she pleaded, referring to the appeal. Qutb responded, "My words will be stronger if they kill me."[2]

It is no coincidence that a man very dispositionally similar to Qutb was a ringleader of the September 11 atrocity. Mohamed Atta is described by Lawrence Wright in *The Looming Tower* using terms such as "extreme rigidity of character" and "very, very scary." Atta was enraged by Israel's 1996 attack on Lebanon, and in response signed a will offering his life to correct what he viewed as an extremely egregious wrong. He was also hateful, misogynistic, and paranoid. This view of Atta squares well with that provided by the psychologist Reid Meloy, who wrote of Atta that he was "confused, angry, lonely, likely depressed, and socially adrift."[3] Loneliness and feeling socially adrift are, according to the interpersonal theory of suicide, key elements of the suicidal mind.

A typical narrative of suicide terrorism is that the perpetrators, though aggrieved, are relatively well educated, well adjusted, of average or above average socioeconomic status, and devoted to a sacred religious cause. Three of these descriptors certainly apply to both Qutb and Atta, though regarding the fourth, they were very far from well adjusted.

This favorable narrative of suicide terrorism that emphasizes supposed adjustment and de-emphasizes how unwell many terrorists are is certainly in accord with the views of the leaders of terrorist organizations, sources of questionable credibility to put it mildly. For example, in 2006 a cofounder of one such organization declared, "These are not suicide operations. This is a despicable term used by the Israelis in order to say that these are suicide operations, knowing that suicide is forbidden in Islam. . . . These are martyrdom-seeking operations."[4] A scholar studying the phenomenon was told by a different terrorist leader, "Those who undertake martyrdom actions are not hopeless or poor, but are the best of our people, educated, successful."[5]

In many cases, however, the reality is very different. These kinds of descriptions offer a far better description of the *leaders* of terrorist organizations, leaders who live on as they repeatedly recruit vulnerable, often suicidal individuals to die on their behalf.[6] Though it is somewhat rare, at least some in suicide terrorism groups are occasionally honest about this reality. The scholar Jessica Stern interviewed a Palestinian Authority general, who stated that they sought as suicide bombers young men who seem "anxious, worried, and depressed" and feel that "life has no meaning."[7] A suicide bomber dispatcher stated of those who recruited potential suicide terrorists, "I asked them to find me guys who were desperate and sad."[8]

It is probably excessive to attribute 100% of the motivation of suicide terrorists to underlying mental disorders and suicidality. Indeed, after reading an earlier draft of this book, Ariel Merari, an internationally renowned expert on this topic, wrote to me, "I have interviewed quite a few suicide bombers who, judging by their clinical interviews and tests, were not suicidal, and actually said that they were afraid of dying and did not want to die, but tried to complete their deadly mission nevertheless because of the commitment they gave to the leader and the group." A complication, however, is that suicidal patients, too, sometimes make similar statements, denying their suicidality and acknowledging their fear of death. Still, as Merari implies, it is complicated, with factors like group pressure, individuals' commitment to the group, and individuals' loyalty to leadership all at play.[9] All these factors, along with denied but nonetheless real suicidality in some cases, can operate together and in fact may scaffold one another.

Of these factors, however, phenomena related to mental disorders and suicidality itself are regularly underemphasized. A woman who was a member of a Palestinian terror group and who was found guilty for her role in facilitating the efforts of suicide bombers said that many of the bombers "think death is better than living the way they do."[10] This last anecdote is reminiscent of the interpersonal theory of suicide, which views the mindset that one's death will be worth more than one's life as central in suicidality.

Those within the Israeli Defense Forces tend to agree that most if not all suicide terrorism is perpetrated by troubled individuals. A senior officer in the forces' Central Command remarked to a *Times of Israel* reporter that most suicide terrorists "have personal problems with their families or they themselves are unbalanced." In the same piece, Israeli psychologist Ariel Merari commented regarding the perpetrators of such acts that they "tended to be people who thought they had disappointed their parents."[11]

The link between socioeconomic status and terrorism has been comprehensively explored by, among others, the late Princeton economist Alan Krueger. He found that there was no link between suicide terrorism and high socioeconomic status, directly contradicting the repeated claims of certain media and suicide terrorist leaders.[12]

In his book *The Knife Went In*, Theodore Dalrymple writes of an aspiring suicide bomber, describing the man as having a long history of drug abuse and criminality.[13] Unsurprisingly in light of Dalrymple's work as a prison psychiatrist and of the individual's substantial criminality, the setting was a prison. Notice in passing the considerable differences in temperament and circumstances between, on the one hand, a man like this and, on the other hand, men like Qutb and Atta (who would disdain drug use, for example). But there were crucial similarities too, in that all three men were psychologically fragile and unwell.

Interestingly, the individual in prison evinced imperviousness to physical pain (and Atta and Qutb both had stoic streaks to their personality as well). That is a potentially important detail. Indeed, my colleagues and I have theorized that suicide can be preceded by a high tolerance to physical pain. To Dalrymple's knowledge, the suicide terrorism aspirant later enacted neither suicide nor any terroristic act. Here, just as occurs with suicide, many contemplate the act—and many speak of it—but far fewer carry through with it.

I rush to caution, incidentally, that speaking of suicide ought not be dismissed as mere talk. Dalrymple has thoughts on this too; in a passage that happens to express my opinions on the matter, he stated, "Even slight (suicidal) gestures had to be taken seriously. . . . It is one of the enduring myths . . . ineradicable by mere evidence and argument," the myth in question being that people who communicate about suicide never enact it. Dalrymple argues further that this myth is the result of mistaken logic, namely, that if many people who talk of suicide never enact it, then it follows that people who die by suicide never speak of it. Of course it does not follow; as noted earlier, as many as three in four people who die by suicide communicate their intent to die in the hours, days, and weeks before their deaths.[14] Dalrymple adds a crucial caveat that none of the foregoing suggests that suicidal talk or gestures are never used as emotional leverage on others, for of course that happens too, turning "diseases into commodity," to use the phrasing of Shakespeare's Falstaff.[15]

To return to the issue of suicide terrorism, the sheer number of terrorist attacks is worrisome.[16] In 2016, a total of 5,650 people perished in suicide attacks in 469 incidents, well over 1,000 more deaths than occurred in 2015, a one-year increase of 30%. Far more than half of this mayhem was caused by ISIS.

Generally speaking, however, and intriguing in light of this book's argument that phenomena like suicide terrorism are at bottom suicide, just as the international suicide rate has drifted downward, and just as the US rate has as well in 2019 and 2020, so has the rate of suicide terrorism. Israel's Institute for National Security Studies reported that 2020 witnessed 127 suicide terror attacks perpetrated by 177 assailants; these resulted in the deaths of 765 people and injured nearly 2,000 more. Though the numbers remain appalling on their own, they do represent a steep decline from 2019, which saw more than two times the number of people killed in suicide terror attacks (the specific toll was 1,855 dead), and from 2015 and 2016, in which years far more perished in suicide terror incidents. As might be inferred from the foregoing, the lethality of attacks has decreased noticeably—for example, the number of people killed per incident in 2019 was approximately 12, about twice the number killed per attack in 2020.[17]

If suicide terrorism is a subspecies of suicide, there should be at least some parallels between the vicissitudes of suicide rates and those of suicide terrorism rates. The data just presented are consistent with such parallels.

Such parallels between suicide decedents and suicide terrorists should also be apparent in the psychology of suicide terrorism as investigated in would-be or thwarted suicide terrorists. There are many near-death scenarios in suicide terrorism in which individuals attempt the act but are thwarted, sometimes by a brave bystander or law enforcement officer, but mostly by flawed explosive devices that fail to detonate (constructing a device that will detonate lethally is harder than most people, including some terrorists, understand; it is like suicide in this regard as well [i.e., harder than most understand]).

In some of the most illuminating research of all on suicide terrorism, some of those who attempted to perpetrate suicide terrorism but who survived have been studied in depth and compared with interesting control samples. For example, Ariel Merari and colleagues compared would-be suicide terrorists with nonsuicidal terrorists.[18] All of the approximately forty interviewees in the study were incarcerated, and all were carefully interviewed and tested, using such tests as a version of the California Personality Inventory and, although it is a little hard to imagine administering these to jailed terrorists, projective tests like the House-Tree-Person Test (in which one is asked to draw a house, a tree, and a person). Impressively, the researchers spent about six hours with each of the incarcerated participants administering the interviews and tests, taking thoughtful steps to mitigate sources of bias, such as the fact that some of the terrorists might be deceitful in interviews.

The general picture that emerges from the interviews and tests on the suicidal terrorist portion of the incarcerated individuals is reminiscent of that described earlier regarding individuals like Mohamed Atta and Sayyid Qutb. A main personality style detected among the jailed attempted suicide terrorists indicated interpersonal touchiness and a tendency to avoid or stand off from others. Psychologically as well as interpersonally, they appeared vulnerable and victimized. For some of them, an element of rashness was combined with vulnerability and avoidance. That they tend to be rash in personality does not mean all their acts are impulsive; acts of suicide terrorism overwhelmingly tend to be planned in detail. This same general personality profile of traits like avoidance and touchiness is recognizable in Atta and Qutb, but, more important in the present context, it regularly emerges in psychological autopsy studies of those who have died by suicide as well.

In interviews, one of the suicide bombers, a twenty-one-year-old man, was asked to describe his childhood. In reply, he described a lonely time, one in which he usually played alone and actively avoided other children. He had no friends. The interviewer's impressions during the evaluation was of a shy individual lacking in vitality.

Strikingly, among the control participants, who were involved in terroristic activities but not of a direct suicidal nature, no individuals displayed signs of suicidality. Among the suicide terrorism sample, several did. A similar pattern emerged regarding depression symptoms: rare in the nonsuicidal comparison group and common in those jailed for suicide terrorism attempts. If these seem like achingly obvious findings, I remind readers of the claim, made by terrorist organizations and others, that suicide terrorism has nothing whatsoever to do with suicide. It clearly does, at least according to the results of this illuminating study.

122 | SUICIDE TERRORISM

The researcher who conducted this study, Israeli professor Ariel Merari, was interviewed regarding Palestinian terrorism, and, as seems to be his wont, he made a penetrating point. He stated, "A first question that has to be asked is not why there are so many attackers, but why there are so few?" He continued, "There is no doubt that the overwhelming majority of the Palestinian population hates Israel. The vast majority are happy when there are terror attacks against Israel. But when it comes down to it, very few are willing to carry out these attacks themselves."[19] Who are these very few? His answer—and mine—is that in large part they are people with substantial underlying suicidality.

My thinking on suicide terrorism has been significantly shaped by the ideas of Adam Lankford, a professor of criminology at the University of Alabama and the author of the book *The Myth of Martyrdom*. It is my habit to sometimes reach out to authors of works I find illuminating, as I did regarding Dr. Lankford. Much of the following material is based on email correspondence with him, though the thesis that animates his remarks is fully consistent with his *Myth of Martyrdom* book as well as his other scholarly published work.

For instance, as Lankford pointed out to me, the United Nations reported that, grotesquely, ISIS has used children with significant developmental delays to carry out suicide terrorism. This is at least as odious, of course, as recruiting young people who are prone to suicidality and depression; the commonality in both practices is the predatory exploitation of the vulnerable. This awful practice, incidentally, paints members of ISIS exactly as they are; they are not altruistic crusaders fighting and willing to die for a sacred cause, but rather depraved and psychopathic serial killers. This is an extreme example of a narrative that truly is apt regarding suicide terrorism; that is, far from being an educated, high-functioning individual that suicide terrorist leaders suggest is the case, the modal bomber is a vulnerable soul, sometimes very much so, on whom leaders have preyed and whom leaders have essentially destined to die and induced to murder others as well.

In this light, it is interesting to further consider the psychological functioning and histories of those who perpetrated the attacks of September 11. As usual, a narrative cropped up around them that they were by and large educated and well functioning, but that is just not true regarding many of them.

I have already noted the numerous psychological difficulties of the atrocity's ringleader, Mohamed Atta. As another example, a report by the Central Intelligence Agency states of one of the attackers that he "suffered from depression and asked for a leave of absence from his job." This episode was not in the terrorist's distant past, but rather occurred within two years of the attacks. Moreover, the episode appeared severe; according to friends who were interviewed later, "It was not just depression, but perhaps even a suicidal tendency."[20]

Of another 9/11 terrorist, one of his flight instructors recalled behaviors and attitudes that approached, if did not count as, frank suicidality. The instructor remarked that the terrorist had "told me about one flight in which he had almost run out of fuel. . . . What struck me most when he was recounting this story was that he did not seem to care. . . . [Subsequently,] on one occasion when [he] and I were about to fly I double-checked the fuel (as all pilots and flight instructors always do prior to a flight) and noticed that there was almost no fuel; [he] was ready to fly. I questioned him about the lack of fuel and again he seemed mildly amused rather than appalled by his possibly life-threatening mistake (again)."[21]

Some individuals were originally intended to be a part of the September 11 plot but, for reasons like failure to obtain a visa, in the end were not involved. At least two of these individuals were plainly psychologically unwell. One seems to have had past suicide attempts as well as past nonsuicidal self-injury. Another has schizophrenia comorbid with major depressive disorder and has likely faced elements of the former illness since his youth. Within the two years prior to the 9/11 atrocity, this individual experienced a severe, suicidal psychotic episode, which involved trying to throw himself into a street and occasioned an involuntary inpatient psychiatric admission. Still another evinced clear signs of mental disorders during his trial for conspiring in the planning of 9/11 attacks. Such conditions run in his family. He has two sisters; both suffer from schizophrenia and, quite appropriately, are taking antipsychotic medications to mitigate and cope with the illness. His father has a different condition—bipolar disorder—and each of these three have been hospitalized for their illnesses in an inpatient psychiatric facility.[22] (Proper treatment for such conditions can be a blessing, at times a life-saving one; there is no shame in having these conditions and treatments.

I sincerely wish that my own father, who had bipolar II disorder, were hospitalized; it may well have averted his death by suicide.)

Interviews with individuals who planned to engage in suicide terrorism but who experienced a bomb malfunction or another impediment to enacting their plan suggest that these individuals feel as though they are a burden to their families.[23] A similar sentiment is expressed by individuals at elevated suicide risk.[24] Crucially, as noted previously, these interviews also reveal that a substantial portion of these suicide terrorists report a history of depression, past suicidal thinking, and/or suicide attempts prior to making the decision to engage in suicide terrorism.[25] This stands in contrast to assertions that suicide terrorists are not psychologically impaired in any way, are entirely mentally healthy, or are even above average in functioning. Further underscoring this important point, interviews with violent terrorists who do not participate in suicide attacks, and even those who train and dispatch suicide terrorists, have revealed that the majority of these individuals would not be willing to carry out a suicide attack themselves, despite being willing to fight and possibly die to defend their cause.[26] This suggests that there is a distinct, genuinely suicidal quality to suicide terrorist activity.

The documentary *Dugma: The Button* portrays the day-to-day lives of young men who are awaiting assignment to a suicide terrorism mission. The IMDb summary of the film suggested that it was mostly about the positive reasons that the young men invoke for their impending deaths (although none of the men depicted in the film are assigned to a mission).[27] Indeed, in one striking portion of the film, a young man waxes on about the elation he felt on a recent mission that was canceled at the last moment. However, there are moments in the documentary that reveal the palpable depression and suicidality of these men. One of them states, "Our aim is death." Another is focused on his own sinfulness (cf. guilt and worthlessness in major depressive disorder) and looks forward to death because it will "wash away [his] sins." One of the men emphasizes the reward that will come to his father as a result of his death, a parallel to the relief of the burden many suicide decedents believe themselves to have been to their families. It is notable how common deep and melancholy sighs are among the young men as they are interviewed for the film. A man recently injured in a mission in which he expected to die exhorts others that their mission cannot be driven by being tired of life, an implicit acknowledgment that this motive is present.

Much of the film is set in a kind of terrorist training camp, and it is interesting to reflect briefly on the similarities such places have to "exit guide" organizations, which will be covered later in depth. These latter groups' purpose is to help people through the stages of assisted dying. A similar process occurs in suicide bomber training centers, with the important exception that the latter are conditioning their trainees not just to die but also to kill others.

The distinctions I am emphasizing here between actual heroism, on the one hand, and the vulnerable being preyed upon to carry out pseudoheroic depravities, on the other, are clearly illustrated by three examples of extreme and genuine heroism in reaction to those perpetrating suicidal violence. In two of these cases, the heroic individuals sacrificed their lives, and thus reduced the number of other people killed.

The gun-involved atrocity perpetrated at a school in Newtown, Connecticut, took the lives of twenty-six people, twenty of them young children (the shooter had killed his mother beforehand and killed himself at the school, bringing the total death toll to twenty-eight). The first person to die at the school was its principal, who was among the first to confront the shooter. The latter raised his menacing weapon at a group of administrators, office staff, and teachers; understandably, the group all cowered. All, that is, except the principal—a physically diminutive woman of just over five feet in height, with no military or law enforcement experience—who unflinchingly ran at the perpetrator. It is somewhat unclear, but given the nature of such situations, it is likely that the woman's behavior rattled the gunman at least somewhat; he killed her nonetheless, and in doing so spent far more of his ammunition than was needed to be lethal. The action cost the principal her life and cost the shooter crucial time, probably several seconds. In an incident in which twenty-six people were killed within a very few minutes, the elapsing of several seconds is potentially highly significant and may well have saved at least one life.

In this same atrocity at Newtown, virtually everyone who heard the gunfire panicked in some manner, again quite understandably. The principal was an exception; so was the school's custodian, who instinctually ran *toward* the gunfire in a full sprint, warning and exhorting people

126 | SUICIDE TERRORISM

toward safety along the way. He survived the ordeal, and he, too, may well have saved lives.

In November 2017 in Kabul, Afghanistan, a suicide bomber appeared at a political rally. His intentions became clear to a police officer, Lieutenant Sayed Basam Pacha, who yelled repeatedly at the attacker. Getting no response, Lieutenant Pacha ran to the attacker and bear-hugged him; within seconds, the attacker's device detonated, killing the attacker, Lieutenant Pacha, and thirteen bystanders. Authorities report that there is no doubt that the death toll would have been substantially higher absent Lieutenant Pacha's heroism.

Consider these heroic acts in the midst of tragedies, in the context of what the heroes-to-be expected of their day. In the principal's and the custodian's cases, just as hundreds of days at the school had come and gone without incident or with the minor day-to-day problems of schools, they very likely expected the day in question to be similar. What the day actually entailed was, I would suggest, literally unimaginable to them, and certainly it is not accurate to characterize their reactions as in any way scripted or thought through. They reacted in the moment, selfless and brave. Much the same could be said about Lieutenant Pacha. Although his military training may have prepared him in general for such scenarios, he too had to act very quickly and in the moment, at great peril to himself.

In these extremely chaotic scenes, only two individuals had fully planned out their actions in advance, the two suicidal perpetrators. In this way, they are characteristic of to-be suicide decedents in general, in that they planned their deaths in detail with considerable forethought. By contrast, the principal, the custodian, and the lieutenant acted as they did absent planning; they initiated or risked their own deaths, but they were not suicidal because they did not primarily intend their death in the moment nor did they plan it in advance.

A detail of the incident involving Lieutenant Pacha deserves further reflection. Specifically, as the lieutenant became aware of the potential attacker, Pacha repeatedly yelled out to him, without success. It would be plausible to suggest that the soon-to-be perpetrator heard the lieutenant but deliberately ignored him—plausible but, I believe, probably wrong. I suspect that the terrorist did not hear the lieutenant at all because he was in the highly peculiar mindset of being focused on death.

When this mental state takes over fully, the focus tends to be absolute and excludes the processing of stimuli that would ordinarily be very salient. In the terrorist's case, he likely did not hear Lieutenant Pacha; in many videotaped cases in which people are entreating a suicidal jumper not to jump from a height, it at least appears that the onlookers' pleadings are not registered; and in cases in which suicidal drivers steer into oncoming traffic and accelerate, the prospect of their own death so fully absorbs their attention that I believe they do not really comprehend that their actions will likely entail the deaths of others. These latter incidents often understandably strike people as monstrously selfish, but what I am suggesting here is a little different: they involve extreme self-focus, specifically on one's own death, so much so that all else is excluded from mental processing.

* * *

I have critiqued the narrative that suicide terrorists are not suicidal at all, but rather are high-minded martyrs. The media are occasionally complicit in propagating this narrative, though they sometimes do so in ways that are implicit or subtle. For example, a *New York Times* piece from October 2016 presents a profile of a reformed suicide terrorist. The individual is a woman whose desperation and depression were noted in the piece, and then were glossed over in favor of themes of her anger at Israel and her thoughts about justice.[28]

In the December 2016 issue of the *British Journal of Psychiatry*, researchers presented their findings on the association between depressive symptoms and sympathy for violent protest and terrorism. In a sample of over six hundred people of Bangladeshi and Pakistani origin, around 10% were very highly sympathetic, and membership in this sympathetic group was significantly associated with prominent depressive symptoms.[29] This connection between depression and sympathy with violent protest and terrorism is consistent with the theme of this chapter that suicide terrorism is an expression of depressotypic suicidality per se.[30]

A later study by this same research group corroborated and added specificity to the results just described.[31] In the later study, this one of 618 white British and Pakistani people in England, sympathy for violent protest and terrorism was associated with several specific mental disorders, particularly (and in this order) what is known as "double depression" (i.e., a major depressive episode superimposed upon a long-standing dysthymia), anxiety symptoms, and post-traumatic stress symptoms. Of interest, the size of the association with double depression was approximately four times the effect size for both anxiety symptoms and post-traumatic stress symptoms, consistent with the depressotypic and suicidotypic characterization of suicide terrorism I have formed here. Indeed, double depression is among the most depressotypic of all phenomena, and tellingly, it stood out in its association with sympathy toward violent protest and terrorism.

A history of criminal convictions was also a significant correlate of sympathy toward violent protest and terrorism. This result leads me to wonder whether the statistical interaction between history of criminal convictions and double depression would be further predictive of sympathy toward violent protest and terrorism (to my knowledge, the researchers did not examine this possibility). I suspect that the form of any such interaction would be such that those with both double depression and a history of convictions have especially high sympathy toward violent protest and terrorism. A result like this would hearken back to the earlier discussion of the difference between those who enact suicide terrorism and those who lead terror groups, with the latter mostly lacking the element of depressivity and suicidality.

Yet another informative aspect of this study were the variables that did *not* significantly relate to sympathy toward violent protest and terrorism. A partial list of such variables includes education and social capital, relevant to the notion, disputed earlier in this discussion, that those most fervent about terrorism are especially educated and resourceful.[32] In this context, an important finding of the study just discussed is that religious belief was not correlated with sympathy toward violent protest and terrorism. Sympathy toward violent protest and terrorism was more common in white British people than in Pakistani people in England, and more common in those born in England than those not.[33]

If suicide terrorism is a form primarily of suicide, as argued here, and given that suicide has a genetic basis, it would follow that suicide terrorism should run in families too.[34] There is, to my knowledge, no systematic study on this question. I have already noted that Sayyid Qutb's siblings shared his religious fanaticism; his sister was incarcerated for related activities as, of course, was Qutb. It is further noteworthy that the

Boston Marathon bombings, the shootings at the *Charlie Hebdo* newspaper offices in France, and a more recent Paris rampage were perpetrated in part by young men who were brothers. In suicide bombing incidents that occurred about an hour apart in separate locations in Brussels, Belgium, it later emerged not only that the two incidents were connected but that the perpetrators were brothers as well.

Much of the foregoing focuses on those who are part of a terrorist group and, like gang members for example, may experience a significant sense of belongingness in relation to the group. Though this can be sustaining, it plainly does not save them all. It is of interest in this regard to compare those who belong to a terrorist group—often selected because they are vulnerable, a vulnerability that may be offset somewhat by connection to the group—to "lone wolves," who are self-selected and who may not experience any buffering connection to a larger group. In fact, there is clear evidence that the lone wolves are even more mentally unstable than group-based suicide terrorists, remarkable in that the latter are often selected specifically for their instability. One estimate puts the risk for mental illness among lone wolves at thirteen times the risk rate of group-based terrorists.[35]

It could be argued, therefore, that, among group-based terrorists, mental disorders are only part of the picture, at least as compared with lone-wolf terrorist individuals. Indeed, I noted earlier that a mix of group pressure, mental disorders, individuals' commitment to the group, and individuals' loyalty to leadership are all relevant in group-based contexts, and that such factors may interact synergistically. There are in fact relevant phenomena in which mental disorders and suicidality per se may not be as influential as these other factors. Consider hunger strikes, for example, a salient example of which occurred in Belfast's Maze Prison in 1981. The cause of the strike involved Irish Republican Army prisoners, and whether their status was that of prisoners of war versus other prisoners (prisoners of war did not have to do the work or wear the uniform of other prisoners). Prisoner of war status was revoked, and in response, several rounds of protest resulted, with the last involving seventeen prisoners who went on hunger strike. Ten of these prisoners starved to death.

It might be argued that it was unlikely for ten individuals, all with underlying suicidality, to have ended up in the same prison at the same time. Rather, it may seem more plausible that what these ten had in common were qualities like commitment to a cause and to each other—a viable perspective. However, it is also the case that, of all prisoners who were affected by the change in status, not all went on hunger strike, and of those who did go on hunger strike, not all died. It remains possible that these ten did indeed share psychological commonalities relevant to suicidality, and that there was a suicidal element to their deaths, just as I have contended is the case in suicide bombing terrorism incidents.

* * *

This chapter has made the case that suicide terrorism is fundamentally suicide. If that is so, then it stands to reason that suicide prevention would be a key lever in the prevention of terrorism. And, it follows that federal agencies interested in the prevention of terrorism, such as the US Department of Homeland Security, would be interested in funding research on suicide prevention. Given its sprawling nature, it is quite possible that the agency is regularly doing just that. In fact, it has within it an Office of Bombing Prevention, and suicide bombing is mentioned in some of its training materials. But if these agencies are supporting research, I am unaware of it, with one exception relating to studying how mental health providers might assess and manage risk for targeted violence and terrorism in community settings.[36] (I would reiterate that there are federal agencies that are very concerned about suicide prevention in general, the leading one, by far, being the Department of Defense.) Yet it seems prudent—indeed, vital—that funding be directed to the suicidal element of suicide terrorism. Such funding may mitigate terror and may also open up new vistas on suicide prevention in general.

5

Is Physician-Assisted Suicide Suicide?
Is Death Row Volunteering?

In John Updike's novel *Rabbit at Rest*, a character muses that we "fill a slot for a time and then move out; that's the decent thing to do: make room."[1] Gifted novelists like Updike tend to pack a lot into a little, though at times imperfectly, and I suggest that he has done this in the quoted lines. He refers to our biological bodies as a "slot," simultaneously understanding the triviality of a particular body in the arc of the infinite and timeless cosmos, though also dismissing the simultaneous wonder that a life—life—exists at all. Similarly, our life spans are rendered "for a time," again perceiving the snap-of-the-fingers nature of our lives within time immemorial, but again underappreciating the potential richness of a life of marriage, friendships, family, children, work, accomplishment, belief, values, and the like. To speak of dying as to "move out" or "make room" is accurate, if cavalier.

But it is the phrase "the decent thing to do" that I find most compelling. Whether "moving out" on purpose is ever proper is eminently arguable, and this chapter takes up that debate. As will become clear, I have a definite view of the matter, and, as I suspect happens with most people on such life-and-death questions, my opinions arose viscerally and then my thoughts were shaped thereafter, not vice versa. Whether one opines that physician-assisted death represents suicide or not, it is hard to deny that this form of dying raises moral and philosophical questions of considerable depth, more so even than the other, deeply tragic types of death covered in this book. Accordingly, as compared with previous chapters, this one contains more moral and philosophical reflections on the matter, proportionate to its moral and philosophical profundity.

As we will see, the debate over physician-assisted suicide tends to be dominated by advocates' emphases on self-determination, the dignity of the self, and autonomy, and opponents' religious and/or moral beliefs.

These are key elements of the issue, to be sure, but they overlook an aspect that is at least as key, which is our deeply interconnected, gregarious, ancestrally "codependent" natures. It is telling that "codependency" became something to be avoided and pathologized in modern times when actually it is an essence of who we are as a species. John Donne understood this clearly; how else could he have penned these timeless lines of poetry: "No [one] is an island . . . any[one's] death diminishes me, because I am involved in [hu]mankind, and therefore never send to know for whom the bell tolls, it tolls for thee"?[2] Without each other and the polities and societies we create together, there is no forum for one's dignity and autonomy in the first place. This is true in general, but it is certainly true in cultures and societies that emphasize *mutual aid*—that is, the obligation to assist travelers and others who may find themselves in need of food, shelter, clothing, and so on and the mutual confidence that one will be provided for similarly should the need arise. Early European observers of Native American societies were impressed by the bedrock nature of mutual aid in those societies and by the fact that it was "seen as the necessary condition for individual autonomy."[3] Autonomy and mutuality are inextricable, a reality that is regularly overlooked in debates about physician-assisted suicide as an inherent individual right.

* * *

In June 2019, news broke of a seventeen-year-old girl who had died in the Netherlands. Initial reports incorrectly stated that she was put to death, legally, at a euthanasia clinic. This caused a predictable furor in light not only of her young age but also of the fact that she did not have a terminal illness; rather, she claimed "unbearable suffering" due to severe PTSD, anorexia nervosa, and depression.

The truth emerged within a day or so: The girl had in fact died, had in fact done so intentionally, and had indeed claimed "unbearable suffering" due to the three psychiatric conditions already noted. But she had not been euthanized; instead, she intentionally died in a hospital bed installed in her home after having refused food and water for many days; no one, including her parents, other relatives, friends, or medical authorities, intervened.[4]

Oddly, the revelation of these facts seemed to calm the public outcry. Is it not still concerning that a young girl died like this? Is it not extremely questionable for her to die without exhausting all possible treatments? On the latter point, she had not received a highly effective treatment for suicidal depression called electroconvulsive therapy. Dutch physicians considered her too young for the remedy of this treatment. She had not received involuntary feeding, a well-characterized approach in the treatment of anorexia nervosa. I have as yet found no evidence that she received robust forms of the two leading treatments for PTSD, prolonged exposure and cognitive processing therapy. For each of the three conditions, then—conditions that undoubtedly did produce considerable suffering—the girl seemed not to have received all possible treatments to their fullest extent. To allow a girl of this age to decide that her suffering was not just substantial but lastingly unbearable, and to do so in the absence of all possible clinical measures, strikes me as at least as much reason for furor as euthanasia (which, incidentally, is legal for a seventeen-year-old in the Netherlands, and which the girl had requested; her request was denied, all the more reason for profound concern regarding her death).

To justify this state of affairs would require two fundamental premises: that self-determination reigns supreme over all other human values, and that psychiatric conditions can be wholly unresponsive to intervention. My sense of grievance about this case and others like it stems not from the first premise; I happen to disagree that self-determination is supreme, but I nonetheless understand and respect how one can come to embrace that view. My qualms are mostly due to the assertion that psychiatric conditions can be irremediable. I am quite fully aware of the very significant misery that may attach to mental disorders and of the very long journeys that may be involved in finding a treatment regimen that works, but literally and completely irremediable? There is currently no convincing evidence that this is so, and to treat it as uncontested truth on which to base a seventeen-year-old girl's death is a senseless tragedy.

* * *

As the woeful tale of this young person's demise amply illustrates, an important factor in decisions involving physician-assisted suicide and related forms of death relates to the indeterminacy of concepts like "intractably unbearable suffering," and, additionally, the inaccuracy that can and often does attach to physicians' determinations of time left to live in patients with actual terminal illnesses. In light of this latter point, consider, for example, the case of J. J. Hanson, a US Marine Corps veteran who served in Iraq.[5] Years after his military service, in the first half of 2014, Hanson was diagnosed with a glioblastoma, a highly aggressive form of brain cancer. At the time of his diagnosis, he was in his early thirties, married, and with a one-year-old son. His doctors believed he would die within four months.

The physicians' estimates of when Hanson would die were off by a factor of about 12; that is, instead of surviving for four more months, he lived for almost four more *years*, his illness having responded unexpectedly well to surgery, chemotherapy, and an experimental treatment. During these years, Hanson's marriage continued, he and his wife had another son, and he became an outspoken and effective opponent of physician-assisted suicide, speaking regularly on the topic in his home state's capital of Albany, New York, and elsewhere. For more than a thousand "extra" days, every day, Hanson lived a full life, including experiencing the birth of his second son, knowing that physician-assisted suicide in the months after his diagnosis would have taken all of this from him and his family; physician-assisted suicide would have prevented Hanson's second son from even existing. It is not hard to understand why he became an ardent opponent of the procedure.

A very different picture seems to surround the May 2018 assisted suicide death in Switzerland of a respected Australian scientist. The media reporting on the man's decision tended to emphasize his age—he was 104 years old—and his stated reasons that he had stopped enjoying life, largely due to decreased mobility and impaired eyesight. The reporting implies that these are understandable and straightforward reasons, but they give me pause. Ceasing to enjoy things is a cardinal symptom of major depressive disorder, and it is in no way clear to me why very advanced age or limitations in mobility and eyesight render life not worth living. I base this less on personal opinion than on the following factual observations: (1) there are approximately half a million people in the world who are more than a hundred years old, with more than sixty-five thousand in Japan alone; (2) there are people who are not just limited in mobility—the Australian scientist could still walk with the assistance of a walker—but are fully immobile and who do not want to die; and (3) there are people who cannot see at all—the Australian scientist's vision was impaired, but the impairment was not total—and still live rich lives. I am not particularly irked by the Australian scientist himself; he is an autonomous person, free to choose as he will, and to add to that, an accomplished and seemingly very nice man. Rather, I am uneasy about the reflexive reporting implying that aged, visually impaired, and/or mobility-challenged populations have obvious reasons to desire death. My view is diametrically the opposite: that they have obvious reasons to desire life, like everyone else.

Passionate advocates of the opposing view—those enthusiastically in favor of broad access to assisted death—are often drawn toward stories of intractable suffering and how physician-assisted suicide undeniably ends such suffering. Inherent in their perspective seems to be the view that suffering calls for death, or almost requires it. But there are other possible attitudes toward suffering. Consider the experiences of Wilhelmina Jenkins, a vocal supporter of increased quality of care and compassion for those suffering from myalgic encephalopathy/chronic fatigue syndrome. The condition is characterized by sapping fatigue that is unimproved by rest, significant concentration problems, and physical pain, among other symptoms. To make matters worse, misunderstanding about the condition is rampant, with some doubting its very existence (analogously to the situation with some psychiatric illnesses).

Sufferers thus have to deal with the daily, grinding physical symptoms sometimes compounded by a lack of sympathy and support. Jenkins knows all this very well from her own experience, about which she regularly blogs. In a recent blog post, specifically addressed to a fellow sufferer who was contemplating suicide as a response to her own misery, Jenkins wrote about the illness that it "is a devastating disease." She continued, "There's no question that it burns to ashes the life that you thought you had and leaves you with sickness and pain and a quality of life lower than any other major disease. Many people, after a long struggle, decide that they can't go on any longer. I understand that. I have felt that way many times. But if you can stay, please stay. . . . I do not care if we agree or disagree about anything—I still want you here. You are unique. You are valuable . . . even when things are darkest, you are a part of a community and you are loved."[6]

Jenkins's counsel is very similar to that which I offer in this book, though I do not claim to have suffered like she has. Specifically, I accept that it is debatable, but the exhortation to stay essentially no matter what has enough merit that it at least deserves reflection. My view of human nature is that self-determination is indeed a main pillar of it, but one that is not more important, and is arguably less important, than our debt to one another (past, present, and perhaps especially future—what the American Founders called "our Posterity" [as pointed out later, their capitalization being purposeful]). Again, the one is not truly possible without the other.

Stipulating that this is true, it follows that physician aid-in-dying should be deeply considered not just from a self-determination angle but also, at least as important, in the context of social duty. Given the significance and the stakes, that is the case under any circumstances, but especially if the main appeal is to self-determination (as it seems to me it often is—and with reason, in that it is an essential value). It is important that this view not be conflated with an inflexible opposition to any and all aid-in-dying; I accept that there are cases in which it maximizes virtues like dignity, duty, and mercy.

One might argue that, even if one has full autonomy and choice and thus should have legal access to the choice to die, once one has a child, autonomy and choice are considerably altered. The child had no choice in the matter of their existence; the parent in a sense abrogates or at least mitigates their own choice by imposing choice on a child. Parents may ignore their debt to their posterity, but that has nothing to with the debt's reality. That suicidal parents come to view their debt to their children as the obligation to die—to remove their burden from their children—illustrates the power of the mental disorders that spur death by suicide.

Advocates for physician-assisted suicide often employ terminology, turns of phrase, and associations that can be seen as revealing. For example, in the podcast *Criminal*, a woman is interviewed who views herself as an "exit guide," by which she means a compassionate companion who stays in the presence of someone who is enacting suicide.[7] She is one of many such "guides" who are part of the organization the Final Exit Network. I have hardly scratched the surface of their choice of words, but already, there is much on which to reflect. The term "guide," for example, has nearly universal positive connotations and brings to mind (albeit to a very fortunate mind) things like a safari trip or a day at the Louvre. This is characteristic of the organization: its words implicitly deny death's defining and essential elements by describing them in phrasing that is euphemistically positive. The organization's name includes the words "Final Exit," as if death were just one more exit along the way of a lifetime full of exits.

The interviewer asked the woman about the method of death involved and, in phrasing the question, asked about a "bag" filled with gas. The woman agreed but rushed to replace the term "bag" with "hood," her intent being, I believe, to make the procedure sound more official. But the object in question really does amount to a bag. Furthermore, as not infrequently happens with this group, its efforts to make the process seem formal and professional can instead underscore its disturbing aspects, for the term "hood" may be more haunting than "bag," bringing to mind images from an American low point at Guantánamo Bay. The procedure, the woman added, is "easy," "peaceful," and "100% effective."

Almost in the same sentence the "exit guide" emphasized that the Final Exit Network is a mostly volunteer organization and that anyone whom they assist in death "must be mentally competent." This glib, in-passing assertion glosses over a towering issue in the debate about assisted suicide: namely, the very real possibility that subtle, hard-to-detect forms of mental disorders exist and, despite their subtlety, can nonetheless be pernicious enough to spur suicide. This is certainly my own considered view after decades in clinical and related arenas, and if it is true, it would be a challenge for a world-class expert to reliably detect all such disorders, and it is not at all plausible that a volunteer organization could, even if its volunteers all go through training regimens.

The woman went to some lengths to emphasize that she and the others of the organization's volunteers are not directly involved in the mechanics of death, stating that they "do nothing," "do not touch anything," and "do not bring them anything." It beggars the imagination that this is literally true; of course they do *something*, in that they show up and offer support, and of course they touch *something*, including very likely the suffering individual in order to show warmth and reassurance, or at least as a conventional greeting. But in another sense, I understand her meaning to a point: she meant that as far as the method of death and its physical aspects like the provision of a "hood" or the placing of it over the individual's head are concerned, volunteers are uninvolved.

That is plausible, but it is also very much beside the point. Analogously, it is quite plausible that someone accused and convicted of conspiracy to commit murder would have nothing hands-on to do with the killing, and yet be very obviously guilty. Aid, abetment, encouragement, and support need not be mechanical to be influential and indeed causal. In fact, the Final Exit Network itself would, I assume, concede the point that support and encouragement can be influential; it is the main reason that the group thinks that compassionate presence during someone's suicide is the right thing to do.

Another reason, in the words of the woman interviewed for the podcast, is "nobody ever should have to die alone." On the one hand, this is moral pablum, a sentiment with which one does not need to struggle to endorse. To take personal examples, when I reflect on my relatives' suicides, as for better or worse I am regularly induced to do, the facets that aggrieve me are legion, but among the most pronounced is that they died so utterly alone in every way.

However, would I feel better if they were accompanied in their deaths by "exit guides"? I cannot say with certainty, but one speculation is that it would add yet one more facet of grief to the deaths in question for our family; speaking for myself, I suspect that I would have been angered that the "guide" colluded in the death, and that I would have been intensely pained that so intimate a moment passed not with our family but with a stranger to our family. I have no question, incidentally, that my relatives in question, now dead by suicide, but who, when living, could be extremely capable and engaging, could have convinced a supposedly discerning "guide" of their mental health. In truth they suffered from mental disorders of such severity and clarity that a genuine mental health expert might be able to diagnose them almost on sight.

Furthermore, the suicides in question and their aftermath are, I can attest, grievous enough already. Our family is in no need of it being pointed out that our relatives should not have died in the way they did—alone, bereft. We are already sufficiently aware of that.

Further still, one wonders how many suicidal crises that were almost but not quite lethal—with the surviving individual still alive years and sometimes decades later—would have instead been suicide deaths were a "guide" present? I do not know, but think it unfathomable that the number is zero—and if it is greater than zero, then I for one regard it as a moral outrage.

In further explaining her rationale, the "guide" continued, "We do not come into this world alone, and we should not have to leave it alone." This too is easily morally digestible, but upon deeper analysis, open to questioning. What is the connection necessarily between how we come into the world and how we leave it? Are there not rare instances in which a child is born to a mother, with just the two of them present, and the mother perishes just before or after the instant of birth, leaving the infant alone? There are also certainly occasions on which a child is born to a mother, with just the two of them there, and the mother immediately abandons the baby.

The "guide's" point may be better served by focusing on the "should not have to leave [life] alone" portion of her assertion. But here, too, according to whom? What of the millions of our forebears who have died alone? Who may have, out of their own sense of dignity or privacy, preferred to die alone?

Advocates of extreme positions can show no moral flexibility regarding their particular passionately held position, yet in the next breath show considerable moral flexibility, even lassitude, regarding others. The "guide" stumbled into this very quandary in discussing the role of family in the work she does. Sensibly enough, she emphasized how important it is for end-of-life decisions to be family affairs, with decisions being made in a process over time of discussion among loved ones. But in the next sentence or so, she turned to a specific case in which she and a fellow "guide" colluded with an eventual decedent to actively deceive someone closely connected to the decedent, someone who disapproved of the plan to die. They did this by waiting for an "all clear" sign from the decedent that the disapproving person was temporarily absent.

As noted earlier, the "guide" from the podcast claimed with confidence that the organization ruled out anyone requesting aid-in-dying who has a mental disorder. Similar, more stringent, and much more believable protections are in place in states like Oregon that have "death with dignity" laws. These protections depend on physicians' regularly referring patients requesting a lethal prescription for psychiatric evaluations. Given that the base rate for major depressive disorder in the general population is approximately 5%, one would expect the referral rate to be at least that, if not several times that, among those requesting death. But it is 3%.[8] This rate, in a group facing severe illness and death, is about half the *population base rate*, not at all credible. Oregon's laws and procedures for physician-assisted suicide are among the most careful in the world, but even they are plainly flawed.

* * *

In 2016, Margaret Battin, a professor of philosophy, and Anna Beck, a professor of oncology, both at the University of Utah, wrote in an op-ed piece about their very seasoned views on the topic of physician-assisted suicide. In this piece, Beck states, "I know that the (cancer) patient I'm trying to help has little kids; and I know that her death will be a loss in so many ways. She will fight, struggle, hang on as long as possible. For a young mother, it's not about autonomy or avoiding suffering. She's the last one who would ask for aid in dying. For her, it's about being the mother of those kids until every last breath is taken." The authors continue, "Sadly . . . ironically . . . her dying legacy may be more difficult for her family because she struggled so mightily."[9]

This last sentence is crucial and loaded, as I believe it at least flirts with the false premise that struggle, even that which is full of suffering, must be viewed by others as negative (e.g., "sad" and "ironic" in Battin and Beck's terms). First, I would suggest that the young mother in question would see her struggle as very definitely including negative aspects but not limited to them. Second, even extreme suffering in medical settings need not be—usually should not be in the twenty-first century—ghastly and regrettable; rather, it should be palliated to the fullest degree possible, about which I should acknowledge these professors know more than I.

Third, compare the sentence "She suffered greatly" to one that situates the sentiment interpersonally: "She suffered greatly *for us.*" A mere two words opens new worlds of meaning, shifting the family's viewpoint from "that was grievous" to align with the young mother's, "that was hard, even at times regrettably so, but I did it for you, and I would do it again." Is the latter not brave and moving? What about it is sad or ironic?

And last, the issue of *alignment of perspectives* deserves emphasis. In Battin and Beck's example, the lack of alignment is between the views of the now deceased young mother and that of her bereaved family. It is true that these can be different perspectives; it is also possible that one party's perspective is mistaken, and that this mistake is the source of the misalignment. It is perilous to question the perspective of the bereaved, but being a human perspective, it is necessarily thus subject to human error, and it is therefore possible that their view is simply not as correct as that of the young mother.

In these scenarios, I have found over the decades a bias against the perspective of the deceased and for that of the living. This bias makes a certain amount of intuitive sense to most people, but that does not transform it from being a bias. Furthermore, this kind of bias can lead to profound misunderstandings. For instance, in many deaths by suicide, the bereaved may feel that their loved one's decision to die was to some degree selfish, and this feeling may color their grief for years, decades, even a lifetime. This would be sad in any event, but it would be made all the more so if their feeling were actually mistaken, if, in reality, their loved one's primary motivation had nothing to do with selfishness but rather involved the wish (albeit a misguided one) to make everyone better off. The latter is easily the more common motivation for suicide than the former, and think of it what one may, it is not selfish.

I publicly debated these matters with Peggy Battin at a conference in April 2018.[10] She argued for self-determination, and I countered that there is more to human nature than autonomy, that our social debt and connections to our ancestors, to the living, and to our posterity are important too. In one of our exchanges, Battin recalled an anecdote regarding the founder of the conference, the late Edwin Shneidman, who is regarded hagiographically within this particular organization. Shneidman had said something like, "No one should have the right to physician-assisted suicide . . . except me." Perhaps Battin mentioned the remark to illustrate a view of physician-assisted suicide critics, who can be high-minded idealists when the matter is abstract, but when it is not—when it involves them personally—ideals recede.

This is undoubtedly true in some instances, as it is, for example, regarding politicians who rigidly disapprove of certain things until they themselves need them. Shneidman's barb does not apply to my position, which is not categorical disapproval but, rather, generally tends toward disapproval leavened by an understanding, apt for most things in human affairs, that exceptions exist, and events could conspire such that anyone comes to view themselves as one of those exceptions.[11]

I return to the example of Wilhelmina Jenkins, the woman who suffers from and advocates for others who suffer from myalgic encephalopathy/chronic fatigue syndrome. Like many, in times of anguish, Jenkins wished for death, but having survived the crisis, she can see in retrospect that her suicide would have been a mistake. Like her, the motto of J. J. Hanson, the US Marine mentioned earlier, was "Every day is a gift, and you can't ever let that go."[12]

From a cosmological perspective, Hanson and Jenkins may have even understated the case. Given the unforgiving physics of the cosmos, the existence of *any* form of life for even an instant cannot be taken for granted, and the existence and survival over eons of our planet's biodiversity, including us, represent an epic and vanishingly unlikely miracle. The facts that the universe is infinite and likely multiple, one might counter, assure that life, including intelligent forms of it, will occur here and there inevitably. Be that as it may, termination of this particular miraculous happenstance of life, and especially premature termination, should therefore proceed with the gravest of caution.

Examples like J. J. Hanson, who survived cancer for years beyond physicians' predictions, clearly illustrate one peril of physician-assisted suicide, specifically, premature death and the attendant and needless robbing from the individual in question and from their loved ones of days, weeks, and months of life. In Hanson's case it was years of life; in other cases, like that of Stephen Hawking's (expanded on more later in this chapter), it was decades. And that is just one of the procedure's dangers; there are others.

From the many examples like this, I reiterate what I think the proper inference is. It is *not* that physician-assisted suicide should be strictly banned, because of course not all cases of terminal illness are the same; some involve such extreme physical pain and psychological anguish in the face of clearly imminent death that even skeptics understand and sympathize. Rather, it is that the potential dangers of the procedure are numerous enough and can be profoundly regrettable enough (such as the nonexistence of Hawking's acclaimed work), that the threshold for triggering physician-assisted suicide should be extremely stringent and, even then, worried over repeatedly and deeply by those considering the procedure, along with their loved ones and their physicians, in consultation with palliative care professionals.

As we have seen, one argument that compels many to support physician aid-in-dying boils down to autonomy; an individual is the owner of their life and thus should be free to determine everything about that life, including how it ends. But is it one's life really? I suppose if anyone owns a life it is the individual in question, but what I am questioning is whether anyone, even the individual who lives a particular life, really owns it. They did not create it; it was not their idea in the first place. Does a star own itself, a galaxy, a universe? A critic of Dutch laws allowing assisted suicide stated, "The myth is that it is purely individual choice, while it always also affects family, the community, health care providers and ultimately society."[13]

Additionally, some feel that physicians do not need more encouragement and emboldening to engage in practices involving assisting death, because some physicians were already worryingly involved, even before Oregon became the first US state to pass laws allowing and regulating physician-assisted suicide. A 1998 article in the *New England Journal of Medicine* reported a fully anonymous survey of physicians in specialties likely to receive requests from patients regarding facilitating death (e.g., internal medicine, oncology, geriatrics).[14] On the one hand, most physicians (more than 90%) reported that they had never facilitated death; on the other hand, the range of involvement was large. Specifically, with regard to actively euthanizing patients, one physician reported killing 150 patients. How many patients has that physician since killed, knowing that physician-assisted suicide is now legal in multiple US states? As another example of worrying readiness on the part of some physicians to hasten death in their patients, a twenty-nine-year-old with no physical illnesses whatsoever died in the Netherlands in January 2018, by ingesting a poison provided by a Dutch physician.[15] The grounds for the physician's actions were 100% psychiatric, within the law in the Netherlands. The woman's own physicians had refused to aid in her dying specifically because the rationale was 100% psychiatric, and so the woman consulted a different clinic, one that is responsible for the vast majority of assisted deaths on psychiatric grounds in the Netherlands.

A prominent psychiatrist associated with the clinic stated the following when interviewed about such deaths: "I've treated patients that I

144 | IS PHYSICIAN-ASSISTED SUICIDE SUICIDE?

knew were going to commit [sic] suicide. I knew. They told me, *I felt it*, and I thought, 'I can't help you.' . . . The ones I know will commit [sic] suicide are terminal in my opinion. . . . That makes me willing to perform euthanasia."[16] I, too, have been responsible for the clinical care of many extremely suicidal patients, and I do not share the psychiatrist's self-confidence. Perhaps I lack her ability, or perhaps one of us is wrong.

My view is captured well by a different Dutch psychiatrist, Frank Koerselman, who in that same report on the twenty-nine-year-old's death was quoted as saying, "How could I know—how could anybody know—that her death wish was not a sign of her psychiatric disease? The fact that one can rationalise about it, does not mean it's not a sign of the disease." He continued, "It is possible not to be contaminated by their lack of hope. These patients lost hope, but you can stay beside them and give them hope. And you can let them know that you will never give up on them."

Wim van Dijk, a Dutch mental health professional, gives up regularly. In October 2021, he publicly attested that he had provided a lethal poison called Agent X to more than one hundred suicidal people. Facilitators of death seem to have a flare for terms that are especially chilling, as I suggest is the case with Agent X. In word choice and phrasing reminiscent of the "exit guide" covered earlier, van Dijk said, "I have carefully provided people who want to maintain control over their own end of life with the means to end life at the time of their choice in the future. *I am a provider.*"

By "provider," one may imagine that van Dijk means "physician." But, no, he explained, "I have provided Agent X to more than 100 people," and he is not a physician; he is a psychologist. The article on Van Dijk concluded that he "revealed [that] he had suggested people attending the organisation's meetings stay on after the moderator left so he could sell them the drug for €50 (£42) a dose"—death in exchange for $55.23.[17]

In February 2022, an article appeared on which van Dijk and the like-minded I imagine would smile favorably, but which I and others I have discussed it with find ghoulish. The article includes three case studies purporting to validate the concept of "terminal anorexia"—that is, the notion that anorexia nervosa could be a literally terminal illness in the same way that a glioblastoma can be. This work proposes specific criteria for "terminal anorexia," namely, (1) a diagnosis of anorexia nervosa; (2) thirty years of age or older; (3) "prior persistent engagement in high-quality, multi-disciplinary eating disorder care"; and (4) "consistent, clear expression by an individual who possesses decision-making capacity that they understand further treatment to be futile, they choose to stop trying to prolong their lives, and they accept that death will be the natural outcome."[18]

When the stakes involve death, the criteria should have an ironclad quality, but the last two criteria are plainly lacking in that quality—for instance, how to operationalize terms like "persistent," "engagement," and "high-quality"? Further, it is odd to leave an essential element of a supposedly clinical entity like "terminal anorexia" up not to a health professional but to the patient, as the last criterion does. Finally, many of my colleagues find the age criterion to be shockingly low, but given my awareness of the material presented throughout this chapter, it did not particularly surprise me.

I will leave to readers to form their own impression of one last aspect of the paper by Gaudiani and colleagues. Referring to "terminal anorexia" and their paper on it, the authors write, "Three case studies elucidate this condition. One patient was so passionate about this topic that she asked to be a posthumous co-author of this paper."[19]

* * *

On March 13, 2018, we lost Stephen Hawking, author of, among many other works, *A Brief History of Time*. Like J. J. Hanson, who outlived by a factor of 12 physicians' projections for his survival with cancer, Dr. Hawking was told he had two years to live when he was diagnosed with amyotrophic lateral sclerosis in 1963, but lived approximately fifty-five more years, outliving physicians' projections by a factor of almost 26. Dr. Hawking was seventy-six years old when he died.

He would have died much earlier, by age forty, if his wish for an early death had been granted back then. He would not have survived to do the prodigious things he did, nor would he have had the chance to say things like "The message of this lecture is that black holes ain't as black as they are painted. They are not the eternal prisons they were once thought. Things can get out of a black hole both on the outside and possibly to another universe. So if you feel you are in a black hole, don't give up—there's a way out." Like black holes, mental disorders are forces of nature; Hawking's point is that despite this, they can be contended with, and not only by surrender via death, but by holding out. Many people escape, if not fully at least partially, and one wonders how many people have surrendered prematurely, as Hawking asked to be done for him decades before his death, when they could have held out and found a way out. Hawking did, and that fact alone should give pause to reflexive advocates of assisted forms of suicide.

Recent scholarship lends credibility to the perspective articulated here. Calati and colleagues reviewed the literature on assisted suicide in psychiatric patients.[20] With one intriguing exception, these authors reported substantial similarities between what they termed "traditional suicide" and assisted suicide in psychiatric patients (e.g., with respect to patterns of mental disorder and levels of psychological pain).

The one exception was gender; these authors noted that women were the majority among those engaging in assisted suicide for psychiatric reasons, whereas the opposite is true for suicide in general. One plausible interpretation of this pattern is that suicide in general and assisted suicide for psychiatric reasons are distinct, thus their differing demographic profiles; this is the preferred interpretation of proponents of physician-assisted suicide. Calati and colleagues, however, interpreted the pattern quite differently. They wrote, "The ratio of women to men among [those engaging in assisted suicide for psychiatric reasons] is what one would find if a random sample of suicide attempters were given reliably lethal means of suicide."[21] This is a significant and disturbing possibility, specifically, that assisted suicide for psychiatric reasons is so lethal a suicide method—more lethal even than self-inflicted gunshot wound—that it is converting those engaging in suicide attempts and much more often than not surviving to those who are, without exception, deceased.[22]

One may counter that the gender difference trends the other way in other incidents in which the person allocates the self-killing to someone else. Indeed, suicide-by-cop, amok, and death row volunteering are overwhelmingly male, and regularly involve severe violence. One may quibble with the notion that death row volunteering is violent; true, but entry into death row is necessarily violent. Physician-assisted suicide is thus the only form of death in which the killing is potentially allocated to others and in which the process of allocation need not involve violence.

It is often assumed—and this assumption is encouraged by proponents—that physician-assisted suicide is almost always and completely about matters like terminal illness and physical pain. The studies from Europe reviewed earlier on assisted suicide for psychiatric reasons belie this point, as does recent work by Silvia Canetto and John McIntosh.[23] In an analysis of over one thousand requests by older adults for physician-prescribed access to lethal medications in Oregon, fewer than one in four gave physical pain, and fewer than half cited loss of control of bodily function, as a reason for seeking access. Most gave psychological reasons, with the top three being loss of autonomy (nearly 90% of the sample endorsed this reason), decreasing ability to do enjoyable things (nearly 90%), and loss of dignity (nearly 70%). Notably, two of these three reasons are synonymous, or nearly so, with explicit criteria for major depressive disorder (the anhedonia and self-concept symptoms). When viewed in this light, virtually all of the sample meets criteria, at a minimum, for what the *DSM-5* calls other specified depression— essentially a subclinical variant of either major depressive disorder or persistent depressive disorder—and yet reports suggests that very few people who go through this process and are prescribed access to lethal medications meet the criteria for a mental disorder.[24] For this to be true, either the *DSM-5* is incorrect to consider other specified depression a mental disorder, or the Oregon process is so honed and precise that access is being granted only to those among the 10% or so who do not specify psychological reasons for dying. On both counts, there is considerable reason for doubt.

Outside of the top three reasons but within the top five is burdensomeness to others. This is a very relevant factor in suicide in general, not just according to the interpersonal theory of suicide but to other frameworks too, going back at least to Durkheim in the late 1800s.

As an American suicide preventionist, already swimming against a tide of heroin, violence, and the like, I confess to moments of deep frustration and moral concern over the regularizing of suicide that is often implicit and sometimes explicit in discourse involving this variety of death, a discourse that can devolve into casual callousness at times. As noted, with proper decorum and seriousness, I accept the occasional,

148 | IS PHYSICIAN-ASSISTED SUICIDE SUICIDE?

deeply considered, and very, very clearly medically indicated need for death. Still, at the very same time that my colleagues and I are fighting against a host of factors that encourage suicide and, despite those factors, are arguably making gains, an individual and others like him are selling ghoulishly named death pellets (Agent X), like a cocaine dealer on a street corner, and with similar illegality and rationale ("people want it"; "it's their right"). What is means safety against this, a kind of death method that is more lethal than a gunshot wound?[25] An occasional impulse toward "eliminate assisted suicide" is perhaps forgivable under the circumstances, especially among those of us determined to temper impulse with the maxim that absolutes are exceedingly rare in matters of the heart and mind.

Death Row Volunteering

There is near-universal consensus that had Stephen Hawking's wish to die been granted when he was in his twenties or thirties, it would have been a mistake. Such mistakes occur when death is invited or induced before its time. This applies to some physician-assisted suicides, essentially all suicides per se, and also when the state executes condemned inmates. On this latter count, executions of the innocent represent the most profound concern, but there are others, including execution of those who are both guilty and suicidal. That is, it is worth asking whether those who drop all appeals and invite their own executions are essentially suicidal, much as are those who die by suicide.

I believe some are, and if they are, then those on death row who welcome, even pursue, execution should be more similar to decedents from suicide than are those on death row who fight death to the end. To my knowledge, this question has not been rigorously addressed in a systematic, quantitative fashion, but there are anecdotal data that bear on the issue. For instance, an inmate named Scott Dozier asked the state of Nevada to kill him. Like many eventual suicide decedents, he had at least one previous suicide attempt; he ingested a massive overdose of the tricyclic antidepressant amitriptyline, which is a very regularly fatal act. It was nearly so for Dozier, who as a result was in a coma for two weeks, but he nonetheless survived.

As has been noted, my theoretical and other work has posited that genuinely suicidal people are focused on the idea that their deaths will be worth more than their lives to others and to themselves. Dozier's wish to be executed fit this pattern, in that he believed that his life would subject his family to needless years of anguish. He was focused specifically on a granddaughter, whom he dreaded would think of him only as a long-term convict.

If Dozier were genuinely suicidal (subsequent events proved that he was), then there is some likelihood that he, like many suicide decedents, would have a significant family history of suicidal behavior. In fact, an investigator discovered not only that Dozier's family history was positive for suicide but that at least five relatives, all on his mother's side, died by suicide. One was his maternal grandfather, who told his relatives that he had received an ominous cancer diagnosis and did not want to put them through the burden of a long illness; he preferred suicide instead. Here, too, the logic of the suicidal mind is based largely on calculations of death being worth more than life, to others and to oneself.

There is a further aspect to Dozier's grandfather's suicide—subsequent investigation revealed that he did not have cancer but had very likely created the story with the hope that it would make his suicide easier to bear for his family. Here yet again, making others better off was in one way or another at the forefront of his mind.[26]

I am far from the only one who thinks that executions like Dozier's have a suicidal character. The Clark County, Nevada, public defender stated, "We don't kill them in Nevada unless they agree to it. What you've got with Dozier is state-assisted suicide." Lawyers attempting to prevent Dozier's execution agreed, saying, "Our view of the phenomenon of the death row volunteer is that it represents a form of suicide that we would never endorse, encourage, or assist."

These same lawyers hired a consulting psychiatrist to interview and evaluate Dozier. The psychiatrist spent approximately twenty hours with Dozier and later asserted that his wish to die stemmed largely from severe depression along with other co-occurring mental disorders, all made significantly worse by his living conditions. Specifically, the psychiatrist wrote, "I have never seen a cell that is more physically alienating and isolating than the cell where [he] has been confined for years."

In addition to theoretical and other work emphasizing the role of perceived burdensomeness in suicidality, I have conjectured that a sense of aloneness characterizes the mindsets of genuinely suicidal people. The psychiatrist's description of Dozier's living situation can be viewed as consistent with this idea. Dozier killed himself in his cell by hanging in January 2019, after the state of Nevada had twice stayed his execution.

Further consistent with the view that some condemned prisoners are frankly suicidal and encourage their execution as a way of enacting their suicides, a prisoner named Charles Rumbaugh stated in a Texas court, "If they don't want to take me down there and execute me, I'll make them shoot me."[27] Soon thereafter, he did precisely that, rushing in a threatening manner at an armed marshal, who reacted by shooting Rumbaugh, an event that combined suicide-by-cop and state-assisted suicide scenarios. Rumbaugh survived the wound; he was executed by the state of Texas two years after this incident.

Legal scholar Meredith Rountree wrote in 2012, "For some imagining life on death row, nothing may seem more understandable and rational than an attempt to end the pains of imprisonment and seize control of the process by ending appeals." Here, Rountree is echoing a theme of this book, namely, that, from the outside, lethal acts can seem other than they really are. She continues, "Nonetheless hastening execution by abandoning appeals is a socially deviant act."[28] Rountree points out that volunteering for execution on death row is rare; volunteers represent about 11% of those who are executed. Being sentenced to die is by no means, ironically, an actual "death sentence." In Texas, a highly lethal state for those on its death row, one has a better than 50% chance of dying a death other than execution, usually from natural causes. This latter fact is quite consistent with the view that actively volunteering for one's execution has plainly suicidal elements.

Rountree argues that death row volunteers appeal to narratives that seem essentially nonsuicidal in motive but that really are suicidal. For example, having acknowledged his guilt, a man sentenced to death in Texas pointed to the justice inherent in his sentence, saying, "I have a debt to pay and I'm ready to pay it."[29] A related refrain among death row volunteers is that drawing out their appeal will waste societal resources. Despite the attempt to deflect a suicidal intention by emphasizing themes like justice and economy, it is striking how similar such prisoners' thinking is to the thinking of those who are frankly suicidal; the latter, too, believe they deserve death and that everyone else will be better off once they remove the burden they believe their life represents—put differently, they pay their (perceived) debt and save everyone the waste of resources they believe their lives are, just like death row volunteers. There exists a significant set of similarities between those who are suicidal and death row volunteers, and I suggest that it derives from the fact that all are, at bottom, suicidal, no matter how they may rationalize that reality.

Some inmates have claimed that continuation of their waivers is frivolous because, whereas they are plainly guilty and their case has no merit, the cases of some of their fellow death row prisoners are meritorious; continuation of their own case would detract and distract from the more meritorious cases of other inmates. In many other contexts such reasoning would be logical and moral; in those who have perpetrated killings, often very heinous ones, it can be hard to fully believe that their overall moral posture has shifted, and hard to fathom that the motive is anything other than frank dissimulation in the service of facilitating their own desired death.

Consider David Cox, who invoked an array of mostly contradictory reasons that the state of Mississippi should put him to death. Reasons he tended to overlook were the savagery of his crime—he shot his ex-wife in the abdomen, leading to hours of physical suffering before her eventual death, during which the ex-wife observed Cox sexually assaulting her daughter—and the fact that he had committed another murder with which he had gotten away and which he had his lawyers reveal after his death. This kind of depravity can coexist in the mind with self-hatred, and Cox's lawyer believed that his client fundamentally hated himself. Self-hatred, in turn, is a signature of the suicidal mindset, consistent with a suicidal character to Cox's insistence that Mississippi execute him, which it did on November 17, 2021.[30]

Still another consideration in death row volunteering is whether it is in a sense *coerced* by the conditions of death row. The actual conditions of death row and their role in volunteering will be returned to shortly, but for now, I will emphasize that courts deliberating prisoners' requests to waive appeals of death row sentences attend to the *autonomy* of the prisoners' wishes; that is, are prisoners acting based on what they truly wish? The answer is often in the affirmative—they are—but so are those who are frankly suicidal.

Mostly with reference to the legal context and culture of Texas but likely applicable beyond it, Rountree avers that, were these kinds of court deliberations as adversarial as the usual American litigation—with, for example, a lawyer or set of lawyers vigorously contending that the motives for volunteering are fundamentally suicidal and not otherwise— then people who volunteer for death would only very rarely be executed. The usual scenario, however, involves the volunteers' own lawyer(s) advocating for their wishes (i.e., to waive appeals and thereby die by execution). The only usual opposition to this advocacy amounts to little more than a judge directly querying the inmate; an example question from such querying in an actual trial cited by Rountree is, "Has anyone threatened you or forced you in any way to answer any of my questions that I have asked you?" Obviously, it is not difficult to imagine even a despairingly suicidal inmate answering with a simple—and in most cases, sufficient—"no." Exacerbating this dilemma is the fact that the death row volunteers' own lawyers cannot advocate for the prisoners' life, because they are obligated by legal ethics rules to advocate for their clients' wishes (unless they are convinced of the clients' mental incompetence, which is not the same thing as their being in suicidal despair). One-on-one they can try to convince inmates to live, but in court they act on behalf of their clients.[31]

All of the foregoing points to similarities between those on death row who actively invite their executions and nonincarcerated people who desire and enact suicide. Writing in the *Michigan Law Review*, law professor John Blume delved into these similarities and provided a systematic treatment of this topic.[32] Blume pointed out that some inmates who initially volunteer for and welcome their deaths change their minds about it later in the process, in some cases too late. This is yet another parallel to suicide per se, in which change of minds and hearts is not rare, as we have seen. In nonincarcerated suicidal individuals, this phenomenon is referred to as an aborted suicide attempt. It is of note that there are aborted death row volunteering attempts too. Bobby Wilcher, like David Cox executed in Mississippi, waived all his appeals and then was executed as he tried reinstate them.[33]

It is of interest to consider the rate of volunteering for death in condemned prisoners, in the context of the suicide rate in the general population. Blume's article presents data on 815 executed inmates, 106 of whom were willing volunteers (i.e., waived appeals and asked to be put to death), for a percentage of around 13%.[34] On the one hand, this is far in excess of the rate observed in the general population (approximately .01%); 13% exceeds .01% by a factor of 1,300. The general population, however, is a highly questionable choice for a comparison group to condemned prisoners, for an array of reasons. As I will turn to shortly, one such reason is that death row inmates are not demographically representative of the general population, and the ways in which they are not (e.g., mostly male) tilts their odds in favor of higher suicide rates (i.e., males have far higher suicide death rates than females). Another reason is that execution on death row is 100% lethal, converting all who might have expressed their suicidality nonlethally to decedents. This is a parallel process to that in physician-assisted suicide, in which a particular demographic (in the case of physician-assisted suicide, women), on average usually nonlethal in their suicidality, shifts to 100% lethality via provision of the most lethal of methods. As in death row execution, once physician-assisted suicide is actually begun, death is the result virtually all the time; not so with other suicide methods, even highly lethal ones like self-inflicted gunshot wound, for which the lethality rate is approximately 90%.

Condemned prisoners often also have many other suicide-related risk factors that are not at all representative of the general population, such as mental disorders. On the point of mental disorders, there are a few candidates for the single truest marker of psychopathology, among them severe psychosis, florid mania, prankish defecation, extreme cruelty to animals, and highly destructive fire setting.[35] In past work, as well as earlier in this book, I have argued that death by suicide is at least as clear a marker as these, and similarly and relatedly that the unsanctioned killing of a human (whether that human is oneself or another) is an unmistakable marker too. With regard to all these markers, they are common in death row prisoners, and by definition, all of them have killed at least one fellow human. In this context, it is no surprise that the overwhelming majority of those on death row have mental disorders (including severe substance use disorders, often co-occurring with non-substance-use mental disorders). The specific figure from Blume's study was that 93 of 106 volunteers for execution had documented mental disorders (88%), a rate that is very similar to those found in psychological autopsy studies of those in the general population who have died by suicide. As alluded to earlier, in studies such as Blume's of death row volunteers, it is highly likely that those without a documented mental disorder nonetheless had one that went unrecorded.

Further to the point of a very high rate of mental disorders in the death row volunteer population, at least 13% had schizophrenia, and many more had psychotic symptoms suggestive of that illness. This is a rate many times that of the population base rate (around 1% in the general population), and it is noteworthy that schizophrenia is well known for its rendering people vulnerable to death by suicide.

If volunteering for death is related to suicide, it would be expected that volunteers have high rates of past suicide attempts. As expected, at least 30 of the 106 volunteers in Blume's series had at least one past suicide attempt, and several had multiple attempts. As Blume noted, this number is likely a vast underestimate. This is a rate far in excess of what would be expected by chance, and I would predict that it is in excess of the past suicide attempt rate in death row nonvolunteers (though to my knowledge this has not been established).

Having killed at least one other person, and in the vast majority of cases having also inflicted other forms of mayhem on others repeatedly and over years and often decades, death row prisoners have an unusual relationship to violence. Therefore, that they also have a far above-average comfort level with violence and death (whether directed outward or inward) seems predictable.

It is worth remembering that prisoners who are condemned to death and volunteer for execution are not directly engaging in killing (though they will be in dying). In this way, there are parallels among volunteer condemned inmates, those who induce suicide-by-cop reactions from law enforcement, and (in certain jurisdictions in Europe) physician-enacted death (i.e., euthanasia; a key distinction between physician-assisted suicide as practiced, for example, in some states of the United States versus physician-enacted euthanasia is that in the latter, a physician is administering a lethal agent, whereas in the former, the lethal agent is self-administered). In those three groups, death is faced, which alone will make it a relatively rare choice (consistent with the 13% figure mentioned earlier); if the considerable difficulty of facing killing is added on, rates would be much lower still (trending more toward the rate for suicide in the general population).

There is thus a sense in which volunteering for execution is one step removed from suicide; put somewhat differently, it has analogous properties as compared to directly taking one's own life. In this light, it is of interest to examine other analogues usable in experimental research on suicidal behavior, two in particular. In the first, participants are presented with two clear containers, each wrapped in plastic as if brand new, and are asked to remove both containers from the wrapping. Then, participants are told that although both containers are perfectly clean, they are to wash each themselves in a sink available nearby. Afterward, participants are instructed to fill each container with water, to a mark on the container corresponding to a few ounces. Finally, in addition to answering some questions about their views of each container, they are asked to choose one from which they will (and do) drink.

One container is marked innocuously, with a term like "sucrose," and the other ominously, with a term or image related to death (e.g., "cyanide," or a skull-and-crossbones symbol). A simple question in research like this is how many participants, unselected for any type of mental health problem, given a free choice, drink from the death-themed container, knowing full well that it is a new, clean container with water they themselves put in the container. Intriguingly, the answer is around 13%, the same figure that emerges in the context of condemned prisoners volunteering for execution.

A second analogue involves virtual reality. Imagine a virtual reality environment in which one steps into an elevator, goes up several floors, and then exits into an area that appears to be under construction. There is a location that seems to be for a floor-to-ceiling window, but the window is missing. Further, there is a narrow plank that extends horizontally outward, several stories above the ground below. The virtual reality task is to walk the plank—during which, it should be reiterated, one's feet are in actuality firmly planted on the floor of a safe, regular room. One is not asked to jump from the virtual height, nor is one pushed or any such thing; one is only asked to walk the plank. Researchers have found that when they ask undergraduates, here again, unselected on any particular characteristic, to walk the plank, the majority refuse. What proportion agrees to do it and then actually does it? Around 13%, the same rate we have now encountered in diverse contexts, all of which are unified by the fact that they are in a sense analogues to death.

Returning to death row, if volunteering for execution is a suicidal phenomenon, then its demographic characteristics should track it. Gender would otherwise be interesting to examine in this context—and indeed the majority of both US suicide decedents and death row volunteers are male—but so much of death row is male that that is not especially informative.

Ethnicity may prove more illuminating. Among US suicide decedents, white people are overrepresented (as are those of Native American descent), whereas Black, Asian American, and Hispanic people are underrepresented. Are the same patterns detectable among death row volunteers?

Clearly. From Blume's article cited earlier, death row overall was made up of 45.5% white inmates, 42.1% Black inmates, and 10.1% Hispanic inmates; the remaining 2.3% were designated as "other" (all inmates included in these figures were male; 3,436 in total). From this overall group, 786 inmates were executed involuntarily, and of these, the ethnic/racial proportions were 52.4% white, 38.9% Black, 6.4% Hispanic, and 2.3% other. Another 103 volunteered for their execution and were put to death, and of these, the ethnic/racial backgrounds were 87.4% white, 2.9% Black, 6.8% Hispanic, and 2.9% other.

Death row is not overwhelmingly white; neither is being executed involuntarily. But voluntary execution certainly is—of the 103 inmates in Blume's series who volunteered for death, 90 were white, whereas only 3 were Black, 7 were Hispanic, and 3 were "other." Like suicide, death row volunteering generally aggregates in white people.

In Blume's study, this latter category for "other" ethnicity may include Native American individuals. Though the numbers are too small to make much of—again there were only three death row volunteers in the "other" ethnicity category—those in the "other" category were the only other group besides white inmates from death row overall to be overrepresented in the execution volunteer group. The inclusion of Native American inmates in this group may have in part accounted for this effect, and if so, it too would mirror the pattern seen in rates of suicide in the nonincarcerated population.

Blume's article also points to similarities between suicide in the nonincarcerated, on the one hand, and death row volunteering, on the other, with regard to "contagious" processes that may be operative in both.[36] With regard to suicides per se, there is little doubt that they cluster to some degree in time and space; in fact, the well-characterized spring–summer peak in suicides worldwide (in April to August in the Northern Hemisphere; in October to February in the Southern Hemisphere) guarantees at least some clustering in time, as does suicide's weekly peak on Mondays and Tuesdays. There is evidence to suggest that there is clustering at play even beyond these weekly and annual peaks.

A tangent into the weekly and annual peaks is perhaps in order. Regarding the annual spring–summer peak, many at first disbelieve this truth, at least in the Northern Hemisphere, having absorbed through various means that the peak occurs near the winter holidays. But truth it is; in fact, the winter holidays (in the Northern Hemisphere) occur during the annual nadir in suicide rates. The fact that, in the Southern Hemisphere, the "winter" holidays and actual summer coincide may have spurred the myth that suicides peak in December and January worldwide. But, no, the peak is truly a spring–summer one, among the more well-replicated effects in suicide research. As to why this is, there are no completely definitive explanations, but I am inclined to think two of them largely account for this phenomenon.

First, for those who suffer from bipolar disorder (with its usually distinct manic and depressive phases), manias are more likely to occur in spring than in other seasons. An important fact about manias is that they are energy-intensive and thus typically not sustainable for more than a few days or weeks. Thus, if someone gets manic in mid-March, there is a substantial likelihood that, by the end of April, the mania will have subsided. Should the person's mania subside into euthymia (i.e., a symptom-free phase with neither depression nor mania), suicide is somewhat unlikely, but should one's mania translate either into a depression or a mixed state that combines elements of depression and mania—and both situations regularly apply as people cycle out of manias—then by midspring and into summer, the person's depression renders them vulnerable to suicide. Thus, the natural seasonal course of bipolar disorder may be one contributor to the suicide spring peak.

Another candidate contributor, perhaps even more prominent than the course of bipolar disorder, involves the fact that the onset of spring–summer serves as at least a mild, natural antidepressant for the majority of people. Reflect on your own experience for a moment. Do you not feel slightly more energetic as spring arrives, particularly in locales far from the equator? Most people do, and for most, the experience is to the good, but for a small subgroup, spring is not only arousing but overarousing, in the form of agitation, edginess, insomnia, and like states—states that are well-characterized suicide warning signs. This explanation is consistent with the six-month shift in suicide rate peaks between the Northern and Southern Hemispheres. If the shift is truly seasonal, it should occur regardless of which months are in the spring–summer, and this is in fact the pattern.

What of the weekly peak on Monday and Tuesday? As with the annual peak, there is to my knowledge no fully definitive explanation, but I have two speculations. Neither of these have much to do with the "I hate Mondays" idea, though I suppose that could be one contributor. I have contended throughout these pages that death by suicide is daunting and thus requires, among other things, planning and preparation. The weekend may represent an opportunity to plan and prepare for an imminent attempt, which occurs within a day or two later (i.e., on Monday or Tuesday). Also, I have argued that a key aspect of the suicidal mindset involves loneliness. Should one be down on one's luck, out of work perhaps, and should this trigger desperation and depression, leading in turn to contemplation of suicide, consider one's situation come Monday morning. Unlike over the weekend, when most everyone is "out of work," everyone typically goes back to work on Monday morning—everyone, that is, except for those genuinely out of work. For the latter, Monday morning can prove isolating and dispiriting, in that one's loneliness is made salient, as may be any feelings of inadequacy for some (cf. perceived burdensomeness).

The weekly and annual peaks in turn are but two contributors to suicide "clustering" or "contagion." "Clustering," I think, is a better term than "contagion" because the former is agnostic with regard to *why* suicides cluster, whereas the latter suggests some contagious mechanism.

Beyond peaks, the actual operative mechanism is not well understood, but a kind of contagion may indeed be at work. If so, it is almost surely not a literal biological contagion (though there is partial genetic transmission), but contagion in the sense that ideas or trends can spread and in that sense be contagious. In previous work and as touched on earlier in this book, my opinion on this is that the idea that death by suicide is feasible is what can be contagious; suicide seeming feasible is relevant because to many, it is unimaginable, and this deters many from translating suicidal thinking into suicidal action. On this view, the reason that suicides cluster at the Golden Gate Bridge is that it is widely known that many have perished by jumping from the bridge (which an installed barrier will soon stop); that is, it is feasible there. Similarly, why do suicide clusters sometimes plague certain schools? One possibility is that one suicide within a student body conveys to other students that death by suicide is feasible for a student like them.

To return to death row and to apply this same logic there, the voluntary execution of one inmate may convey to other inmates that volunteering is a feasible option. Indeed, Blume wrote, "Part of the conventional wisdom among capital defense attorneys is that when one death-row inmate waives his appeals, others frequently do so as well, or put differently, one volunteer begets another."[37] Blume's article documents spates of volunteering that occurred in the 1990s on death rows in the states of Texas, South Carolina, and others as well.

Like suicide in the nonincarcerated, volunteering for execution does not seem to be evenly distributed geographically. In the United States, rates for suicide are high in the Mountain West and Alaska, and generally more moderate in other areas of the country. In Blume's analysis of death row volunteering, a somewhat similar pattern emerged: The top state for volunteering was Utah, with a rate ten times that of the national average. Second on the list was Washington, which, though not a Mountain West state per se, abuts one; in addition, its eastern portion shares some cultural similarities with the Mountain West. Moreover, rates for suicide in the state of Washington are above the national average.

Volunteering occurred infrequently in Alabama, Florida, Georgia, and California; in Louisiana and Mississippi, there were no examples at all at the time of Blume's analysis.[38] Of these six states that are low in death row volunteering, none are in the top twenty for general population suicide rates; in fact, all are below the median except the highest of these six, Alabama, which is twenty-fourth. These states have fairly low suicide rates, despite the fact many are popular retirement destinations, and such destinations tend to be associated with elevated suicide rates via suicide's connection with older age.

What is more, the death row conditions in these six states with low volunteering rates are above average in their harshness, and in some cases are deplorable. By contrast, the state with the highest rate of death row volunteering—Utah—has among the best death row conditions of any state. There thus seems to be no general connection between death row volunteering and the harshness of the environment (though in some cases it seems to play some role, as we have seen); a similar pattern (or lack of one) is detectable with regard to states' socioeconomic conditions and general suicide rates. This is not to say that death row environments anywhere are particularly humane, just that some are clearly harsher than others, and that this difference seems to have little overall bearing on the phenomenon of death row volunteering. Neither is it to deny that with regard to some health problems, harshness of conditions and socioeconomic factors are certainly implicated.

Further to the disconnect between death row conditions and death row volunteering, in Blume's analysis there were no volunteers in Mississippi, a candidate for the country's worst death row conditions. The conditions have been described as follows in an article by Elizabeth Bruenig: "Vermin ran rampant inside the prison walls . . . : rats, mice, spiders, cockroaches, snakes, opossums. There was no air-conditioning during the long southern summers. The humidity control was so poor . . . that when it rained outside, it rained inside, with water falling from the ceiling."[39]

Those who object to the idea that death row volunteering amounts to suicide might argue that volunteering is distinct because its motivation is different from that in suicide. Specifically, volunteering may stem from a clear-eyed acceptance of one's own guilt and of a proportionate punishment. There are, however, at least two problems with this argument. First, Blume's article notes a survey that was administered to death row attorneys; of forty-four cases, attorneys in sixteen of the cases believed that acceptance of one's guilt was a primary motivation for their condemned client's volunteering—a percentage of 36%. This seems a low percentage for a supposedly primary motivation. Second, and perhaps more important, even stipulating that an acceptance of irredeemable guilt and the need for requisite, extreme punishment are implicated as motives, this does very little to distinguish volunteering from suicide. In the latter phenomenon, it is very common for soon-to-be decedents to record or express to others in the time frame leading up to suicide their opinion of their extreme guilt, self-loathing, and self-disgust, along with the view that it is right and proper for them to die. Suicidal people can hold to this view very tightly, even when loved ones and others earnestly try to disabuse them of the notion (which, it should be noted, can work and should be tried, but like pretty much everything else in human affairs, is not always effective).

* * *

The American Founding Fathers, as imperfect as they plainly were, articulated a vision of freedom never before or since matched for its eloquence and profundity. These days, their vision of freedom is usually and understandably enough cast as one not just of freedom but also of related concepts like self-determination, individual rights, and autonomy. The Founders *did* indeed care about, write about, and endorse such themes. In this modern context, it is of interest to linger over the words of three of the most famous and important passages in the founding documents:

1. We hold these truths to be self-evident, that all men are created equal, that they are endowed by their Creator with certain unalienable Rights; that among these are Life, Liberty, and the pursuit of Happiness.
2. We the People of the United States, in Order to form a more perfect Union, establish Justice, insure domestic Tranquility, provide for the common defence, promote the general Welfare, and secure the Blessings of Liberty to ourselves and our Posterity, do ordain and establish this Constitution for the United States of America.
3. [W]e mutually pledge to each other our Lives, our Fortunes and our sacred Honor.

The first and the third, from the Declaration of Independence and styled by committee but largely by Thomas Jefferson, does in fact emphasize individual rights and freedom, but even here the emphasis is not just on the freedom of the individual (singular) but also on the equality of individuals (plural). Inherent to equality is the implicit demand of responsibilities, duties, and obligations to each other; justice demands as much. It is noteworthy that the Declaration of Independence is not really about the formation of the United States; rather, it is on the individual states' independence from Great Britain. Nevertheless, it still concludes with selflessness; the third quote pledging the Founders' honor, their fortunes, indeed their very lives is how the Declaration ends.

The second of the quotes, from the US Constitution and also a collaboration but here heavily influenced by James Madison, picks up on this theme of selfless togetherness and mutual obligation. It is significant that in opening the signal document of the country's actual founding, the Founders relegated the self and elevated the polity. Indeed, it is hard to find mention of individual freedom, whereas every line except perhaps the last teems with selflessness and ignores self-interest.

Even the choice of which words to capitalize—more an art form than a systematic grammar in the eighteenth century—conveys sentiments of togetherness and selflessness. In the Declaration's incomparable sentence on the self-evident truth of equality, words such as "Rights," "Life," and "Liberty" are capitalized, whereas "men" is not (capitalization aside, the choice of this word is a blatant shortcoming because of its lack of inclusiveness; some of the Founders had a somewhat more inclusive view than others of the *eventual* spread of freedom and equality, though none of them could fathom how or when). Returning to the details of capitalization, the opening lines of the US Constitution and the closing lines of the Declaration capitalize the following: We the People of the United States, Order, Union, Justice, Tranquility, Welfare, Blessings of Liberty, Posterity, Constitution for the United States of America, Lives, Fortunes, Honor. In these same lines, the Founders had the chance to capitalize words that were personal to them, like "our" and "ourselves," but they usually did not.

In my book *Mindlessness: The Corruption of Mindfulness in a Culture of Narcissism*, I bemoaned that, from when the Founders were writing until the present day, much has changed regarding citizens' self-views.[40] Whereas back then, even the plainly accomplished Founders took opportunities to promote the common good over individual feeling, now even the least accomplished—perhaps *especially* the least accomplished—but not just them, liberally and serially take opportunities for self-promotion. Anything that ranks the self over values like honor, dignity, sacrifice, and endurance tends to be reflexively preferred, to all our detriment. In that same book I show that these trends are evident in many ways, including regarding aging, death, and dying. Consider in this context these words from Herb Hendin's book *Seduced by Death*: "In a culture that fosters narcissism, aging and death are harder to bear."[41]

If that is true, as I discussed at length in *Mindlessness*, it should be demonstrable in multiple ways that more recent generational cohorts stand in different stead to themes of aging and death than do older cohorts. One reflection of that exact shift can be seen in the habits of census takers. As noted by Atul Guwande in his book *Being Mortal*, generations ago census professionals knew to adjust age figures *downward*, because people used to value being older and more respected, and so routinely *overreported* their age. "The dignity of old age was something to which everyone aspired," wrote Guwande.[42] These days, census workers also adjust age figures, but now *upward*, because people routinely *underreport* their age, the supposed virtue now being youthfulness.

As another reflection of this trend, my colleagues and I studied a concept called "maturity fears"—fears of aging and of the consequences of aging—and we did so in college students tested in 1982, 1992, 2002, and 2012 (i.e., new cohorts of late adolescents collected every ten years over the course of thirty years). As each decade passed, maturity fears significantly increased.[43] Still another reflection of this same trend can be seen in life insurance purchasing patterns. The purchase of life insurance has a selfless aspect, in that one is spending money in the present to benefit others in the future (granted those others may share one's genes, but do not always). In fact, the purchase of life insurance is a much less frequent occurrence in the twenty-first than in the twentieth century.

Two fundamental aspects of human nature are our sociality and our self-determination. The former immerses the self within the larger matrix of human discourse and favors responsibility, duty, and obligation to others. In tension to it, self-determination emphasizes the self, in all

164 | IS PHYSICIAN-ASSISTED SUICIDE SUICIDE?

its (potential) dignity and with all its inherent rights. The management of this tension is key to individual, societal, political, and cultural well-being. Trends toward self-interest and narcissism risk this balance.

*　*　*

Might these same kinds of trends be involved, at least somewhat, in the growing momentum behind death with dignity legislative efforts? That the latter have momentum is clear: recent polling from Gallup and other organizations shows approval by approximately two-thirds of American adults, double the approval rating from a few decades ago. Approval by a majority is a consideration, but it neglects the possibility that the majority may be wrong. In the same polling, the change in attitudes toward physician-assisted suicide has occurred in lockstep with *decreases* in patriotism, in social trust, and even in belief of physicians' expertise. I suppose it is arguable whether decreased patriotism and social trust are warranted—I personally believe they are not and are actively malignant—but I see it as unassailable that physicians know more about medicine than their patients. The same majority who want to be able to direct their physicians to aid them in dying mistrust those same physicians, which is cause for reflection on and skepticism regarding the majority's opinions, at least in some cases. Not that physicians' opinions and decisions are unerring. We have already encountered evidence of questionable opinions (e.g., a psychiatrist who can "feel" in advance which patient will die by suicide; physicians informing cancer sufferer J. J. Hanson of his very few remaining months to live, when he survived far longer).

Supportive opinions related to assisted suicide in physically well people on psychiatric grounds—and, crucially, also in physically well people on *nonpsychiatric grounds*—are prominent in certain European countries. A revealing study by Verhofstadt and colleagues examined euthanasia requests made on the basis of unbearable suffering, and on that basis alone. These authors state, "Only in Belgium, Luxembourg and The Netherlands can requests for euthanasia be legally granted on grounds of untreatable and unbearable suffering."[44] It is important to reiterate what this means; specifically, it is perfectly legal and increasingly common for people in these countries to engage euthanasia services on the basis of their own reports of internal distress, with no physical illness at all, never mind a terminal one.

With regard to Belgium in particular, in 2014 and 2015, almost four thousand people died as a result of euthanasia, almost two thousand per year in each of those years. Of all deaths from all causes in Belgium, euthanasia accounted for almost 2% in 2014 and 2015.[45] For context, in many countries (including the United States), suicide accounts for approximately 2% of all deaths and is often in the top ten causes of mortality. On this logic, euthanasia may soon be in the top ten causes of mortality in countries like Belgium.

Of the approximately four thousand Belgian euthanasia deaths in 2014 and 2015, in one out of every seven (approximately 15%) the basis was a nonterminal illness. A nontrivial number of these patients had a psychiatric condition.[46]

Belgian law dictates that "a physician has to come to 'a level of mutual understanding' with the patient about the extent of their unbearable suffering."[47] How is unbearable suffering operationalized? How is it measured? The article by Verhofstadt and colleagues addresses the question thus: "The extent to which the suffering is unbearable is patient-related, which means that it can only be determined from the perspective of the patients themselves."[48] This answer is a logical extension of the principle of radical self-determination; a literature review from 2010 provides a compatible perspective: "Unbearable suffering in the specific context of a euthanasia request is provisionally defined as 'a profoundly personal experience of an actual or perceived impending threat to the integrity or life of the person, which has a significant duration and a central place in the person's mind.'"[49] In addition to being consistent with an emphasis on radical self-determination, such definitions are also, at least in my opinion, obvious recipes for multiple instances of suicidal people dying when their underlying conditions could have been mitigated. Such mitigation may not always be total (though often enough it is), but nevertheless sufficient to reinstill a will to live (if given time to do so, that is).

Patient testimonials accord with this concern. A patient whose desire to die was approved on psychiatric grounds stated, "I have to admit that since my request to die was considered to be acceptable, I'm experiencing better moments and I'm also in doubt now. I'm still in therapy and there we discuss other available options."[50] Right-to-die proponents may view anecdotes like these favorably, in that validating the person's suffering allowed for less distress and better functioning. That is one possible outcome, to be sure; another one, it should be emphasized, is needless, premature death.

The phenomenon of the approval of one's euthanasia paradoxically giving hope deserves further consideration. Marieke Vervoort, a highly successful wheelchair racer and Paralympic gold medal winner, stated exactly this regarding her own life and eventual death. Vervoort had a degenerative spine condition, and some of its consequences sometimes prevented her, for example, from sleeping; her physical pain levels were at times extremely intense. Referring to the documents from her native Belgium that officially approved her request to die, she stated, "If I didn't have the papers, I think I would have already [died by] suicide." She continued, "I think there will be fewer suicides when every country has the law of euthanasia. I hope everybody sees that this is not murder, but it makes people live longer."[51]

That is a plausible view, but the tragic fact is that Vervoort died—by euthanasia in October 2019—about thirty months after she made those statements. Had Vervoort said "it *can* make people live longer," it would be quite defensible, as her case can be viewed as showing and as others seem to show more definitely. But plainly it does not always make people live longer, as illustrated, for example, by the assisted suicides of very young people referred to earlier. I have already referenced a companion principle that can be operative in suicide—namely, that when people see an array of options in their future, even if one of those options is suicide, that is a far less dangerous mindset than when they see only one option and it is suicide.

Returning to the article by Verhofstadt and colleagues containing testimonials from psychiatric patients contemplating euthanasia in Belgium, consider the following summary of such patient testimonials: "[A] personal social shortcoming was the perceived burdensomeness of one's presence. For example, the impact of patients' suffering experiences on family members was described as so omnipresent or exigent that it led to disruption within the family. The impact (consequences) of a patient's mental disorder(s) could also lead to the patient wanting to relieve their loved ones and believing that their loved ones would be better off without them."[52] This is precisely the basis for many decisions to die in suicide, and to see it as a legitimate reason for death in the context of assisted suicide but not in other forms of suicide is difficult for proponents to reconcile.

The authors who assembled these testimonials concluded, "The results show that the unbearable suffering experienced by psychiatric patients has a wider variety of sources than the psychological symptoms of a patient's disorders alone."[53] This conclusion is not necessarily true—patients' reports of distress from "a wider variety of sources" can and regularly do arise directly from their psychiatric conditions—and it will give comfort to those who want to argue that conclusions about one's unbearable distress are separable from mental disorders, when that is not at all clear.

To their credit, Verhofstadt and colleagues stated, "Note that extreme care in the euthanasia decision-making processes should be applied, as a request for euthanasia can be a symptom of a patient's mental disorder."[54] They remark that there is a "precarious ambiguity" in many such cases; this is an apt phrase, and that it appears in an article describing people already having been killed on the basis of psychiatric unbearable suffering, is notable.

* * *

The attitude of this chapter is intended to be, at least to an extent, questioning, because as with other vexed issues relevant to life and limb (e.g., gun rights in the United States), definitive answers, unlike impassioned opinions, are scarce. In a time when we can manage death in a compassionate and painless way, shouldn't we do so?

In a recent visit to a medical school, I met with a group of bright psychiatry residents. The conversation turned to the question of what counts, and what does not count, as suicide. I commented that a cardinal feature of suicide is the serious intent to die—notice all that the word "intent" carries with it: ideas about suicide, plans for it, resolve, will—and I suggested that any death not characterized by such intent does not qualify as suicide. We turned to examples; some of the most illustrative involve self-starvation in anorexia nervosa, and the continuation of addictive behaviors that one understands are likely to result in death.

Except for those anorexic patients who explicitly intend and enact suicide and almost always do so using means that do not involve starvation, people with anorexia nervosa do not intend that their behavior culminate in death. Rather, it is intended to culminate in thinness, the desire for which is hard to overstate among patients with anorexia nervosa. It is true that their plans for thinness may backfire and lead to death—this is the case in some premature deaths in those with the illness, the others being from suicide—but in their minds, that is beside the point of thinness and a small price to pay for a deeply coveted quality. Suicidal people desire suicide; anorexic people, thinness.

Similarly, life-threatening behaviors done to ingest an addictive substance are usually intended not to bring about death but to satisfy the addiction. It is true that the indulgence of the addiction may risk death, but in the minds of those addicted, that is beside the point and a small price to pay for a deeply desired substance. Here again, suicidal people want death; addicted people intend to heed the call of their addiction.

One of the residents asked about an example in her awareness of a psychotic patient who believed he could create with his mind spans between high, inner-city buildings and walk across them. He fell to his death attempting to do just that. Was this suicide, she asked? I answered that I did not think so, that it struck me as an accidental death, much as if the patient fell by accident off an actual span between buildings. There was no intent to die. She reflected for a moment and responded, "I wonder if his family would be reassured by that, that he did not die by suicide, that his illness killed him." My response was perhaps so, but had it been suicide, I would suggest that in this case, too, the illness killed him.

A thought occurred to another resident, who said, "You have been talking about self-caused deaths that are not suicide because death was not intended, but surely there are intended deaths that are not suicide, like physician-assisted suicide? There are cultures in which older people kill themselves in order to free their families of the responsibility to care for them." I noted that here we had reached the junction between clinical and scientific knowledge, on the one hand, and one's own personal values and ethics, on the other, and that therefore the residents needed to figure much of this out on their own. I added one question that may guide their thinking; namely, of all terminally ill people, and of all older people in the cultures referred to, do all choose to enact their own deaths? Given that the answer is plainly no, then two other questions arise: Are there systematic differences between those who do and those who do not choose to initiate death in end-of-life scenarios? If so, how do those differences relate to phenomena like depression and suicidality itself?

* * *

I will return to these essential questions in due course. Their answers will be shaped to a degree at least by particular cultures' views of death in general, not just of humans but of nonhumans too.

In this context, I found an article that appeared in the *New Yorker* in January 2017 to be noteworthy.[55] The article describes a giraffe that had been kept in zoos in Denmark for all its life. The animal was young and healthy and was also genetically redundant with other giraffes. There is a need within zoos worldwide for population control of certain animals, giraffes being one. In the judgment of zoo officials, the giraffe in question could not be released into the wild because it would suffer a death within days that would entail more agony than what officials had planned, which was a controlled euthanization of the animal. Once that had occurred, they reasoned that (1) there was a considerable educational opportunity in allowing the public to witness the giraffe's dissection; and (2) after that, the remains would be wasted unless they were fed to other animals, in this case lions, which was also something the public could witness.

Though the incident eventually led to an unsurprising worldwide backlash against the zoo officials, it initially caused relatively little consternation within Denmark itself. This led me to assume, perhaps wrongly it turns out, a Danish cultural mindset toward death, including that physician-assisted suicide of humans must surely be legal in Denmark, as it is in some European countries relatively nearby (i.e., Belgium, Luxembourg, the Netherlands; it is common in Switzerland but not clearly allowed or forbidden by formal law there; rather, it is thus legal by omission in Switzerland). My assumption about Denmark was wrong in that physician-assisted suicide is currently illegal in Denmark, but my intuitions about the Danish mindset were perhaps not fully mistaken. In a September 2016 poll taken by the Danish newspaper *The Local*, around eight in ten Danish citizens supported legalizing *active euthanasia* (i.e., a person, almost always a physician, actively administering a lethal agent to another person, as opposed to a more passive approach, such as occurs in some American states, in which a physician prescribes the lethal agent but thereafter may have little or nothing to do with the act of the patient ingesting or injecting it; I would suppose that even more than eight in ten Danish citizens would approve of the latter). The title of the newspaper article, "Why Denmark Could Be the Next 'Right to Die' Battleground," also suggests that my intuitions about Denmark may not have been totally misguided.

* * *

It is perhaps jarring to see physician-assisted suicide considered side by side, as I do in this book, with forms of violence such as suicide terrorism, murder-suicide, and suicide-by-cop, not to mention the obscenities of individuals like Anders Behring Breivik and Joseph Duncan, described earlier. Indeed, these latter are considered atrocities, very obviously in violation of the law, whereas physician-assisted suicide is legal in several jurisdictions (e.g., Oregon, the state of Washington, Belgium) and is understandably viewed by many as combining virtues like compassion and self-determination. A dispassionate look at the logic and evidence regarding physician-assisted suicide, however, at least suggests that it, too, shares basic elements with other types of suicidal violence, perhaps especially suicide-by-cop and death row volunteering. This will be—and should be—hotly debated, but entered into the debate should be facts such as these: (1) Many physicians who have been directly involved in facilitating a requested death later find themselves traumatized by the experience and express profound regret about their involvement.[56] (2) "Slippery slopes" have developed in this domain, in which originally stringent criteria for who is eligible for physician-assisted suicide deteriorate to include categories like "mental disorder" and "weariness of life."[57] A study from Belgium on euthanasia requests in those with psychiatric disorders showed that almost half of the requests were approved on purely psychiatric grounds; a clear majority of the requests were carried out.[58] (3) There are documented similarities between frankly suicidal people and those who request physician-assisted suicide (vs. similarly ill people who do not, who are the vast majority, incidentally); those requesting physician-assisted suicide resemble suicide decedents in several telling ways. Specifically, although it is controversial, there is evidence that what differentiates terminally ill patients who seek such services versus those who do not are subclinical manifestations of mood pathology.[59]

A year or so before his death, the astrophysicist Stephen Hawking voiced his support for physician-assisted suicide, stating that he would like to have the choice should he have nothing more to contribute to science. He neglected to mention that he not only had said similar things in the 1980s, but he also asked his then wife to turn off his respirator during a particularly punishing bout of physical illness, so that he could die. She refused. He felt unbearable suffering, that he could contribute no more, and that he burdened others excessively. An essential point is that he genuinely felt these sentiments and viewed them as unchangeable—and then they passed. Even if he did not understand his state's temporary (if agonizing) quality, his then wife did.[60] This allowed him to live on, serve as an inspiration to millions, contribute massively to science, and write, among other things, *A Brief History of Time*, as already noted. These very clear facts show that Hawking was mistaken about his assisted suicide in the 1980s; was he now right in 2016?

* * *

A report by Kim and colleagues in *JAMA Psychiatry* examined cases of psychiatric patients who had died by either euthanasia or assisted suicide; the report included sixty-six cases from 2011 to 2014 in the Netherlands.[61] Those numbers alone are worth dwelling on—over the course of four years in Holland, more than fifteen psychiatric patients per year are dying via assisted suicide or euthanasia, absent any nonpsychiatric medical condition, let alone a terminal one. The figure of fifteen per year is a bare minimum, in that there were almost certainly more cases than those officially available to these authors.

One quite remarkable aspect of this sample of deceased psychiatric patients was their age; 25% were younger than fifty, and 14% were in their thirties. Another notable feature was the sample's psychiatric presentation; the paper's abstract reads, "Most had chronic, severe conditions, with histories of attempted suicides and psychiatric hospitalizations. Most had personality disorders and were described as socially isolated or lonely. Depressive disorders were the primary psychiatric issue in 55% (n = 36) of cases."[62] What affects me most about this passage, and I expect may similarly strike some clinically active readers, is how similar this description is to my own clinical caseload, for whom the thought of something like euthanasia is so far from my mind—and theirs—as to make reading those lines from the article's abstract harrowing.

Still another informative aspect of the article is the relationship of patients to their physicians, and also the conduct of the physicians. In more than a quarter of the cases, the physicians performing the procedure were new to the patients, and most of these (fourteen of eighteen patients) were conducted by a mobile euthanasia clinic. When there was external consultation with other physicians, disagreement was not rare (i.e., it occurred in almost a quarter of such cases); in more than 10% of cases, there was no consultation at all.

I noted earlier that some of the patients in the article's series were remarkably young, but none younger than thirty. In this context, one might wonder just how far down the age range assisted suicide practitioners are prepared to go. The answer, at least in Belgium, is very far. In the last few years, Belgium extended its laws allowing euthanasia to minors, and since then, at least three youths have died in this fashion.[63] Their ages were seventeen, eleven, and nine.

Related to the other end of the age spectrum, a proposed law called the Completed Life Bill is under consideration in the Netherlands.[64] The law would legalize assisted suicide for anyone over the age of seventy-five—in some versions of the proposal, there actually is no minimum age—including perfectly physically and psychiatrically healthy individuals, simply on the basis that they feel they have lived a full life. The Dutch health minister stated that the law was needed for "older people who do not have the possibility to continue life in a meaningful way, . . . and who have a sense of loneliness, partly because of the loss of loved ones, and who are burdened by general fatigue, deterioration and loss of personal dignity." It is notable how similar this description is to those of outpatient psychotherapy patients suffering from major depressive disorder—until the episode remits, that is, and then their view changes back toward an appetite for life. Indeed, a critic of the bill commented, "We cannot allow people who are needy or lonely to be talked into dying . . . combatting loneliness—and investing in dignity and focusing on our elderly—is always the best option." It should be emphasized that, to my knowledge, the Dutch Completed Life Bill has not yet passed, but its continued and serious consideration in Holland lends credence to those who worry about slippery slopes in this domain.

The American Psychiatric Association adopted a policy aimed toward guarding against just such slopes. The policy reads in part that psychiatrists "should not prescribe or administer any intervention to a non–terminally ill person for the purpose of causing death."[65] A psychiatrist in favor of the policy pointed out that, with one exception, in every country that has made physician-assisted suicide legal, the law eventually was extended to include non–terminally ill patients as well. The one exception, to date, is the United States.

In 2017, I had the pleasure of visiting Riga, Latvia, and attending a suicide prevention meeting organized by the North Atlantic Treaty Organization (NATO).[66] Among the meeting's charms were discussions with other attendees, during one of which I learned that the World Health Organization (WHO) at the time was working on an initiative to officially code physician-assisted suicide as distinct from suicide. The American Association of Suicidology (AAS), an organization in which I participate and which I support, has adopted a similar view. As this chapter has argued, this is premature; the evidence for assertions by WHO and the AAS of a distinction is not persuasive, a fact that should factor in to the thinking of organizations that purport to attend and regularly do attend to science on behalf of public health.

Conclusion

How to Stop a Plague

Some of us who work in the field of suicide prevention conceivably run the risk of becoming inured to and callous about the individual and family tragedies produced by suicide deaths. In my observations of the field over the course of thirty years or so, I see that as a problem in principle but not really in practice. Put differently, I am hard-pressed to think of even one colleague in the field whom I would describe as calloused to the calamities of suicide, likely because it is so common to have a personal connection, either via one's own experience or via the death by suicide of a loved one.

A problem I have observed is in a sense the opposite one—namely, emotional immersion in the tragic aspects of the phenomenon to such a degree that logic and rational thought become challenging. While this is very understandable, I nonetheless view it as an obligation to avoid this pitfall, and instead to steer a kind of middle course that combines a dispassionate, sleeves-rolled-up approach to scientific work on the topic with a compassionate sensibility.

I have tried to do just that in the pages of this book, and if I have erred, it is by overemphasizing a dispassionate approach to events that truly are tragic and at times even utter atrocities. To the degree that I have erred in this and perhaps other ways, it is with the purpose of quicker understanding so that future deaths can be averted, not with any intention to be unsympathetic to the deceased, the bereaved, and those who have been suicidal and survived.

Preventing future deaths is my own professional goal, and that goal alone easily represents enough of one to be sufficient. But, I would suggest, the study of suicidal varieties of violence returns even more dividends. To ponder why someone would want to die in the throes of a grave physical illness whereas someone else desperately wants to live in the midst of that very same illness enriches the understanding of human nature itself. To understand the tensions inherent in end-of-life decisions between human essentials like dignity, debt to others, self-determination, and sociality does the same. Suicide is undeniably a somber topic and it also provides a unique window into the meaning of life.

For example, much can be learned about the will to live from those who are in the midst of a suicide attempt and who find that their self-preservation instinct is sparked and revived at the last moment, sometimes in circumstances that allow self-rescue, and sometimes not. Jumps from a height are paradigmatic of this latter category; I have for many years asserted in both print and aloud that midair experiences among those intentionally jumping from a height very likely share features related to mortal terror. Many seem to, but there is at least some reason for doubt because other reports of midair experiences are distinctly different. Consideration of these other reports will allow for a full and balanced treatment, enabling readers to make up their own minds in possession of a fuller knowledge of the topic.

In a classic, perhaps underappreciated paper, a geologist reported his and other people's experiences of accidental falls from considerable heights. The author being a geologist (and Swiss), his focus was mostly on falls from mountain cliffs (but the principles apply to other accidental near-death scenarios too, including near drownings).

According to this paper, almost all such experiences share these features: a profound slowing of time, extreme acuity of perception, rapidity of thought, some feelings of peace and serenity, and no physical pain. On the latter point of pain, the author made two intriguing observations: (1) accidental fall victims often hear but never feel impact; and (2) physical pain regarding the event does not apply even upon regaining consciousness, and sometimes does not start until hours later (when it can be considerable of course).

Some suicide jumpers who have survived report similar reactions. Indeed, this is the predominant theme in a series interviewed in the 1970s, and one can infer that because some of these survivors had such experiences, so did some of those who purposefully jumped to their deaths.

I wish it were clear that all who died in that fashion had that experience. Of course, one hopes that the decision to die is not taken in the first place. But given that they have decided in their misery to die by jumping and have irrevocably done so, one hopes that at least their last seconds brought not even more anguish and alarm but at least some solace. Alas, it is fairly clear that that is not always the case. Multiple reports from the few who have jumped from the Golden Gate Bridge and survived indicate considerable midair regret and fear.[1]

What might account for these differences in midair experiences between those who jump purposely and those who fall by accident? I would suggest at least two possible sources. First, the accidental fall victims are, to put it mildly, surprised by their predicament, and it may be that the suddenness of the experience is implicated in the brain reactions of acuity, calm, and analgesia. By contrast, at least according to the view of death by suicide articulated here, those who have purposefully jumped to their deaths are far from surprised, in that they have been planning it and preoccupied by it for long stretches of time before the incident. The lack of surprise may prevent the brain response seen in the accidental scenarios. Second, the states of mind and of brain in accidental fall victims versus to-be suicide decedents are almost entirely distinct. In the moments before the incident, the fall victims can almost to a person be described as engaged, active, and in harmony with nature and their fellow climbers. In stark contrast, the suicidal group is anguished and alienated, and most if not all have been suffering from some variant of a mood disorder, often co-occurring with other mental disorders like schizophrenia, borderline personality disorder, or anorexia nervosa. The states of mind and brain in the latter group may suppress the brain reaction seen in the accidental fall victim group.

* * *

In the 2018 documentary *Three Identical Strangers*, genetically identical triplets, separated into different families early in life, find one another later in life. Given their identical genes, it is no surprise that they share many phenotypic similarities, such as appearance, attitudes, preferences, and so on, despite their having been reared apart in very different families for most of their first two decades of life. Nevertheless, there are differences between them too, including very profound ones having to do with ultimate outcomes like the timing and causes of mortality.

Diversity is thus considerable even among the genetically identical, and it is all the more so among those who, far from being genetically

178 | CONCLUSION

literally the same, are merely phenotypically similar. In the latter case, whether the grouping variable is demographic (e.g., gender, ethnicity), temperamental, clinical, or having to do with mortality, the diversity within the group tends to be striking.

This rather obvious truth bears emphasis, for at least two reasons. First, it underscores the individuality—the lived experience—of those within the group, according them the individual respect and dignity that are due everyone; we all have our narratives, our viewpoints, our beliefs, and our values. They are irreducible. This point is highly resonant with a modern sensibility highlighting things like autonomy and self-determination, as noted in chapter 5. It is so resonant that it has the potential to crowd out another important principle, which brings me to the second of the two reasons to reflect on diversity within groups of individuals selected to be similar to one another.

Grouping variables range from the completely arbitrary and useless to the very meaningful and practical, and that is—or can be—true regardless of the amount of diversity within the group. A grouping variable such as "everyone whose first name starts with the letter 'G'" will reliably identify the same group of people, with considerable diversity between them, and to no valid or useful end. The diversity in this arbitrarily selected group may be similar to that in a group selected on a different grouping variable, and, importantly, this latter grouping variable may nevertheless be highly valid and useful. In both grouping scenarios, that is, diversity is considerable, yet the enterprise of grouping is only useful under the one scenario of a valid, nonarbitrary grouping variable.

I suggest that the grouping variable "died by suicide" is of this nonarbitrary, valid character, as may be the grouping variables "attempted suicide and survived" and "seriously considered suicide but did not attempt." As alluded to earlier, there is a vibrant community of those in the latter two groups; they prefer the term "lived experience," meaning that they have lived the experience of thinking about and/or attempting suicide, and they can be a powerful source for change in suicide prevention within societies like the American Association of Suicidology and beyond. They can also be sources of inspiration for new conceptual ideas and directions; it falls to science to arbitrate the ultimate value of any new idea or direction.

One of the emphases of the lived experience of suicidality community is on the uniqueness of their individual experiences, an emphasis that warrants respect. It is for this reason that some of them take issue with terms like "suicide attempter" because such phrasing reduces identity and experience in all their diversity into a term referring just to a sliver of their experience, usually a very small one at that if the metric is the amount of time spent actually having that specific experience.

The persuasive power of these points regarding individuality has the potential to obscure the *possible* validity and utility of a grouping variable involving suicidality. It strikes me as eminently achievable to be open to this possible validity *and* to simultaneously be respectful of individual lived experience, although I acknowledge that that has not always been achieved by researchers or clinicians—two grouping variables in their own right, incidentally, that also have some validity and utility while containing diversity within them.

Much rides on the phrase "possible validity." The validity of a grouping variable having to do with suicidality is a matter open to scientific arbitration. Valid grouping variables identify nonarbitrary commonalities that group members share. In chapter 1 of this book, I described one theoretical effort, the interpersonal theory of suicide, that proposes one set of commonalities, specifically, the conjunction of capability for suicide with feelings of aloneness and burdensomeness that feel intractable to the person experiencing them. In that chapter and elsewhere, my group and I have taken pains to pay attention to both the robustness of the supportive evidence and the limitations to that evidence base.

If this model and ones like it have merit—and I encourage further scientific scrutiny along these lines—then it suggests that there is a common signature to suicide, one that is often obscured by, but is nevertheless detectable through, all the diversity that those who die by suicide plainly have. The identification of such signatures has straightforward prevention and intervention implications, such as those, touched on in the opening chapter, emphasizing increased belonging through caring contact and enhanced relationship functioning. Common signatures also have potential relevance to the identification of those at risk.

An overarching claim of this book can be viewed as a generalization of the common signature perspective of the interpersonal theory. That is, the theory attempts to explain suicide; the current effort makes the case that included within the category of suicide are phenomena like murder-suicide, suicide-by-cop, amok, spree killings ending or potentially ending in suicide, suicide terrorism, death row volunteering, and, perhaps controversially, physician-assisted suicide. If this is so, the elements of the interpersonal theory should be detectable across all these diverse forms of violence, a nonarbitrary and valid commonality observable despite substantial diversity. A related prediction would be that to the degree that a form of violence departs from suicide, the involvement of the interpersonal theory variables should be muted.

For example, many would argue that a line should be drawn such that physician-assisted suicide is located outside of the realm of suicide. As I articulated earlier, I do not agree, but stipulating the point for a moment, if that is so then the interpersonal theory variables should be demonstrably less relevant regarding physician-assisted suicide than regarding other forms of suicide. This logic may hold and be useful regarding any conceptual effort that attempts to identify common signatures of suicide, regardless of whether it is the interpersonal theory or another theoretical model.

A more agnostic version of a "common signature" approach is descriptive. One such perspective is to see suicide as a unitary thing in nature, defined by features such as very high intent to die and determined and effortful focus on a detailed plan to do so, always or almost always spurred by some form or combinations of forms of mental disorders. Regarding this latter aspect of mental disorders, as was emphasized at the outset, an unnuanced conception of exactly what constitutes a mental disorder is very likely to distort or prevent understanding. I have considerable sympathy for this kind of descriptive approach, as attested to by my group's delineation and testing of what we think of as a heretofore uncharacterized mental disorder, acute suicidal crisis disorder, also described as acute suicidal affective disorder.[2]

This descriptive approach to a "common signature" view is not at all mutually exclusive of one like that articulated by the interpersonal theory of suicide. Indeed, my view is that the latter theory is designed to understand the same descriptive outcomes as those emphasized in an atheoretical, descriptive perspective. In the context of an integrated interpersonal theory–descriptive approach, work is ongoing regarding the role of interpersonal theory elements in a syndrome like acute suicidal crisis disorder.

There are of course challenges to this "common signature" approach, and I would like to reflect further on two. First, there may be subtypes of suicide. Even if there are—and I am aware of no persuasive evidence to that effect—it remains possible that one overarching theory could explain them, but it also opens up the possibility that a particular theory is only relevant to one or some subtypes.

A second challenge to the "common signature" conceptual approach involves a priori prediction. That is, if a true common signature exists in advance of a suicide, that signature should at least potentially be detectable to a high enough degree of fidelity to be actionable (e.g., to intervene on a truly at-risk person and to not intervene with regard to someone else). As things stand, the degree of fidelity is high enough to be detectable in a theory-testing, research context, but not at all high enough to be useful regarding person-specific, time-specific prediction in a real-world, actionable context *in advance*.

By contrast, useful, real-world comprehension *in retrospect* is currently possible, and just as such understanding can inform the future prevention of misfortunes like plane crashes and home fires, so may they regarding suicide prevention. The material covered near this book's outset on means safety, obstacles to danger, and active measures is illustrative.

My reaction to the current difficulty in a priori prediction is that it is far from surprising given the state of the art in measurement and also given the extreme challenges of finding a specific signal within the world of noise generated by human nature in interaction with other humans. One source of signal-swamping noise is deception and dissimulation, as was covered in the opening chapter. This source of error has been prominent enough that I believe it has led some in the field to make gross miscategorizations, such as seeing amok as dissociative and nonsuicidal, to take one example. This is far from the only source of such error and noise, and it may not even be the most prominent. Detecting potentially subtle signals against that kind of noise can seem so daunting as to be impossible—until, that is, someone does it, as the history of physics, to take but one example, has repeatedly shown.

182 | CONCLUSION

If, as I have argued, the point of departure for all forms of suicidal violence from amok to physician-assisted suicide is suicide, a clear applied implication is that current, standard suicide prevention is also prevention of these other forms of suicidal violence. There is a reassuring aspect to this assertion, in that we already know how to prevent many suicides; it is no mystery (i.e., means safety, frequent and caring follow-up, access to quality mental health care, education and training of the primary care workforce), though it is a travesty that we fail to implement what we know. There may be no need for a separate set of clinical approaches to the various forms of suicidal violence because the prevention of the one entails the prevention of the others. Prevention of one suicide is a bounty of inestimable value to the individual and to the family in question; prevention of multiple suicides compounds that gift; and, in the course of human affairs, prevention of suicides that would also entail the needless and senseless deaths of our fellow world citizens is among the greatest goods of all.

NOTES

INTRODUCTION

1 "Suicide" is not an apt enough word to use as a term of art throughout the book, nor are others like "conventional suicide" or "usual suicide." To solve this conundrum, at least partially, I will refer to "suicide" as "suicide" and other forms of suicidal violence by their specific terms (e.g., "murder-suicide," "suicide terrorism").

2 Indeed, this same phenomenon occurs with regard to those who have attempted suicide, survived, and harmed no one else. That researchers, clinicians, and others readily believe such disavowals has produced what in my opinion are misunderstandings of the true suicidal mindset, such as the misunderstanding that it is fairly common for people to attempt suicide absent ideation. Multiple studies have indeed found that people who have attempted suicide deny a history of ideation, but that is a wholly different matter than that they really had no ideation.

3 In the chapters that follow, I advocate a particular perspective and in so doing may unknowingly alter or omit a detail.

4 Kormann, 2016.

5 Dalrymple, 1994, p. 58.

6 Dalrymple, 1994, p. 94.

7 Dalrymple, 1994, p. 95.

8 I write not as a critic of the sport but as a former player (I know its violence intimately) and a current, very enthusiastic fan.

9 Jamieson and Romer (2021), for example, linked the increase in media coverage of violence to the youth *homicide* rate. They did not link it to suicide in youth or otherwise; I am suggesting that they might have done so.

10 Cf. Wolfgang, 1958.

11 There were earlier movies and games that were violent, but none received widespread attention.

12 Finkel, 2017.

13 Anestis, personal communication.

14 The paper by Franklin et al. (2017) is often regarded as novel or seminal. I see the work, rather, as a highly competent updating of a long-known fact (e.g., in my first year of graduate school in 1987, we were assigned a paper that, back then, was already fifteen years old and made this same point [Murphy, 1972], and Murphy was responding to an earlier paper that made a similar point in the 1950s [Rosen, 1954]).

184 | NOTES

15 Murphy, 1972, p. 356.

16 Pokorny, 1960, p. 317.

17 This is a paraphrase of Mao, words that he later lamentably and catastrophically betrayed. It is important, I think, to source such paraphrases and catchphrases when possible. For instance, a phrase for buying into a belief or a movement is "drinking the Kool-Aid." Many or even most who use it now forgot or never knew that it is a reference to a grievous crime and an utter tragedy, the Jonestown massacre that took the lives of over nine hundred people. Another example—this one less a phrase than an ideology—is that suicide is or at least can be a revolutionary act of autonomy and protest against oppressive forces (notice how different this view is from one that attributes most or all suicides, in part or full, to mental disorders). On the one hand, this is thought-provoking. On the other hand, who used virtually the same words to exhort? We return to Jonestown: Jim Jones was recorded minutes before the disaster began saying exactly this.

18 My own answer to the former question is in the single digits, and the answer forty to fifty years ago was in the dozens.

19 Pelletier, 2007.

20 This story was covered by the news site 13WGME, on June 30, 2017; see wgme. com.

21 Pirkis et al., 2013.

22 Seiden, 1978.

23 Centers for Disease Control and Prevention (2018).

24 Stares, 2016.

25 An interesting point about guns in America—certainly relevant to obvious suicides but also to the several suicide-involved types of violence pondered in this book—is that the percentage of American homes with guns declined from approximately 46% in 1980 to around 32% more recently (Ramchand, 2022). On the other hand, gun sales have increased dramatically over the last couple of years, and there are more guns in the United States than people. Most of the change in percentage of homes with a gun occurred before 2000, before suicide rates began to relentlessly rise from 2000 to 2018. Thus, during the American suicide surge, the percentage of homes with guns remained roughly steady, and the overall number of guns increased.

26 Robins, 1981.

27 Rogers et al., in press.

28 See Rogers et al., in press.

29 Anestis et al., 2014.

30 Manel, 2016.

31 This and subsequent passages are based on a comprehensive treatment of this topic provided by Stack (2015).

32 *Carter v. Massachusetts*, 2020.

33 One may point out, as a reviewer of this book did, that I seem to believe some instances of anecdotal evidence but not others. I acknowledge that this is true.

For example, I believe Mr. Hines's largely anecdotal account, but in other passages of the book I warn against unquestioning belief in anecdote. My rationale is that some examples of anecdotal evidence are more believable than others, largely because the webs of circumstances, corroborating accounts, and data around some incidents are extensive, whereas in other incidents they are not.

34 I led a Department of Defense–funded initiative called the Military Suicide Research Consortium, the activities of which can be tracked at msrc.fsu.edu.

35 See McNulty et al., 2019.

36 US Department of Defense, 2020.

37 See Comtois et al., 2019.

38 Motto, 1976.

39 Pew Research Center, 2010.

40 See Franklin et al., 2016.

41 Stack, 2005.

42 Cf. Thaler & Sunstein, 2008.

43 Joiner, 2005; Van Orden et al., 2010; Joiner et al., 2016; Olson et al., 2022.

44 It would be ideal if I could support my impression of audiences' reactions using public opinion poll results on beliefs about alcohol's role in suicidality, as well as other topics like the roles of impulsivity and selfishness in suicidality. A search for such data proved unsuccessful, however.

45 Anestis et al., 2014.

46 Cavan, 1928.

47 Chitty et al., 2017.

48 E.g., Hamilton & Opler, 1992.

49 Hames et al., 2012. It occurs to me that a similar principle may be operative in cases of postpartum homicidal ideation, in which mothers of newborns think of killing their baby. I view it as possible that a protective impulse along the lines of "someone might harm my baby" is getting rendered in the mind as "harm my baby."

50 Pascal, 1670, Thought #425.

51 See Winslow, 1840, p. 229.

52 Stefan, 2016.

53 Robins, 1981. Our paper was Joiner et al., 2017.

54 Joiner et al., 2017, p. 1750.

55 Stefan, 2016, p. 33.

56 Lester and Frank, 2008.

57 All US states but one have witnessed very clear increases in suicide rates over those years; the one exception is Nevada, and studying why Nevada is the only such state—it actually saw a small *decrease* in suicides over that interval—strikes me as a useful avenue for future research.

58 Orri et al., 2022.

59 Tong et al., 2022.

60 Cuddehee, 2017. The activist is Marc Hyden.

186 | NOTES

61 It still is there; for example, a recent ruling in South Carolina (the case is *Wicker-sham*) repeatedly used the term "commit."

62 Joiner, 2005; Van Orden et al., 2010; Joiner et al., 2016; Olson et al., 2022.

CHAPTER 1. SUICIDE

1 Joiner, 2005; Van Orden et al., 2010; Joiner et al., 2016.

2 Klonsky & May, 2015; O'Connor, 2021. Cf. fluid vulnerability theory (see Bryan, 2021).

3 Dewey, 2004; Grossman, 1995.

4 There are instances in which a creature's death is worth more to that creature—specifically to that creature's genes—than its life. These are instances of what is called "inclusive fitness," which operates according to Hamilton's rule (i.e., $rB - C > 0$), in which B is benefit, C is cost, and r is the degree of genetic relatedness. For instance, if one saves the lives of three first-degree biological relatives, $r = .50$, $B = 3$, and $C = 1$; .50 × 3, or 1.5, is greater than 1, satisfying the rule.

5 This case was tried in front of a judge and jury in state court, a public proceeding. None of my remarks about this case or others I mention in the book reveal confidential or privileged information.

6 Buss, 2006.

7 Centers for Disease Control and Prevention, 2016.

8 Centers for Disease Control and Prevention, 2016.

9 N. Smith, 2018.

10 Joiner, 2005.

11 On suicide contagion, see Hecht, 2013; on deaths of bystanders, see Joiner, 2014; on the deprivation of choice and life to one's future self, see Hecht, 2013; on causing a state of often lasting bereavement, see Cerel et al., 2015.

12 E.g., Joiner, 2014.

13 Van Orden et al., 2010.

14 These quotes were brought to my attention by the psychologist John Richters, PhD.

15 Van Orden et al., 2010.

16 Joiner et al., 2016; Olson et al., 2022.

17 Joiner 2005.

18 Van Orden et al., 2010.

19 Joiner et al., 2016.

20 Chu et al., 2017; Van Orden et al., 2010.

21 Pokorny, 1960.

22 Durkheim, 1897.

23 Chu et al., 2017.

24 This is spelled out at length by Olson et al., 2022.

25 Nock et al, 2010.

26 McNulty et al., 2019.

27 Colt, 2006, p. 19.

NOTES | 187

28 All of this was conducted in partnership with Florida State University's regulatory officials.

29 See, e.g., the review on divorce and suicide by Stack, 2021.

CHAPTER 2. PERVERTED VIRTUES TRANSFORM SUICIDE INTO MURDER-SUICIDE AND SPREE KILLING

1 Joiner, 2014.

2 See Fridel & Zimmerman, 2019, for an alternative perspective.

3 The book is called *A Mother's Reckoning* (Klebold, 2016a).

4 See Klebold, 2016b.

5 With conditions red in tooth and claw, being salvageable likely had to accompany true vulnerability. There is evidence for this uncomfortable speculation in nonhuman social species as well as in certain human groups. For instance, regarding the latter, Leighton and Hughes (1955) cited the following quote from a Netsilik Eskimo: "For our custom up here is that all old people who can do no more, and whom death will not take, help death to take them. And they do this not merely to be rid of a life that is no longer a pleasure, but also to relieve their nearest relations of the trouble they give them" (p. 328). This perhaps disquieting view has modern currency, in that some form of it is regularly invoked regarding physician-assisted suicide, to be explored in depth in chapter 5.

6 Reid, 2018.

7 It is partial because it is based on my three decades of (mere) clinical experience—the word "mere" can be lingered on or skipped over depending on your own philosophical bent.

8 Many of the students in the vicinity of the 2018 shootings at Parkland were in ninth grade at the time, and thus as I write in the fall of 2022, many are now in their first or second year at state universities in Florida, including Florida State University. Enough of these students with PTSD have come to our clinic's attention that we are considering forming a trauma-focused group intervention specifically for those whose index trauma was the Parkland incident.

9 Scofield & Jones, 2018.

10 Wible, 2018.

11 See Joiner, 2014.

12 Joiner, 2014.

13 Joiner et al., 2016.

14 An illuminating book on the group's theology is Benjamin Zeller's *Heaven's Gate: America's UFO Religion* (2014).

15 Zeller, 2014.

16 Given that bus drivers are so regularly in the public square, it is perhaps unsurprising that they regularly are involved in detecting such incidents. I have formed the anecdotal impression over the years that they not only frequently detect such incidents but also often serve as Good Samaritans in them.

17 See Truesdell, 2017.

18 Reuters Staff, 2016.

19 I am indebted to Thomas Anthony of the University of Southern California for this information on number of people killed.

20 Seierstad, 2015.

21 Seierstad, 2015, p. 302.

22 Seierstad, 2015, p. 394.

23 Skeem et al., 2016; Seierstad, 2015.

24 Seierstad, 2015, p. 358.

25 McVeigh later claimed that he was unaware of the day care center, and that had he been, he might have chosen another target. The FBI viewed this as implausible, however, given the extensive scouting of the site that McVeigh is known to have conducted.

26 Michel & Herbeck, 2001.

27 Blair et al., 2014.

28 Ilic & Frei, 2019.

29 Hempel et al., 1999.

30 Such interviews can be found, for example, in Hines, 2013.

31 Wulsin & Goldman, 1993, p. 152.

32 Bill et al., 2012.

33 Krakow et al., 2001.

34 Raskind et al., 2018. The reason that prazosin is effective at all is not well understood, though it may have to do with the physiological calming associated with somewhat lower blood pressure.

35 Joiner et al, 2016.

36 Keefe, 2015.

CHAPTER 3. KILLING ONESELF WITHOUT KILLING ONESELF

1 Stack et al., 2012.

2 Pyers, 2001.

3 Pyers, 2001.

4 Thorough data are needed on people who identify as nonbinary, gender-nonconforming, and trans. Encouragingly, work in this area appears to be accelerating.

5 Anestis et al., 2014. I am a coauthor of this paper.

6 Weinglass, 2016.

7 Baumeister, 1999.

8 For soldiers unable to kill, see Grossman, 1995; for soldiers who kill but are marred by the experience, see Dewen, 2004; for physicians disturbed by their participation in assisted suicide, see Hendin, 1997.

9 Dewey et al., 2013.

10 See Mohandie et al., 2009; Dewey et al., 2013.

11 Pyers, 2001, p. 4.

12 Pyers, 2001.

NOTES | 189

13 Pyers, 2001.
14 Schram, 2016.
15 Berman, 1979.
16 I am indebted to an anonymous reviewer for alerting me to this topic as well as guiding me toward some useful references on it.
17 Wolfgang, 1957, p. 3.
18 Anestis et al., 2014.
19 Wolfgang, 1959.
20 Suonpää & Savolainen, 2019.
21 Polk, 1997.
22 "Beginning in 2003 the CDC collected state data from seven states. Between 2004 and 2006 additional states were added. By 2006 the data were collected in seventeen states: Alaska, California, Colorado, Georgia, Kentucky, Maryland, Massachusetts, New Jersey, New Mexico, North Carolina, Oklahoma, Oregon, Rhode Island, South Carolina, Virginia, West Virginia, and Wisconsin" (Wasserman & Stack, 2011, p. 36).
23 The work of Ian Rockett and colleagues is of clear relevance (e.g., Ali et al., 2022).
24 Anwar, 2015; Skeem et al., 2016.
25 Skeem et al., 2016.
26 Seierstad, 2015, p. 372.
27 E.g., Gimlette, 1901.
28 Ellis, 1893.
29 Gaw & Bernstein, 1992.
30 American Psychiatric Association, 2000, p. 845.
31 On punishing amok by execution in Britain, see Carr & Tann, 1976.
32 Anestis et al., 2014.
33 Shays, 1994.
34 Poindexter et al., 2015.

CHAPTER 4. SUICIDE TERRORISM
1 L. Wright, 2006, p. 31.
2 L. Wright, 2006, p. 31.
3 Meloy, 2004, p. 143.
4 See Lankford, 2013a.
5 Atran, 2010, p. 362.
6 E.g., Lankford, 2013b.
7 Stern, 2003.
8 Berko, 2016, p. 1.
9 Cf. Ohnuki-Tierney, 2002, p. 169; Merari & Ganor, 2020.
10 Berko, 2016, p. 25; see also Stern, 2003, p. 50
11 Weinglass, 2016.
12 As noted in Apuzzo, 2016.
13 Dalrymple, 2017.

14 Robins, 1981.
15 Dalrymple, 2017. I was reminded of the Shakespeare quote by a passage in Dalrymple's book.
16 Isaacharoff, 2017.
17 Dudley, 2021.
18 Merari et al., 2009.
19 Weinglass, 2016.
20 Sennott, 2002.
21 Emerson, 2002, p. 160.
22 Wilkinson, 2011.
23 Baer, 2008; Berko, 2016.
24 Brown et al., 2002; Joiner et al., 2002.
25 Lankford, 2013b; Merariet al., 2009; Merari, 2010.
26 Lankford, 2013b; Merari et al., 2009; Merari, 2010.
27 The review (with no author attributions) is at www.imdb.com.
28 Baker & Nazzal, 2016.
29 Bhui et al., 2016.
30 However, it should be acknowledged that the association between depression and sympathy for violent protest and terrorism is not wholly driven by suicidality; the association remains when it is examined absent the suicidality item on the depression measure (Bhui et al., 2016).
31 Bhui et al., 2020.
32 Groups like ISIS are responsible for a disproportionate number of terrorist attacks worldwide, accounting in part for the fact that a number of incidents included in this book were perpetrated by such groups. The notion that Islam particularly leads to mental illness, suicidal tendencies, or suicide terrorism is not intended and is patently ludicrous.
33 Bhui et al., 2020.
34 E.g., Brent & Mann, 2005.
35 Corner & Gill, 2014.
36 The exception is an effort being led by psychologist Emma Cardeli of Boston Children's Hospital/Harvard Medical School.

CHAPTER 5. IS PHYSICIAN-ASSISTED SUICIDE SUICIDE? IS DEATH ROW VOLUNTEERING?

1 Updike, 1990, pp. 24–25.
2 Donne, 1624/1923, p. 98. It would surprise me if American colonists in the mid-eighteenth century were unaware of this poem, in light not just of their erudition—literacy rates were astonishingly high in the colonies (90% or higher by the late 1700s), one reason I suspect for their success, as alloyed as it admittedly was—but also because Donne's words are resonant with those in the founding documents, to which I return later in this chapter.
3 Graeber, 2021, p. 131.

NOTES | 191

4 A report on this case can be found at Aldersly, 2019.
5 See Hughes, 2017.
6 Jenkins, Wilhelmina (@minadjenkins). Accessed June 5, 2023. https://twitter.com/minadjenkins/status/1031571383476793344
7 The episode, titled "Final Exit," appeared on March 13, 2015. https://thisiscriminal.com.
8 Oregon Health Authority, 2018.
9 Battin & Beck, 2016.
10 The conference was the annual meeting of the American Association of Suicidology.
11 To her credit, and I like to think to mine, Battin and I had a drink together later that day, a very pleasant coda to the debate in this age of vilification of the other side.
12 Quoted in M. Wright, 2017.
13 Bilefsky & Schuetze, 2016.
14 Meier et al., 1998.
15 See The Christian Institute, 2019.
16 BBC News, August 9, 2018, www.bbc.com (emphasis added).
17 Boffey, 2021 (emphasis added).
18 Gaudiani et al., 2022.
19 Gaudiani et al., 2022, p. 1.
20 Calati et al., 2021.
21 Calati et al., 2021, p. 170.
22 Nicolini et al., 2022, make a similar point.
23 Canetto & McIntosh, 2022.
24 Oregon Health Authority, 2018.
25 On the view that means safety is in principle always possible, an answer to this mostly rhetorical question is that it would be possible to attend the meetings after which these sordid transactions of cash for death take place, and to confront the transactants.
26 Many of the details of Dozier's life and family history are available at the website of the Marshall Project, in a story filed on January 18, 2018. See www.themarshall-project.org. See also thenevadaindependent.com.
27 Rountree, 2012, p. 589.
28 Rountree, 2012, p. 594.
29 Rountree, 2012, p. 601.
30 The details of Cox's case can be found in Bruenig, 2022.
31 Rountree, 2012.
32 Blume, 2004.
33 See Bruenig, 2022.
34 Blume, 2004.
35 Extreme cruelty to animals, prankish defecation, and destructive fire setting are characteristic of conduct disorder/antisociality. The memorable phrase "prankish defecation" is from Hervey Cleckley's classic book *The Mask of Sanity* (1941).

36 Blume, 2004.

37 Blume, 2004, p. 963.

38 David Cox, mentioned earlier, was executed in Mississippi, but well after the time frame on which Blume was focusing.

39 Bruenig, 2022.

40 Joiner, 2017.

41 Hendin, 1997, p. 182.

42 Guwande, 2014, p. 18.

43 See A. Smith et al., 2016.

44 Verhofstadt et al., 2017, p. 238.

45 Federal Control and Evaluation Committee on Euthanasia, 2016.

46 Federal Control and Evaluation Committee on Euthanasia, 2016.

47 Ministry of Justice, 2002.

48 Verhofstadt et al., 2017, p. 239.

49 Dees et al., 2010, p. 350.

50 Verhofstadt et al., 2017, p. 241.

51 CNN, September 12, 2016, Rio de Janeiro (CNN), www.cnn.com.

52 Verhofstadt et al., 2017, p. 241.

53 Verhofstadt et al., 2017, pp. 242–243.

54 Verhofstadt et al., 2017, p. 243.

55 Parker, 2017.

56 Hendin, 1997.

57 Fischer et al., 2008; Joiner, 2014.

58 Thienpont et al., 2015.

59 Ganzini et al., 2003.

60 Elgot, 2015.

61 Kim et al., 2015.

62 Kim et al., 2015.

63 Hodjat, 2018.

64 Bilefsky & Schuetze, 2016.

65 *Psychiatric News*, January 3, 2017; American Psychiatric Association, 2016.

66 Candor compels me to admit that I had forgotten or never knew that Latvia is a member country of NATO, as, of course, is the United States, facts with new poignancy in light of Russia's invasion of Ukraine in 2022.

CONCLUSION

1 Noyes & Kletti, 1972.

2 The syndrome includes features like rapidly escalating suicidal intent; self-hate/ self-disgust; social alienation; and overarousal symptoms such as agitation, insomnia, nightmares, and/or marked irritability. See Rogers et al., 2019, for further information.

BIBLIOGRAPHY

Aldersly, M. (2019, June 4). Dutch girl, 17, who was sexually abused at 11 and raped as a 14-year-old is legally allowed to die after contacting "end-of-life" clinic because she felt her life was unbearable due to depression. *Daily Mail*. www.dailymail.co.uk.

Ali, B., Rockett, I. R. H., Miller, T. R., & Leonardo, J. B. (2022). Racial/ethnic differences in preceding circumstances of suicide and potential suicide misclassification among US adolescents. *Journal of Racial and Ethnic Health Disparities, 9*, 296–304. https://doi.org/10.1007/s40615-020-00957-7.

American Psychiatric Association. (2000). *Diagnostic and statistical manual of mental disorders, text revision, fourth edition*. Washington, DC: Author.

American Psychiatric Association. (2016). *Position statement on medical euthanasia*. www.psychiatry.org.

Anestis, M., Joiner, T., Hanson, J., & Gutierrez, P. (2014). The modal suicide decedent did not consume alcohol just prior to the time of death: An analysis with implications for understanding suicidal behavior. *Journal of Abnormal Psychology, 123*, 835–840.

Anwar, Y. (2015, May 11). Psychotic hallucinations, delusions rarely precede violence. *Berkeley News*. https://news.berkeley.edu.

Apuzzo, M. (2016, March 28). Who will become a terrorist? Research yields few clues. *New York Times*. www.nytimes.com.

Atran, S. (2010). Pathways to and from violent extremism: The case for science-based field research. Statement before the Senate Armed Services Subcommittee on Emerging Threats & Capabilities, 10.

Baer, R. (2008). *The cult of the suicide bomber* [DVD]. London: Many Rivers Films.

Baker, P., & Nazzal, R. (2016, October 28). Once devoted to suicide bombing, she now embraces a peaceful jihad. *New York Times*.

Battin, M. P., & Beck, A. C. (2016, February 27). Op-ed: End-of-life bill is about honoring dying patients' wishes, not a "right to kill." *Salt Lake Tribune*.

Baumeister, R. (1999). Evil. New York: Holt.

Berko, A. (2016). *The smarter bomb: Women and children as suicide bombers*. New York: Cambridge University Press.

Berman, A. L. (1979). Dyadic death: Murder-suicide. *Suicide and Life-Threatening Behavior, 9*, 15–23.

Bhui, K., Otis, M., Silva, M., Halvorsrud, K., Freestone, M., & Jones, E. (2020). Extremism and common mental illness: Cross-sectional community survey of white British and Pakistani men and women living in England. *British Journal of Psychiatry, 217*(4), 547–554. https://doi.org/10.1192/bjp.2019.14.

Bhui, K., Silva, M. J., Topciu, R., & Jones, E. (2016). Pathways to sympathies for violent protest and terrorism. *British Journal of Psychiatry, 209,* 483–490.

Bilefsky, D., & Schuetze, C. (2016, October 13). Dutch law would allow assisted suicide for healthy older people. *New York Times.*

Bill, B., Ipsch, L., Lucae, S., Pfister, H., Maragkos, M., Ising, M., & Bronish, T. (2012). Attempted suicide–related posttraumatic stress disorder in depression—An exploratory study. *Suicidology Online, 3,* 138–144.

Blair, J. P., Martaindale, M. H., & Nichols, T. (2014, January 4). Active shooter events from 2000 to 2012. *FBI Law Enforcement Bulletin.* http://leb.fbi.gov.

Blume, J. H. (2004). Killing the willing: Volunteers, suicide and competency. *Michigan Law Review, 103,* 939–1009.

Boffey, D. (2021, October 25). Dutch psychologist says he sold "suicide powder" to over 100 people. *The Guardian.* www.theguardian.com.

Brent, D. A., & Mann, J. J. (2005). Family genetic studies, suicide, and suicidal behavior. *American Journal of Medical Genetics, 133C*(1), 13–24. https://doi.org/10.1002/ajmg.c.30042.

Brown, M. Z., Comtois, K. A., & Linehan, M. M. (2002). Reasons for suicide attempts and nonsuicidal self-injury in women with borderline personality disorder. *Journal of Abnormal Psychology, 111*(1), 198–202. https://doi.org/10.1037/0021-843x.111.1.198.

Bruenig, E. (2022, November 22). A history of violence. *The Atlantic.* www.theatlantic.com.

Bryan, C. (2021). *Rethinking suicide.* New York: Oxford University Press.

Buss, D. M. (2006). *The murderer next door: Why the mind is designed to kill.* New York: Penguin.

Calati, R., Olié, E., Dassa, D., Gramaglia, C., Guillaume, S., Madeddu, F., & Courtet, P. (2021). Euthanasia and assisted suicide in psychiatric patients: A systematic review of the literature. *Journal of Psychiatric Research, 135,* 153–173.

Canetto, S. S., & McIntosh, J. L. (2022). A comparison of physician-assisted/death-with-dignity-act death and suicide patterns in older adult women and men. *American Journal of Geriatric Psychiatry, 30*(2), 211–220.

Carter v. Massachusetts, 149 U.S. 910 (2020). www.scotusblog.com.

Case, A., & Deaton, A. (2020). *Deaths of despair and the future of capitalism.* Princeton, NJ: Princeton University Press.

Cavan, R. (1928). *Suicide.* New York: Russell and Russell.

Centers for Disease Control and Prevention. (2016). WISQARS: Web-Based Injury Statistics Query and Reporting System. www.cdc.gov.

Centers for Disease Control and Prevention. (2018). National Violent Death Reporting System. www.cdc.gov.

Cerel, J., Van De Venne, J. G., Moore, M. M., Maple, M. J., Flaherty, C., & Brown, M. M. (2015). Veteran exposure to suicide: Prevalence and correlates. *Journal of Affective Disorders, 179,* 82–87.

Chitty, K., Dobbins, T., Dawson, A., Isbister, G., & Buckley, N. (2017). Relationship between prescribed psychotropic medications and co-ingested alcohol in intentional self-poisonings. *British Journal of Psychiatry, 210,* 203–208.

The Christian Institute. (2019). "We must give hope to patients asking for euthanasia"—Dutch doctor. www.christian.org.uk.

Chu, C., Buchman-Schmitt, J., Stanley, I., Hom, M., Tucker, R., Chiurliza, B., Hagan, C., Patros, C., Podlogar, M., Rogers, M., Michaels, M., Ringer, F., & Joiner, T. (2017). The interpersonal theory of suicide: A systematic review and meta-analysis of a decade of cross-national research. *Psychological Bulletin*, *143*, 1313–1345.

Cleckley, H. (1941). *The mask of sanity*. St. Louis: Mosby.

Colt, G. H. (2006). *November of the soul: The enigma of suicide*. New York: Simon and Schuster.

Comtois, K. A., Kerbrat, A. H., DeCou, C. R., Atkins, D. C., Majeres, J. J., Baker, J. C., & Ries, R. K. (2019). Effect of augmenting standard care for military personnel with brief caring text messages for suicide prevention: A randomized clinical trial. *JAMA Psychiatry*, *76*(5), 474–483.

Corner, E., & Gill, P. (2014). A false dichotomy? Mental illness and lone actor terrorism. *Law and Human Behavior*, *59*, 425–435.

Cuddehee, M. (2017, March). A matter of life: The death penalty as a conservative conundrum. *Harper's*. https://harpers.org.

Cullen, D. (2009). *Columbine*. New York: 12 Books.

Dalrymple, T. (1994). *If symptoms persist*. London: Carlton Books.

Dalrymple, T. (2017). *The knife went in: Real-life murderers and our culture*. Gibson Square. Kindle Edition.

Dees, M., Vernooji-Dassen, M., Dekkers, W., & van Weel, C. (2010). Unbearable suffering of patients with a request for euthanasia or physician-assisted suicide: An integrative review. *Psycho-oncology*, *19*, 339–352.

Dewey, L. (2004). *War and redemption*. Burlington, VT: Ashgate.

Dewey, L., Allwood, M., Fava. J., Arias, E., Pinizzotto, A., & Schlesinger, L. (2013). Suicide by cop: Clinical risks and subtypes. *Archives of Suicide Research*, *17*, 448–461. https://doi.org/10.1080/13811118.2013.801810.

Donne, J. (1624/1923). *Devotions upon emergent occasions*. London: Cambridge University Press.

Dudley, D. (2021, January 12). Number of suicide attacks fall again in 2020 and they are getting less deadly. *Forbes*. www.forbes.com.

Durkheim, É. (1897). *Suicide*. Paris: Alcan.

Elgot, J. (2015, June 3). Stephen Hawking: "I would consider assisted suicide." *The Guardian*. www.theguardian.com.

Ellis, W. (1893). The amok of the Malays. *British Journal of Psychiatry*, *39*, 325–338.

Emerson, S. (2002). *American jihad*. New York: Free Press.

Federal Control and Evaluation Committee on Euthanasia. (2016). *Seventh report to the Parliament (2014–2015)* [in Dutch].

Finkel, M. (2017). *The stranger in the woods*. New York: Knopf.

Fischer, S., Huber, C., Imhof, L., Imhof, R., Furter, M., Zeigler, S., & Bosshard, G. (2008). Suicide assisted by two Swiss right-to-die organisations. *Journal of Medical Ethics*, *34*, 810–814.

Franklin, J. C., Fox, K. R., Franklin, C. R., Kleiman, E. M., Ribeiro, J. D., Jaroszewski, A. C., . . . & Nock, M. K. (2016). A brief mobile app reduces nonsuicidal and suicidal self-injury: Evidence from three randomized controlled trials. *Journal of Consulting and Clinical Psychology, 84*(6), 544–557.

Franklin, J. C., Ribeiro, J. D., Fox, K. R., Bentley, K. H., Kleiman, E. M., Huang, X., Musacchio, K. M., Jaroszewski, A. C., Chang, B. P., & Nock, M. K. (2017). Risk factors for suicidal thoughts and behaviors: A meta-analysis of 50 years of research. *Psychological Bulletin, 143*(2), 187–232.

Fridel, E., & Zimmerman, G. (2019). Examining homicide-suicide as a current in the stream analogy of lethal violence. *Social Forces, 97*, 1177–1204.

Ganzini, L., Dobscha, S. K., Heintz, R. T., & Press, N. (2003). Oregon physicians' perceptions of patients who request assisted suicide and their families. *Journal of Palliative Medicine, 6*(3), 381–390.

Gaudiani, J., Bogetz, A., & Yager, J. (2022). Terminal anorexia nervosa: Three cases and proposed clinical characteristics. *Journal of Eating Disorders, 10*, 1–14.

Gaw, A. C., & Bernstein, R. L. (1992). Classification of amok in *DSM-IV. Hospital and Community Psychiatry, 43*, 789–793.

Gimlette, J. D. (1901). Notes on a case of amok. *Journal of Tropical Medicine and Hygiene, 4*, 195–199.

Graeber, D. (2021). *The dawn of everything.* New York: Farrar, Straus and Giroux.

Grossman, D. (1995). *On killing.* New York: Little, Brown.

Guwande, A. (2014). *Being mortal: Medicine and what matters in the end.* New York: Henry Holt.

Hagan, C., Podlogar, M., & Joiner, T. (in press). Murder-suicide: Bridging the gap between mass murder, amok, and suicide. *Journal of Aggression, Conflict, and Peace Research.*

Hames, J., Ribeiro, J., Smith, A., & Joiner, T. (2012). An urge to jump affirms the urge to live: An empirical examination of the high place phenomenon. *Journal of Affective Disorders, 136*, 1114–1120.

Hamilton, M. S., & Opler, L. A. (1992). Akathisia, suicidality, and fluoxetine. *Journal of Clinical Psychiatry, 53*(11), 401–406.

Hecht, J. M. (2013). *Stay: A history of suicide and the philosophies against it.* New Haven, CT: Yale University Press.

Hempel, A. G., Meloy, J. R., & Richards, T. C. (1999). Offender and offense characteristics of a nonrandom sample of mass murderers. *Journal of the American Academy of Psychiatry and the Law, 27*, 213–225.

Hendin, H. (1997). *Seduced by death.* New York: Norton.

Hines, K. (2013). *Cracked, not broken.* New York: Rowman and Littlefield.

Hodjat, A. (2018, July 15). Belgium approved euthanasia of 3 minors, report finds. *Voice of America.* www.voanews.com.

Hughes, C. (2017, December 30). J. J. Hanson, opponent of assisted suicide, dies. *Times Union.*

Ilic, A., & Frei, A. (2019). Mass murder and consecutive suicide in Switzerland: A comparative analysis. *Journal of Threat Assessment and Management, 6*(1), 23–37. https://doi.org/10.1037/tam0000121.

BIBLIOGRAPHY | 197

Isaacharoff, A. (2017, January 6). 2016 was the deadliest year ever for suicide bombings worldwide. *Times of Israel*. www.timesofisrael.com.

Jamieson, P. E., & Romer, D. (2021). The association between the rise of gun violence in popular US primetime television dramas and homicides attributable to firearms, 2000–2018. *PLoS ONE 16*(3): e0247780. https://doi.org/10.1371/journal.pone.0247780.

Joiner, T. (2005). *Why people die by suicide*. Cambridge, MA: Harvard University Press.

Joiner, T. (2014). *The perversion of virtue: Understanding murder-suicide*. New York: Oxford University Press.

Joiner, T. (2017). *Mindlessness: The corruption of mindfulness in a culture of narcissism*. New York: Oxford University Press.

Joiner, T., Buchman-Schmitt, J., & Chu, C. (2017). Do undiagnosed suicide decedents have symptoms of a mental disorder? *Journal of Clinical Psychology, 73*, 1744–1752.

Joiner, T., Hom, M., Hagan, C., & Silva, C. (2016). Suicide as a derangement of the self-sacrificial aspect of eusociaity. *Psychological Review, 123*, 235–254.

Joiner, T. E., Pettit, J. W., Walker, R. L., Voelz, Z. R., Cruz, J., Rudd, M. D., & Lester, D. (2002). Perceived burdensomeness and suicidality: Two studies on the suicide notes of those attempting and those completing suicide. *Journal of Social and Clinical Psychology, 21*(5), 531–545. https://doi.org/10.1521/jscp.21.5.531.22624.

Keefe, P. (2015, September 7). The worst of the worst. *New Yorker*.

Kim, S., De Vries, R., & Peteet, J. (2015). Euthanasia and assisted suicide of patients with psychiatric disorders in the Netherlands 2011 to 2014. *JAMA Psychiatry, 73*(4), 362–368. https://doi.org/10.1001/jamapsychiatry.2015.2887.

Klebold, S. (2016a). *A mother's reckoning: Living in the aftermath of tragedy*. New York: Crown.

Klebold, S. (2016b). My son was a Columbine shooter. This is my story. TEDMED. www.ted.com.

Klonsky, E. D., & May, A. M. (2015). The three-step theory (3ST): A new theory of suicide rooted in the "ideation-to-action" framework. *International Journal of Cognitive Therapy, 8*, 114–129.

Kormann, C. (2016, October 18). A shocking suicide, a long-lost friend, and a movie trailer. *New Yorker*.

Krakow B., Hollifield, M., Johnston, L., Koss, M., Schrader, R., Warner, T. D., . . . & Prince, H. (2001). Imagery rehearsal therapy for chronic nightmares in sexual assault survivors with posttraumatic stress disorder: A randomized controlled trial. *JAMA, 286*, 537–545.

Lankford, A. (2013a, February 17). Exposing false martyrs as suicidal. *Jerusalem Post*. www.jpost.com.

Lankford, A. (2013b). *The myth of martyrdom*. New York: Oxford University Press.

Leighton, A. H., & Hughes, C. C. (1955). Notes on Eskimo patterns of suicide. *Southwestern Journal of Anthropology, 11*, 327–338.

Lester D., & Frank, M. (2008). How do American undergraduates view suicide bombers? *Psychological Reports, 103*, 713–714.

Manel, J. (2016, June 12). "Body on the moor." BBC News.

McNulty, J., Olson, M., & Joiner, T. (2019). Implicit interpersonal evaluations as a risk factor for suicidality: Automatic spousal attitudes predict changes in the probability of suicidal thoughts. *Journal of Personality and Social Psychology, 117*(5), 978–997.

Meier, D. E., Emmons, C. A., Wallenstein, S., Quill, T., Morrison, R. S., & Cassel, C. K. (1998). A national survey of physician-assisted suicide and euthanasia in the United States. *New England Journal of Medicine, 338*(17), 1193–1201.

Meloy, J. R. (2004). Indirect personality assessment of the violent true believer. *Journal of Personality Assessment, 82*(2), 138–146.

Merari, A. (2010). *Driven to death: Psychological and social aspects of suicide terrorism.* New York: Oxford University Press.

Merari, A., Diamant, I., Bibi, A., Broshi, Y., & Zakin, G. (2009). Personality characteristics of "self martyrs"/"suicide bombers" and organizers of suicide attacks. *Terrorism and Political Violence, 22*(1), 87–101. https://doi.org/10.1080/09546550903409312.

Merari, A., & Ganor, B. (2020). Interviews with, and tests of, Palestinian independent assailants. *Terrorism and Political Violence, 34*(8), 1595–1616. https://doi.org/10.1080/09546553.2020.1821668.

Michel, L., & Herbeck, D. (2001). *American terrorist.* New York: Regan Books.

Ministry of Justice. (2002, June 22). Law on euthanasia of May 28, 2002 [in Dutch and French]. *Belgian Official Gazette.* www.npzl.be.

Mohandie, K., Meloy, J. R., & Collins, P. I. (2009). Suicide by cop among officer-involved shooting cases. *Journal of Forensic Sciences, 54*(2), 456–462.

Motto, J. A. (1976). Suicide prevention for high-risk persons who refuse treatment. *Suicide and Life-Threatening Behavior, 6*(4), 223–230.

Murphy, G. (1972). Clinical identification of suicidal risk. *Archives of General Psychiatry, 27*, 356–359.

Nicolini, M., Gastmans, C., & Kim, S. (2022). Psychiatric euthanasia, suicide and the role of gender. *British Journal of Psychiatry, 220*(1), 10–13. https://doi.org/10.1192/bjp.2021.95.

Nock, M. K., Park, J. M., Finn, C. T., Deliberto, T. L., Dour, H. J., & Banaji, M. R. (2010). Measuring the suicidal mind: Implicit cognition predicts suicidal behavior. *Psychological Science, 21*(4), 511–517.

Noyes, R., & Kletti, J. (1972). The experience of dying from falls. *Omega, 3*, 45–52.

O'Connor, R. (2021). *When it is darkest.* New York: Random House.

Ohnuki-Tierney, E. (2002). *Kamikaze, cherry blossoms, and nationalisms.* Chicago: University of Chicago Press.

Olson, M. A., McNulty, J. K., March, D. S., Joiner, T. E., Rogers, M. L., & Hicks, L. L. (2022). Automatic and controlled antecedents of suicidal ideation and action: A dual-process conceptualization of suicide. *Psychological Review, 129*, 388–414.

Oregon Health Authority. (2018). Oregon Death with Dignity Act 2017 data summary. www.oregon.gov.

Orri, M., Vergunst, F., Turecki, G., Galera, C., Latimer, E., Bouchard, S., . . . Côté, S. (2022). Long-term economic and social outcomes of youth suicide attempts. *British Journal of Psychiatry, 220*(2), 79–85. https://doi.org/10.1192/bjp.2021.133.

Parker, I. (2017, January 8). Killing animals at the zoo. *New Yorker.* www.newyorker.com.

Pascal, B. (1670). *Pensées*. Paris: Chez Guillaume Desprez.

Pelletier, A. R. (2007). Preventing suicide by jumping: The effect of a bridge safety fence. *Injury Prevention, 13*, 57–59.

Pew Research Center. (2010, September 2). Cell phones and American adults. www.pewinternet.org.

Pirkis, J., Spittal, M. J., Cox, G., Robinson, J., Cheung, Y. T. D., & Studdert, D. (2013). The effectiveness of structural interventions at suicide hotspots: A meta-analysis. *International Journal of Epidemiology, 42*(2), 541–548.

Poindexter, E., Mitchell, S., Jahn, D., Smith, P., Hirsch, J., & Cukrowicz, K. (2015). PTSD symptoms and suicide ideation: Testing the conditional indirect effects of thwarted interpersonal needs and using substances to cope. *Personality and Individual Differences, 77*, 167–172.

Pokorny, A. (1960). Characteristics of forty-four patients who subsequently committed suicide. *Archives of General Psychiatry, 2*, 314–323.

Polk, K. (1997). A reexamination of the concept of victim-precipitated homicide. *Homicide Studies, 1*, 141–168. https://doi.org/10.1177/1088767997001002004.

Putnam, R. (2000). *Bowling alone*. New York: Simon and Schuster.

Pyers, L. (2001). Suicide by cop—the ultimate "trap." *FBI National Academy Associates Magazine, 3*, 4. www.theppsc.org.

Ramchand, R. (2022, July 11). Personal firearm storage in the United States: Recent estimates, patterns, and effectiveness of interventions. www.rand.org.

Raskind, M., Peskind, E. R., Chow, B., Harris, C., Davis-Karim, A., Holmes, H. A., . . . & Huang, G. D. (2018). Trial of prazosin for post-traumatic stress disorder in military veterans. *New England Journal of Medicine, 378*, 507–517.

Reid, W. H. (2018). *A dark night in Aurora: Inside James Holmes and the Colorado mass shootings*. Skyhorse Publishing. Kindle Edition.

Reuters Staff. (2016, September 12). Taiwan bus bursts into flames, killing 26, including 24 tourists from China. Reuters. www.reuters.com.

Robins, E. (1981). *The final months*. New York: Oxford University Press.

Rogers, M., Chu, C., & Joiner, T. (2019). The necessity, validity, and clinical utility of a new diagnostic entity: Acute suicidal affective disturbance (ASAD). *Journal of Clinical Psychology, 75*, 999–1110.

Rogers, M., Gai, A., & Joiner, T. (in press). Fluctuations in and associations between physical and psychological distance to suicide methods, fearlessness about death, and suicidal intent. *Journal of Psychopathology and Clinical Science* (formerly *Journal of Abnormal Psychology*).

Rosen, A. (1954). Detection of suicidal patients: An example of some limitations in the prediction of infrequent events. *Journal of Consulting and Clinical Psychology, 18*, 397–503.

Rountree, M. (2012). "I'll make them shoot me": Accounts of death row prisoners advocating for execution. *Law and Society Review, 46*, 589–622.

Schram, J. (2016, March 14). Detective killed by friendly fire in "suicide by cop" shootout. *New York Post*.

Scofield, D., & Jones, B. (2018, March 1). Teen planned school shooting before suicide. *News 5 Cleveland.*

Seiden, R. H. (1978). Where are they now? A follow-up study of suicide attempters from the Golden Gate Bridge. *Suicide and Life-Threatening Behavior,* 8(4), 203–216.

Seierstad, A. (2015). *One of us.* New York: Farrar, Straus & Giroux.

Sennott, C. (2002, August 4). Fighting terror: The investigation. *Boston Globe.*

Shays, J. (1994). *Achilles in Vietnam.* New York: Scribner.

Skeem, J., Kennealy, P., Monahan, J. Peterson, J., & Appelbaum, P. (2016). Psychosis uncommonly and inconsistently precedes violence among high-risk individuals. *Clinical Psychological Science, 4,* 40–49. https://doi.org/10.1177/2167702615575879.

Smith, A., Keel, P., Bodell, L., Holm-Denoma, J., Gordon, K., Perez, M., & Joiner, T. (2016). "I don't want to grow up, I'm a [Gen X, Y, Me] kid": Increasing maturity fears across the decades. *International Journal of Behavioral Development, 41*(6), 655–662.

Smith, N. (2018, January 24). South Korea makes suicide pacts a criminal offence in effort to reverse world's second highest rate. *Telegraph.* www.telegraph.co.uk.

Stack, S. (2005). Suicide and the media: A quantitative review. *Suicide and Life-Threatening Behavior, 35*(2), 121–133.

Stack, S. (2015). Suicide in the Grand Canyon National Park. In D. Lester & S. Stack (Eds.), *Suicide as a dramatic performance* (pp. 129–149). New Brunswick, NJ: Transaction Publishers.

Stack, S. (2021, November). Contributing factors to suicide: Political, social, cultural and economic. *Preventive Medicine, 152* (pt. 1), 106498. https://doi.org/10.1016/j.ypmed.2021.106498.

Stack, S., Bowman, B., & Lester, D. (2012). Suicide by cop in film and society: Dangerousness, depression, and justice. *Suicide and Life-Threatening Behavior, 42,* 359–376. https://doi.org/10.1111/j.1943-278X.2012.00096.x.

Stares, J. (2016, May 17). Families of suicide victims who kill themselves on train lines must pay compensation to rail firms to cover the cost of damaged trains, Belgian courts have ruled. *Daily Mail.* www.dailymail.co.uk.

Stefan, S. (2016). *Rational suicide, irrational laws: Examining current approaches to suicide in policy and law.* New York: Oxford University Press.

Stern, J. (2003). *Terror in the name of God: Why religious militants kill.* New York: HarperCollins.

Suonpää, K., & Savolainen, J. (2019). When a woman kills her man: Gender and victim precipitation in homicide. *Journal of Interpersonal Violence, 234,* 2398–2413. https://doi.org/10.1177/0886260519834987.

Thaler, R., & Sunstein, C. (2008). *Nudge.* New Haven, CT: Yale University Press.

Thienpont, L., Verhofstadt, M., Van Loon, T., Distelmans, W., Audenaert, K., & De Deyn, P. (2015). Euthanasia requests, procedures and outcomes for 100 Belgian patients suffering from psychiatric disorders: A retrospective, descriptive study. *BMJ Open, 5,* 7. http://dx.doi.org/10.1136/bmjopen-2014-007454.

Tondo, L. (2014). Brief history of suicide in Western cultures. In S. Koslow, P. Ruiz, & C. Nemeroff (Eds.), *A concise guide to understanding suicide: Epidemiology, pathophysiology and prevention* (pp. 3–12). Cambridge: Cambridge University Press. https://doi.org/10.1017/CBO9781139519502.003.

Tong, B., Devendorf, A., Panaite, V., Miller, R., Kashdan, T., Joiner, T., Twenge, J., Karver, M., Janakiraman, R., & Rottenberg, J. (2022). Future well-being among U.S. youth who attempted suicide and survived. *Behavior Therapy, 53*, 481–491.

Truesdell, J. (2017, November 22). Mom says murder-suicide attempt on her 2 children was a "harmless" cry for help. *People*. www.yahoo.com.

Updike, J. (1990). *Rabbit at rest*. New York: Random House.

US Department of Defense. (2020). Department of Defense suicide event report. https://health.mil.

Van Orden, K. A., Witte, T. K., Cukrowicz, K. C., Braithwaite, S. R., Selby, E. A., & Joiner, T. E., Jr. (2010). The interpersonal theory of suicide. *Psychological Review, 117*(2), 575–600. https://doi.org/10.1037/a0018697.

Verhofstadt, M., Thienpont, L., & Peters, G.-J. Y. (2017). When unbearable suffering incites psychiatric patients to request euthanasia: Qualitative study. *British Journal of Psychiatry, 211*, 238–245.

Wasserman, I., & Stack, S. (2011). Race, urban context, and Russian roulette: Findings from the National Violent Death Reporting System, 2003–2006. *Suicide and Life-Threatening Behavior, 41*, 33–40. https://doi.org/10.1111/j.1943-278X.2010.00014.x.

Weinglass, S. (2016, January 31). Are Palestinian teens committing "suicide by soldier"? *Times of Israel.*

Wible, P. (2018, January 13). What I've learned from my tally of 757 doctor suicides. *Washington Post.*

Wilkinson, P. (2016). *Terrorism versus democracy*. New York: Routledge.

Winslow, F. (1840). *The anatomy of suicide*. London: Renshaw.

Wolfgang, M. E. (1957). Victim precipitated criminal homicide. *Journal of Criminal Law and Criminology, 48*, 1–11.

Wolfgang, M. E. (1958). Delinquency and crime as part of a course of social studies. *Social Studies, 49*, 20–24. https://doi.org/10.1080/00220973.1940.11018139.

Wolfgang, M. E. (1959). Suicide by means of victim-precipitated homicide. *Journal of Clinical and Experimental Psychopathology, 20*, 335–349.

Wright, L. (2006). *The looming tower*. Knopf Doubleday Publishing Group. Kindle edition.

Wright, M. (2017, December 31). JJ Hanson, opponent of assisted suicide, dies at age 36. *Daily Mail*. www.dailymail.co.uk.

Wulsin, L. R., & Goldman, L. (1993). Post-traumatic stress disorder following a suicide attempt. *Journal of Traumatic Stress, 6*, 151–155.

Zeller, B. (2014). *Heaven's Gate: America's UFO religion*. New York: New York University Press.

INDEX

9/11, 122–23
911, 2, 27
988, 2

AAS. *See* American Association of Suicidology
Achilles in Vietnam (Shays), 115
acute suicidal affective disorder, 180
Adams, John, 50
Agent X, 144, 148
agitation, 82, 112, 158, 192n2
airplane incidents, fatality ratios, 86n19. *See also* Germanwings disaster; suicidal violence: proposed unified view
alcohol, 40, 101; blood alcohol content at time of suicide, 31, 100–101; excessive intake of, 9; intoxication, 115; misuse in lethal behaviors without actively killing, 33; role in suicidality, 31, 33, 185n44
Aldrin, Buzz, 8
alienation, 9; social, 192n2
altruistic. *See* suicide: subtypes
ambivalence, 22–25, 54; aspect by precipitating others to do the killing, 24; following desensitization, 24; toward suicide, 84
American Association of Suicidology (AAS), 173, 178, 191n10; "Integrating Science, Experience, and Political Will: Informed Action to Prevent Suicide," 2018 annual meeting, 13
American Civil Liberties Union, 25

American: colonists, 8, 190n2; football, 8, 55; gun policy, 75; revolutionaries, 8; values, 11; violence, 8
American Founding Fathers, 161
American Psychiatric Association, 113, 173
amok, 34–35, 46, 98, 110–13, 115, 146, 180–82; as dissociative episode, 113; as dissociative syndrome, 1; punishing of, 189n31; running, 112
amyotrophic lateral sclerosis [ALS], 82, 145. *See also* Ice Bucket Challenge
analgesia, 177
anaphylactic suicide, 33. *See also* suicide attempt(s): nonlethal
ancestral environs, 59
"and-the-next-thing-I-knew-doctor" event, 4, 110, 112
Anestis, Michael, 11, 18, 100
Anna Karenina (Tolstoy character), 34
anomic. *See* Durkheim, Émile; suicide: subtypes
anorexia nervosa. *See under* mental disorder(s); diagnoses associated with suicide
anterior cingulate cortex, 63–64
Anthony, Thomas, 188n19
anti-death penalty activist, 44
anti-psychiatry, 39
antidepressant, 72
antiscience obstruction to suicide prevention, 13–14
antisocial personality disorder. *See under* diagnoses associated with suicide; mental disorder(s)

204 | INDEX

anxiety symptoms. *See under* diagnoses associated with suicide; mental disorder(s)

Apollo 1, 8

Apollo 11, 8

Applewhite, Marshall, 81

Armstrong, Neil, 8

Asperger's syndrome, 105

Atta, Mohamed, 117, 119, 121, 123

attitudes toward gun safety. *See* gun safety

Augusta Mental Health Institute, 14

automatic: affective response, 62; behavior, 51; cognition perspective contribution to suicide theory, 57; suicides, 33

autonomy, 131–32, 161, 178, 184n17; of the prisoner's wishes, 151

Battin, Margaret, 140–41, 191n11. *See also* physician assisted deaths

Bay Bridge, 22. *See also* Golden Gate Bridge

Beachy Head, Princess Diana and, 63

Beck, Anna, 140. *See also* physician assisted deaths

behavioral-cognitive interventions, 94

behaviors: fundamentally suicidal, 35; post hoc explanations for, 5

Being Mortal (Guwande), 163

Belfast's Maze Prison hunger strikes (1981), 129

Belgium railway suicide compensations policy, 17

belief(s), source and variety of, 178; of physicians' expertise, 164

bereaved by suicide, 34–35, 56, 186n11. *See also* suicide and bereavement

Berman, Lanny, 15

bipolar disorder. *See under* diagnoses associated with suicide: bipolar spectrum disorder; mental disorders

black holes, Hawking's figurative use of, 145–46

blame externalization, 114

blink rate: as indication of imminent suicide risk, 81–82. *See also* suicide risk

blogs, 135

blood alcohol content (BAC). *See* alcohol

Blume, John, 152–54, 156–57, 159–60

borderline personality disorder. *See under* mental disorder(s); diagnoses associated with suicide

Boston Children's Hospital/ Harvard Medical School, 190n36

Boston Marathon bombings, 129

Bowling Alone (Putnam), 9

Breivik, Anders Behring, 87–88, 96, 111–12, 170

bridge, 51; barriers, 15; cost of barriers, 14; of lethal height, 49; suicidal crises at, 35. *See also* suicide intervention. *See also* Bay Bridge; Golden Gate Bridge; suicide intervention

A Brief History of Time (Hawking), 145, 171

British Journal of Psychiatry (journal), 127

Bruenig, Elizabeth, 160

burdensomeness, 42, 179. *See also* perceived burdensomeness

Buss, David, 54

bystanders, 56, 186n11

Calati, Raffaella, 146

California Personality Inventory, 121

cancer, 30

Canetto, Saliva, 147

capitalism, 9

Captain Cook, 112

carbon monoxide poisoning, 24, 56, 84

Cardeli, Emma, 190n36

caring: contact, 179; follow-up, 182; letters, 28–29, 62; memories, 63; messages, 30; text, 29–30, 32, 62

Carter v. Massachusetts, 184n32

Case, Ann, 9

catatonia, 38

INDEX | 205

CDC. *See* Centers for Disease Control and Prevention

Centers for Disease Control and Prevention (CDC), 41–42, 109, 189n22

Central Intelligence Agency (CIA), 123

Chaffee, Roger, 8

Charlie Hebdo (newspaper offices), 129

Chu, Carol, 60–61, 64

Chubbuck, Christine, 3

Churchill, Winston, 14

CIA. *See* Central Intelligence Agency

cirrhosis deaths, 9

Cleckley, Hervey, 191n35

CNN, 41–42

cognitive processing therapy, 133

Columbine (Cullen), 67

Columbine school shooting, 52, 68–69, 76–77, 89

Completed Life Bill (Netherlands), 172

complexity theory, 43

Comtois, Kate, 28–30; replication project of, 29

Cosmos perspective, 131, 142

COVID-19 pandemic, 9

Cox, David, 151–152, 192n38

Cracked, Not Broken (Hines), 26, 93

Criminal (podcast), 136

criminal(ity), 119; conviction of involuntary manslaughter for encouraging suicide, 24; as distinct from suicide, 4–5, 45; outlawing of suicide pacts in South Korea, 55

Cullen, Dave, 67–69

culture of: safety, 11; violence, 10, 13, 75

"cyanide," 155

Cyberball, 63–65

Dahmer, Jeffrey, 102

dairy farmer. *See* perversion: of mercy; of virtue,

Dalrymple, Theodore, pseud. *See* Daniels, Anthony

Daniels, Anthony, 5, 119, 190n15

A Dark Night in Aurora (Reid), 71

Darwin, Charles, 51

death instinct, 50–51, 106

death row prisoners, 151

death row volunteer(ing), 1, 24, 44, 46, 54, 109, 146, 149, 154–55, 157, 180; aborted attempt, 152; legal ethics in representation abiding by client's wishes, 152; potential suicidal aspects of, 150–56; and prevalence of mental disorders, 153

death with dignity, 164; laws, 139

deaths of despair, 9

Deaths of Despair and the Future of Capitalism (Case and Deaton), 9

Deaton, Angus, 9

Declaration of Independence, 162

"demand characteristics," 110–11

depressed individuals, 82

depression, 72, 97, 103, 132, 149, 157, 168, 190n30; double depression, 127–28; examinations as public policy during health checkups, 55; impaired concentration as a cardinal symptom of depression, 85; suicidal depression, 107

depressive: disorders, 171; symptoms as preceding homicidal ideation, 71

depressotypic suicidality, 127–28

diagnoses associated with suicide: anorexia nervosa, 26–27, 39, 132–33, 167–68, 177; bipolar spectrum disorder, 26, 39, 124, 157–58; borderline personality disorder, 39, 177; dysthymic disorder, 128; eating disorder, 145; major depressive disorder, 39, 123–24; mood disorder, 177; persistent depression disorder, 147; schizophrenia, 39, 106, 123, 154, 177; substance use disorder, 154

Diagnostic and Statistical Manual of Mental Disorders (*DSM-IV*), 112–113

Diagnostic and Statistical Manual of Mental Disorders (*DSM-5*), 91–92, 112, 147

206 | INDEX

dignity, 176; of the self, 131
dissociation, 111; occurrence of, 6
dissociative, 118; phenomenon, 35
diversity, 177–79
divorce, 65
domestic violence, 107
Donne, John, 132
Dozier, Scott, 148–50
drugs, misuse of, 31
DSM-IV and *DSM-5*. *See* Diagnostic
 and Statistical Manual of Mental
 Disorders
Duffy, Mary, 82
Dugma: The Button (film), 124
Duncan, Joseph, 95–96, 170
Durkheim, Émile, 33–34, 147; on potential
 suicide, 86, 61
"dyadic death," 106
dysexecutive suicidality, 33. *See also* suicide attempt(s), nonlethal
dysthymia. *See under* diagnoses associated with suicide; mental disorder(s)

eating disorder. *See* diagnoses associated
 with suicide; mental disorder(s)
egoistic. *See* suicide: subtypes
electroconvulsive therapy, 133
Ellington (DC area bridge), 15–16
emergency room settings, intoxicated
 suicide attempters in, 32–33
emergency services, 27
end-of-life decisions, tensions inherent
 in, 176
Epistles of Horace (Horace), 50
Esquirol, Jean-Étienne, 38
ethics of studying suicide. *See* Interpersonal Needs Questionnaire
ethnicity. *See* race and ethnicity
euthanasia, 132–33, 143–44, 154, 164–67,
 170–72; active and controlled, 169
euthymia, 157
"exit guide," 81, 136–38, 144; organizations,
 125

The Exorcist (film), 10
"extrapyramidal-induced suicidal dysphoria," 33. *See also* suicide attempt:
 nonlethal

Falstaff (Shakespeare character), 119
fatigue syndrome. *See* myalgic encepha-
 lopathy/chronic fatigue syndrome,
 135, 142
FBI. *See* Federal Bureau of Investigation
fear of guns as dangerous. *See* gun safety
fearing death, 50, 54
fearlessness, about death, 26; and hesitation to enacting suicide death, 51
Federal Bureau of Investigation, 77,
 188n25
fentanyl, 109
filmmakers, 97
Final Exit Network, 136–38, 191n7
Finkel, Michael, 183n12
fire codes, 23
fitness, 60; inclusive, 186n4
Florida State University, 23, 27, 76, 187n8,
 187n28
Fluid Vulnerability Theory, 186n2
football, 8, 55. *See also* American football
Franklin, Joe, 11–12, 29–30
free speech, 25
Freud, Sigmund, 50–51
Friday the 13th (film), 10
"full-court press," 30

Gallup (research organization), 164
gaming culture. *See* video games
garden hose case, 83–84
Gaudiani, Jennifer, 145
gender, 178
genes, 59, 177
genetically identical triplets, 177
Germanwings disaster, 79–80, 86–87
Germany's Social Democratic Party, 53
giraffe, genetically redundant, 169. *See
 also* euthanasia

glioblastoma, 134, 144
Golden Gate Bridge, 16, 18, 22, 26–27, 91, 93, 159, 177; suicide attempt survivors relate last-minute regrets, 91. *See also* other named bridges
Grand Canyon, as site of multiple-method suicide, 23–24
grassroots activism, 97
Grissom, Gus, 8
Guantánamo Bay, 137
gun ownership; increased access to, 13, 18; increased likelihood of fatality if suicidality emerges, 20; rights in the US, 167; sales, 184n25; Tallahassee, Florida, 18
gun safety, 11, 18, 19; conversations, 18; malleable attitudes toward, 19; messaging, 18
Guwande, Atul, 163

Hagen, Chris, 61
Hale-Bopp comet, 81
Halloween (film), 10
Hammock, Liz, 64
Hanson, J. J., 134, 142, 145, 164
Harper's (magazine), 44
Hawking, Stephen, 142, 145–46, 148, 171
Heaven's Gate, 79–83
Heaven's Gate: America's UFO Religion (Zeller), 187n14
Hendin, Herb, 163
heroin, 109
heroism, 8
Hines, Kevin, 26–27, 93, 185n33, 188n30
Holmes, James, 71–72
Homer, 115
homicide, 95; concealed ideation of, 6; as less difficult to enact than suicide, 53; postpartum ideation of, 185n49; victims, 101. *See also* victim
House-Tree-Person Test, 121
human nature, 4, 176
Hume, David, 37

humiliation, preceding suicide attempt, 62
hunger strikes, 129–30; Belfast's Maze Prison, 129

Ice Bucket Challenge, 82
If Symptoms Persist (Dalrymple, pseud.), 5
imagery rehearsal therapy, 94
IMDb, 124
The Imp of the Perverse (Poe), 34
implicit: messaging, 22; psychological processes, 62
"Incel," 114
index trauma, 92; and powerlessness, 93
individual right(s), 132, 161
individualism, 9; definition of, 8
inpatient psychiatry, 49, 93
insomnia, 40, 158, 192n2
instinctual character, 51
insurance policy: purchasing patterns, 163; and suicide, 87
integrated volitional-motivational model, 50
"Integrating Science, Experience, and Political Will: Informed Action to Prevent Suicide," (2018). *See* American Association of Suicidology (AAS)
Internet, as forum for suicidal individuals planning death, 16
Interpersonal Needs Questionnaire, 61
interpersonal rejection, 62; as motivation to restore social connection, 64. *See also* humiliation, preceding suicide attempt
interpersonal theory of suicide, 24, 36–37, 42, 47, 50, 58–60, 62, 65–66, 117–18, 147, 179–81; observations of varieties of self-directed violence as a starting point, 50; major theoretical components, 31, 57; primary hypothesis of, 59
involuntary feeding, 133
irritability, 192n2
ISIS, 120, 122, 190n32

208 | INDEX

Israel's Institute for National Security Studies, 120
Israeli Defense Forces, 118

JAMA Psychiatry (journal), 171
Jefferson, Thomas, 162
Jenkins, Wilhelmina, 135–36, 142, 191n6
Jones, Jim, 80, 184n17
Jonestown, 30, 79–80, 184n17
Juliet (Shakespeare character), 34
justice-motivated, 70. *See also* perversion: of virtue

kerosene, 108
key drivers for suicidal behavior, 8, 17, 127; examples, 9
killing: extremely difficult, 74; fear of, 50; of pets or farm animals, 79. *See also* euthanasia
Kim, Scott, 171
Kingdom of Us (film), 72
Klebold, Sue, 69, 187n3
Klonsky, David, 50; three-step theory, 50
The Knife Went In (Dalrymple, pseud.), 119
knife wounds, 32
Knight, Christopher, 11
Koerselman, Frank, 144
The Kreutzer Sonata (Tolstoy), 4
Krueger, Alan, 118

Lankford, Adam, 122. *See also* ISIS
law enforcement, 3, 101, 154; officer, 49–50, 77, 99, 102, 105, 110–11, 120
legal liability, 26
lions, 169
Live TV, 4
lived experience, 12, 44, 178–79; definition of, 43
The Local (newspaper), 169
lone wolves, 129
loneliness, 9, 62, 116, 117, 158, 172

long-term marriage outcomes, 62. *See also* marital satisfaction
The Looming Tower (Wright), 117
low belonging, 42. *See also* thwarted belongingness

Madison, James, 162
major depressive disorder, 39, 123–24, 134, 147, 172; episode, 35, 128. *See also under* diagnoses associated with suicide; mental disorder(s)
Malaysian Airlines Flight 370, 87
Man against Himself (Menninger), 5
mania, 38, 153, 157
marital satisfaction, 27–28, 30
Maron, Marc, 72
Marshall Project, 191n26
martyrdom-seeking operations, 117
The Mask of Sanity (Cleckley), 191n35
mass: killing, 1; shooting, 67
maturity fears, 163
McIntosh, John, 147
McNulty, Jim, 27, 29–30, 62
McVeigh, Timothy, 52, 68–69, 88–89, 188n25
meaning of life, 176
means safety, 191n25; defined, 14; effect, 11, 15, 17, 21–24, 26, 36, 74, 181–82; efforts, 22; substitution phenomena, 16; temporariness-heavy messaging, 19. *See also* bridge: barriers
means substitution, 15; defined, 16; statistical support for, 16
measurement imprecision, 60
media, 10, 13, 63, 80, 105; commentators, 74; coverage of violence, 183n9; reports of, 67; suicide stories, 30
Meloy, Reid, 117
Memoirs (Adams), 50
Memorial Bridge, 14
memories: of caring and being cared for, 62
Menninger, Karl, 5

mental disorder(s), 26, 28, 33, 38, 39–45, 47, 129, 177, 180, 184n17; anorexia nervosa, 26–27, 39, 132–33, 167–68, 177; antisocial personality disorder, 114; anxiety symptoms, 128; bipolar, 26, 39, 124, 157–58; borderline personality disorder, 39, 177; dysthymia, 128; as key distal causal factors associated with suicide, 42; mood disorder, 177; persistent depression disorder, 147; schizophrenia, 39, 106, 123, 154, 177; speculation on role in suicide, 38; subclinical manifestation of, 7, 41; substance use disorders, 154; as related to suicide, 4, 37, 81; treatability of, 36; among those volunteering for execution, 154

mental health, 38, 48; care, 182; professionals, 3, 6, 41

mental illness, 39, 75, 111

Merari, Ariel, 101, 118, 120, 122

mercy-motivated, 70. *See also* perversion: of virtue

meta-analysis, 11, 16, 32, 60–61, 100

Michigan Law Review, 152

midair experiences following from a height, 176–77. *See also* Golden Gate Bridge

military, 27; life and culture, 27; service members, 11

Military Suicide Research Consortium, 27, 185n34

Milk cows. *See* perversion of virtue, of mercy

Mindlessness: The corruption of Mindfulness in a Culture of Narcissism (Joiner), 162–63

mobile devices, 29

mood disorder. *See under* diagnoses associated with suicide; mental disorders

moral: flexibility, 139; pablum, 138

mortal: combat, 115; fear, 26; terror, 92, 176; threat, 63

mortality, 178

motherly love, 106

A Mother's Reckoning (Klebold), 187n3

Motto, Jerome, and "caring letters" study, 28

multiple-method suicide. *See* Grand Canyon

The Murderer Next Door (Buss), 54

murder-suicide, 1, 6, 46, 50, 54, 67, 70–74, 76, 78–80, 84–85, 89, 98, 114, 180, 183n1; among physicians, 78; potential partially antidepressant properties of planning, 71; rates, 77; as type of suicide, 81; as a variant more of suicide than murder, 2

Murphy, George, 12

mutual aid, 132

myalgic encephalopathy/chronic fatigue syndrome, 135, 142

The Myth of Martyrdom (Lankford), 122. *See also* ISIS

narcissism, 163–64

narcotics detective, 105

Nasser, Gama Abdel, 116

National Rifle Association, 75

natural selection, 52, 63

near-death self-injury, 41

negative suicide-related images, 30

Neo-Popperian philosophy of science, 7

New England Journal of Medicine, 143

New York Times, 127

New Yorker (magazine), 169

nightmares, 192n2; treatment for, 94. *See also* post-traumatic stress disorder: nightmares

Nock, Matt, 62

Norse literature, 115

North Atlantic Treaty Organization (NATO), 173, 192n66

Norwegian law, and Breivik spree killing, 88

"nudge" perspective, 15–17, 30, 52

INDEX

obstacles to danger, 181
O'Connor, Rory, 50
Office of Bombing Prevention, US Department of Home Security, 130
Oklahoma City bombing, 52, 88. *See also* McVeigh, Timothy
opiates, 109
opioid(s), 9; crisis, 10, 13
Oregon, 143, 147; Health Authority, 191nn8, 24
organ donor programs, 30
ostracism, 64. *See also* social exclusion/ostracism

Pacha, Sayed Basam, 126–127
pain tolerance, 58–59
palliative care professionals, 143
pandemic. *See* COVID-19 pandemic
paralympic gold medal winner, 166
Parkland shooting, 75–76, 187n8
Pascal, Blaise, 36–37
patriotism, 164
Penobscot Narrows Bridge, 14
perceived burdensomeness, 36–37, 42, 57–61, 150, 158, 166
perceived virtue, 73
persistent depressive disorder, 147. *See also under* diagnoses associated with suicide; mental disorder(s)
perversion: of duty, 78, 90; of justice, 76, 78, 114; of loyalty, 90; of mercy, 78–79, 85–86, 90; of virtue, 68, 70–71, 79
The Perversion of Virtue: Understanding Murder-Suicide (Joiner), 67, 79
phenotypic similarities, 177
physician-assisted deaths, 1, 24, 39, 41, 44, 47, 98, 102, 131–33, 143, 170–71, 180, 182; op-ed exploration of issues, 140–41; physician-prescribed access to lethal medications, 147; physicians disturbed by their participation, 188n8; roots in suicidality, 2

physics, 181
perceived intractability, 61
Pirkis, Jane, 16
pistol, murder with, 5
Poe, Edgar Allan, 34
Pokorny, Alex, 12
police involvement, 49; in suicide-by-cop incidents, 103. *See also* suicide-by-cop
Pong (1972), 10, 63
positively valenced images, 28
post-traumatic stress disorder (PTSD), 17, 91–94, 102, 104, 115, 132–33, 187n8; nightmares, 93–94
post-traumatic stress symptoms, 128
prazosin, 94, 188n34
precarious ambiguity, 167
predator threats, 94
predicting suicide-related outcomes, 11–12, 58; a priori prediction, 181
predictive accuracy, 12–13; prediction is no better than a coin flip, 12
premature death, 166, 168
Princess Diana, 62
prison: psychiatrist, 4; settings, 4
prisoner abuse, 40
prolonged exposure, 133
prominent model of suicidal behavior, 50
proverbial pitchforks, 50
pseudoheroic depravities, 125
psychiatric: nomenclature, 40; status prior to suicide attempt, 53
Psycho (film), 10
psychological: autopsy, 20, 39–40, 64–65, 121, 154; distance, 19–20, 23; pain, 146
psychopathology, 52, 56; suicidal behavior as among the truest markers, 43
psychosis, 38, 111, 153
puritanism, 46
Putnam, Robert, 9

quasi-suicidal mindset (Breivik), 88
Qutb, Sayyid, 116–17, 119, 121, 128

Rabbit at Rest (Updike), 131
race and ethnicity, 10, 156, 178; Asian
    American, 156; Black, 156; Hispanic,
    156; Native American, 113, 132, 156;
    White, 9–10, 127–28, 156
railroad tracks, 49
rampage killings, 46
ratio: of murder to attempted murder, 54;
    of suicide death to attempted suicide,
    54
real-life gun violence, facilitators of, 9
Reid, William, 71–72
religious experiences: fundamental com-
    monalities to, 1
reluctance to kill, 95–96, 102; as inherent
    to humans, 88
reputational miscalculations, 108
responsibility for one's own behavior, 4
retirement: destinations, 160; savings
    plans, 30
revenge: misunderstood role in suicidal
    behavior, 68; as motive, 90. *See also*
    suicide myths
"revolutionary suicide," 80–81
right-to-die proponents, 165
risk factor, of suicide, 65
risk falsification, 7
Robins, Eli, 20, 39–40
Rodger, Elliot, 114
romantic relationship: strife as common
    triggers for suicide death, 27
Romeo (Shakespeare character), 34
Rountree, Meredith, 150, 152
rugged: definition of, 8; rugged individu-
    alism, 8–9, 11
Rumbaugh, Charles, 150rural, 18
Russian roulette, 109, 115

safety messaging, 19; as a philosophy for
    destigmatizing suicide, 45
schizophrenia. *See under* diagnoses asso-
    ciated with suicide; mental disorder(s),
    schizophrenia;

scientific: arbitration, 179; research, 46
Second Amendment, 18
Seduced by Death (Hendin), 163
self-: asphyxiation, 57; burdensomeness,
    37 (*see also* perceived burdensome-
    ness); destruction, 32; determination,
    131, 133, 136, 141, 161, 163, 165, 170, 176,
    178; directed violence, 8; disgust, 161,
    192n2; harm, 30; hatred, 151, 192n2; in-
    flicted death, 57; inflicted knife wound,
    31; interest, 164; killing, 38; loathing,
    161; poisoning, 33; promotion, 163; res-
    cue, 176; sacrifices, 60; derangement of
    behavior, 59
self-inflicted gun-shot wound, 5–6, 22, 55,
    77, 79, 153; on local TV, 3
self-preservation, 26, 51, 176; instinct, 51–
    52, 103; motive, 21
service dog, 105
severe abuse, 40
shahid (hero), 101
Shays, Jonathan, 115
Shneidman, Edwin, 141
Skeem, Jennifer, 88
skull-and-crossbones symbol, 155
slippery slopes, 170, 172
smoking, 97
snakes, 30
social: connectedness, 65; debt, 141; duty,
    136; isolation, 26; pressure, 2, stressors,
    42, trust, 164
social exclusion/ostracism: neurobiology
    of its pain, 63–65
socially acceptable, 35
socially relevant neuropeptides; oxytocin,
    64
socioeconomic factors preceding suicide,
    42, 160
soldiers, 102, 188n8
South Korea suicide policies, 55
space: craft, 81; exploration, 8; travel, 7
spiders, 30
spree killing, 1, 2, 95, 180

212 | INDEX

Stanley, Ian, 76, 91
staring down death, 82–83
Stefan, Susan, 39, 41
Stern, Jessica, 117
stigma, 38, 45, 56, 75
stoicism, 119
The Stranger in the Woods (Finkel), 11
strychnine poisoning, 21
substance use. *See under* diagnoses associated with suicide; mental disorder(s)
sucrose, 155
suicidal mind, 22, 27, 33, 149; ambivalent debate characteristic of, 21
suicidal violence: diverse forms of, 47–48, 50, 182; proposed unified view, 46; varieties of, 1, 3, 14, 175
suicide: active desire for, 57; common locations of, 16–17; complex, 23; deaths as primarily, 1, 3; defined, 7; escape from misery as motivation for, 4; genuine, 109; as misfiring of evolutionary adaptive behavioral suite, 60; instinctual aspect of, 4; sequela, 31; subtypes, 61; traditional, 146; traumatic stress in witnessing, 25; true, 1, 183n2
suicide and bereavement, 34–35, 56, 186n11; longstanding impact of, 56
Suicide and Life-Threatening Behavior (journal), 45
suicide as unitary phenomenon, defined with gradations and stages of severity, 58, 61
suicide attempt(s), 25; aborted, 85, 152; history of, 60; multiple, 103, 105; nonlethal, 33; predicting the occurrence of, 11; survivors, 26, 34–35, 43
suicide-by-cop, 1, 6, 24, 33–34, 46, 50, 54, 97–102, 104–6, 109–10, 112, 115, 146, 150, 180; as involving planning and intent, 103; statistics, 98
"suicide-by-other," 106
suicide capability, 58–60, 179

suicide clusters. *See* suicide contagion
suicide contagion, 56, 158–159, 186n11
suicide copycat effect, 30
suicide deaths: annual and weekly peaks in, 157; male majority of decedents, 98, 156; state-assisted, 150
suicide decedents, 20, 24–25, 31–33, 36–37, 39–42, 83, 177
suicide intent, 19, 58, 60, 75,192n2: communicated prior to death, 20, 100
suicide intervention, 11, 25, 27; cost of, 26; to de-escalate suicidal crises, 2, 29, 63
suicide legal consulting work, 25
suicide literature, 60
suicide method(s), 20, 23, 26, 32; bridge, 14, 35; defined, 14; by hanging, 25
suicide myths: of impulsivity, 3, 21, 33–36, 51; of selfishness, 36
suicide note(s), 6, 102–3, 109
suicide pacts, 54
suicide plan/planning, 35, 49, 51
suicide prevention, community, 9, 12–14, 43; prevention research, 27; as naturally occurring control condition, 15; prevention strategies, 2, 17, 19. *See also* means safety
suicide qua suicide, 107
suicide rate, 41, 55, 120; international comparison, 7–8, 13; recent declines, 2; trend overview, 9–10, 185n57; in US military, 27
suicide risk, 2, 28; considering suicide as the only option as indicator of, 72; high, 50; imminent, 59; intent to die as cardinal feature of suicide, 19, 167; preoccupation with death as, 35
suicide terrorism, 1, 2, 46, 53, 98, 101, 117–119, 130, 180, 183n1; suicidal element of, 52
suicide terrorist(s), 21, 41, 97, 120, 127–129
suicide warning signs, 82, 158
surveillance cameras, 26
survival of the fittest, 51

The S-Word (film), 44
Szasz, Thomas, 39

taboo of suicide, 56
Taft (bridge), 15, 16
terminal illness, 40, 147; myth of terminal anorexia, 144–145; patients with, 170
terror(ism), 2; attack, 2, 190n32; politically motivated, 53
Thelma and Louise (film), 24
Three Identical Strangers (film) 177
thwarted belongingness, 57–61
Times of Israel (online newspaper), 101, 118
tobacco, 97
train(s), 49, 51
tricyclic antidepressant amitriptyline, 148
TV news anchor, suicide of, 3

United States: recent advances in national suicide prevention, 2; suicide deaths, 9
Updike, John, 131
US Constitution, 162
US Department of Defense, 27, 130, 185n34
US Department of Homeland Security, Office of Bombing Prevention, 130
US Marines, 29
US Supreme Court, 25

Van Dijk, Wim, 144
Van Order, Kimberely, 58, 60
Varieties of Religious Experience, The (James), 1

Varieties of suicidal experience, 21, 23, 33, 50
Verhofstadt, 164–65, 167
Vervoort, Marieke, 166
Victim(s), 3, 57, 67, 70, 76, 83, 87, 89, 96, 101, 176–77; blaming, 109; precipitated homicide, 106–7, 109
Video game(s), 10, 29–30, 63
Vietnam War, 115
violence, 180; as suicidal, 1–3. *See also* suicidal violence
virtual reality, 155

walk the plank, 155
war-related phenomenon, berserk, 115
Washington Post (newspaper), 78
whack-a-mole, 46
wheelchair racer, 166
White, Ed, 8
Why People Die by Suicide (Joiner), 55, 57
Wible, Pamela, 77–78
Wickersham (legal case), 186n61
Wilcher, Bobby, 152
will to live, 50, 90, 176
Wolfgang, Marvin, 107–9
World Health Organization (WHO), 173
Wright, Lawrence, 117
WTF (podcast), 72

YouTube, 105

Zeller, Benjamin, 187n14
zoo, 169

ABOUT THE AUTHOR

THOMAS JOINER is the Robert O. Lawton Distinguished Professor of Psychology at Florida State University and author of *Why People Die By Suicide*.

Printed and bound by CPI Group (UK) Ltd, Croydon, CR0 4YY

17/11/2024

14594038-0002